The Crimes in Time
Journal
Volume I

First Edition

Written by

Dr. Hollis A. Palmer

Deep Roots Publications
Saratoga Springs, N. Y.

The Crimes in Time Journal
Vol. 1

Published by:

Deep Roots Publications
P. O. Box 114
Saratoga Springs, NY 12866

Library of Congress Number 00191948

ISBN 0-9671713-1-8

Palmer, Hollis Albert.
The crimes in times journal. Vol. I / Hollis A. Palmer. -- 1st ed.
p. cm.
LCCN 00-191948
ISBN 0-9671713-1-8

1. Crime--New York (State)--History--19th century.
I. Title.

HV6795.N5P35 2000 364.1'09747
QBI00-901483

This book is dedicated to my son

Scott Eaton Palmer

who doesn't waste time dreaming about tomorrow
or regretting yesterday
but instead enjoys the time from sunrise
to sunrise for all that it brings.

... I envy him

Special thanks to

NICOLE STEIN

Without whom, I would not have sounded even this eloquent.

Table of Contents

Dear Reader,

The tale told in **To Spend Eternity Alone** is now a play performed at dinner theaters and as a fundraiser. The story begins the night before the trial with Jesse Billings telling the jailer (the audience) why the trial should never happen. The next act is in two parts. First, the prosecutor reviews the evidence and testimony for the jury (the audience). The defense attorney follows with his summation. In Act II the judge charges the jury to secure a verdict in the case. After the audience has had a chance to discuss the case it renders a verdict. After the verdict, Jesse returns to the stage as a seventy-two year-old man coming home from his daughter's funeral. He relates what happened to each of the characters.

The Crimes in Times Journal vol. I is the first, in what is anticipated to be a series of books dedicated to recounting some of the more interesting but forgotten crimes of the Victorian Era. To be included in these books there has to be something unusual in the crime or it has to remain unsolved. The spin could occur in the motive, method or outcome. An example would be the case of the Borne brothers where in 1819 (I know not the Victorian Era), a man was convicted of murder and, while he waited for the hangman's noose, the alleged victim turned up alive.

We hope you enjoyed this book and will want to read the future books in the series. The next book is anticipated to be out June 4, 2001. This is again on the anniversary of one of the crimes reported. In this particular case we examine the question; doesn't a Civil War Calvary General have the right to shoot a man who made unwanted advances to his wife while he was out defending the union.

If you know of a crime that may fit the classification of this series, please let us know.
We may be reached by writing to:

Deep Roots Publications
P. O. Box 114
Saratoga Springs, NY 12866.

Or by e-mail eternity.alone@worldnet.att.net

You may also be added to our mailing list through either address above.

Keep up with the play and publications by visiting our web site www.eternityalone.com.

Sincerely,

Hollis

Waterford:

Crime Pays

(Somebody)

Waterford

According to the markers posted on the edge of town, Waterford is the oldest incorporated village in the United States. The community is fortunate to have retained most of the historical elements from the time when it had a dominant economic presence. There are numerous reminders of the past including many of the fine brick homes and businesses. Most of these structures were built as a result of the village's strategic commercial location. Waterford is, after all, at the junction of two of the leading thoroughfares of the 1800s - the Erie Canal and the Barge Canal. The community is also at the junction of the Hudson and Mohawk Rivers. The water from each was essential for the industrial development that took place during the Victorian era. By the 1870s, when this story took place, railroad tracks had been constructed along the same general paths as the waterways, continuing Waterford's economic dominance. Even today, from the shores of Waterford one can get to any place in the world. Although access to all forms of transportation from the village was not essential to the events in this story, the ability to escape from Waterford probably played heavily on the minds of the men who broke into the Saratoga County Bank.

One night in the fall of 1872, 10 burglars, dressed as members of the Ku Klux Klan, committed one of the biggest and most daring robberies in the history of the United States.

The Scene

The night of Sunday, October 13–14 was rainy and bleak. Modern storm sewer systems had not yet been installed, so the streets of the quaint historical village were flooded with water several inches deep. It was the kind of cold rain that kept even the most ardent adventurer in for the evening. It was the kind of damp darkness that caused families to retire early, seeking the warmth and comfort that only a sympathetic bed can offer. It was the kind of weather that caused people to completely close up their homes to keep the elements out. It was a constant rain, creating a background sound that drowned out all but the loudest disturbances. It was a night perfectly suited for the most despicable of misdeeds. It was a time for crime.

The Bank

The Saratoga County Bank of Waterford was in the brick building that still stands at the northeast corner of Broad and Second Street. The bank's business offices were housed in the two rooms directly on the corner or the left side of the first floor, as one faces the building. The bank was comprised of two main rooms and a third space that was referred to as the vault. The main business room, where the tellers took in deposits, was in the front of the building. There was a second room in the back referred to as the counting room. Between the rooms was an oversized hallway constructed to be a vault.

Cashier

David Van Hovenbergh was the cashier at the bank. The position of bank cashier was one to aspire to in the 1870s. David's compensation package included a very, special residence. David and his family lived in an apartment, which comprised the remainder of the bank building. In the days before security cameras, motion detectors, and time locks, having a trustee reside in the bank building was considered the ultimate in asset protection.

The Van Hovenbergh family used the two rooms on the first floor that were not part of the bank, the entire second floor and part of the raised basement as its residence. To help the home remain cool in the summer, there was a center hall, on both floors, that ran the entire width of the building. The family used its portion of the first floor as two parlors. The second floor consisted of four bedrooms. The kitchen and dinning room were in the raised basement. There were no bathrooms inside the house. The family's outhouse was inside a fenced-in yard that surrounded the bank and limited grounds. The fence had been built to afford seclusion when the family walked to the outhouse. To provide its patrons with a sense of security, the bank had installed iron bars over the widows of the raised basement and over the windows of the bank area. Most of the iron bars remain on the windows even today.

The location of the bank was perfect for a business engaged in commerce. Just two blocks east was the bridge to Lansingburgh and the entrance to the Champlain Canal. Directly down the street to the south was the entrance to the barge canal and the railroad line. The train station was only two short blocks north. Going west, the road led to Cohoes, one of the major industrial centers of the country. As good as the site was for a commercial location, it was even a better spot for a robbery, as these same routes could be used in the event anyone wanted to escape the scene!

The Family

The Van Hovenbergh family consisted of Mr. David Van Hovenbergh, his wife, Sarah his 18 year-old-twin daughters, Mary and Sarah, and his son, Mulfred. Little "Freddie" was turning eight on October 14th, the day of the crime. The parents shared one room on the second floor. The children each had their own bedchambers. There was a servant; a girl named Ann Driscoll. Ann slept in a small room off from the kitchen in the basement. At the time of the robbery, Ann had been employed by the family for less than a week

The Break In

It took several days to determine, with even reasonable accuracy, the manner in which the dastardly crime was committed. This much is known. Sometime after midnight, all but one member of the gang climbed over the fence that surrounded the backyard of the bank/home. The remaining member of the gang took a position near a post on the corner. He would spend the night standing sentry in the pouring rain.

When all the gang members were inside the enclosed backyard, several pulled at the various sets of welded metal bars covering the basement windows. As they had suspected, one set of bars was loose. Believing the rain would cover any sounds from the prying ears of neighbors, the group wrenched the loose set of bars from the sill. Positioning the welded bars against the house, the band converted what was supposed to be a security shield into a makeshift ladder. Two of the rain soaked gang members used the "ladder" to climb up the five and a half feet into the unprotected and unlocked window, leading into the back parlor of the Van Hovenbergh apartment. Once inside the two immediately unlocked the rear door, letting in their associates. Within a minute of the first person entering through the window, all the confederates were in the warm, dry apartment. Fearing some sound may have been heard in the basement, two of the men slipped silently down the backstairs to detain the servant.

The Maid

Ann awakened to the sight of two hooded men standing over her bed. One held a black lantern (the type used as a flashlight); his cohort pointed a revolver at her head. While she was staring into the black tunnel of the barrel, Ann was told that if she uttered the faintest cry they would kill her immediately. Silently, and with the skill of rodeo cowboys, they bound her in tarred ropes. The ropes around her arms were so tight she was virtually incapable of any movement. One of the men demanded to know who slept in each room on the second floor. Out of fear for her life, Ann told the truth as to the location of the inhabitants but tried a little lie in an attempt to deter the thieves. Ann told her assailants that Mr. Van Hovenbergh's brother was also staying in the house. The gang member with the gun immediately pointed the pistol to her forehead and told her that the brother had been gone for over a week. In no uncertain terms, Ann was told that any further lies would result in her being killed instantly. To defend her story, Ann told the men she had spent the afternoon in Troy and was perhaps incorrect as to the whereabouts of the cashier's brother.

Weapons

"Where's the ax?" one of the captors asked of the frightened maid. Whether by plan or improvisation, this man apparently wanted to limit the number of potential weapons available to be used against the band. Homes at this time were heated by wood or coal. It was a logical assumption that a family would have an ax to split wood.

"There isn't any ax," the terrified girl responded. The implication to the gang members was clear. Mr. Van Hovenbergh was so wealthy and frivolous that he had his wood already split before it arrived. This was an economic status that each of the thieves hoped to attain, as a result of this night's efforts.

Assured that they had all the information they needed, the two men pulled Ann's hands behind her back, placing metal handcuffs on her wrists. To guarantee themselves of her silence, they then tore her sleeping garments and used the strips of cloth as gags. They were rough as they pulled the cloth firmly into her mouth. Throwing her back on the bed, Ann was ordered to remain quiet or an instant death would be her penalty.

In all, the two men had threatened Ann with death at least three times.

Upstairs

When the two who had tied up Ann reached the second floor, there was a total of nine men gathered in the center hallway. The thieves split into three teams. Each group had come prepared with a crowbar. Two crouched at each of the twin sisters' bedroom doors. Four crouched outside the sleeping chamber of the parents. They had not planned to enter the son's room at this time. To be sure they would all respond at the same instant, the final member, who was also the leader of the group, boldly lighted the gaslights in the center hallway. At the signal, the group broke into the three sleeping chambers. The person in charge immediately joined the four who had entered the parents' room.

For many years after, the use of crowbars was evident in the casings surrounding the doors. The beautiful dark cherry wood of each frame was fractured in the assault.

Like all mothers whose ears are tuned for strange sounds, Mrs. Van Hovenbergh was the first to wake up. Still groggy from only having been asleep for a little while, she felt the touch of a hand around her throat and opened her eyes to see the barrel of a revolver pointed at her head. Despite the rough grasp, she was able to utter a cry, asking to be spared. Looking to her right, Mrs. Van Hovenbergh saw a second man with his hand on her husband's neck. When the tension of the man's grip awoke him, David immediately realized the situation and shouted for help. Instantly, the clutch was tightened, depriving the cashier of air. Realizing his predicament, Van Hovenbergh was silent. Two of the men pulled David from the bed and began to bind him.

The Boy

The only person who was awakened by Mr. Van Hovenbergh's brief outcry was his son. The boy hastened to his parents' room only to be confronted by a terror greater than any his eight-year-old mind had ever imagined. Both his parents were in the act of having their legs and arms bound by rope and their wrists handcuffed. His father, who had been pulled from the bed, was being held up by several men. The boy was so scared he began to cry uncontrollably. One of the confederates took Freddie by the nightgown that covered his thin chest and held a knife to his throat. In a calm demanding voice the man told the boy, "Stop screaming or I'll cut your throat."

Like any mother in this situation, Mrs. Van Hovenbergh cried for mercy. Reaching deep into his constitution the boy was able to muffle his outburst. Feeling that further noise from Freddie was no longer a threat, the man with the knife threw the lad into a clothespress in the center hallway. To insure the boy would not be heard, the man tossed blankets on top of him.

The Twins

The twin daughters, Sarah and Mary, were awoken just like their mother and the maid. Each girl reported her fear at opening her eyes and looking down the barrel of a pistol. Like the other members of the family, the girls were bound with tarred rope. Sarah, who would prove to be a feisty demon, at first struggled with her captors. Despite her valiant efforts, Sarah soon realized her strength was no match for her assailants.

Sarah, the bolder of the sisters, went so far as to ask her assailants, "Do you mean to hurt me?" She was assured by one of the men that they would not hurt her as long as she behaved. It was interesting that as violent and traumatic as this crime was, throughout the act, the women were consistently treated as ladies.

The Parents

As Sarah was being tied to the bed, in her own room, things were proceeding as planned in the parents' bedchamber. One of her captors asked Mrs. Van Hovenbergh, "Where is the revolver?"

She responded that she didn't know where it was. Under the mask the questioner rolled his eyes as he responded sarcastically, "Doesn't matter, you didn't get to use it, did you?"

At first, the band completely bound Mr. Van Hovenbergh in the tarred ropes. This was one of the few errors in the gang's scheme. Realizing he could not walk down the stairs to the bank area, they were forced to free his legs. Throughout the long night, his arms remained tied behind his back.

Surrounded by seven members of the contingent, David Van Hovenbergh was escorted from the sleeping chamber. As the cashier was taken from the room his wife called out, "Do not kill him; he's all I've got."

One of the band responded, "He won't be hurt, only he must obey orders."

Of the seven men who accompanied the cashier down the stairs to the bank area, three were responsible for making him feel threatened. Two, one on each side, held guns to his temples. The third was behind him with a "dark knife," the tip of which was kept pricking the skin of the cashier's neck. Once they had him down in the banking rooms, the men demanded that he open the vault. Mr. Van Hovenbergh's actions for the next hour were bold and brassy. Many would later hold that he had not resisted enough. It would have been interesting to see how long these same critics would have defied the thugs if they had a weapon poised at their heads and their families at the mercy of other members of the gang.

Holding the Women

Two men were left on the second floor to guard the boy and the women of the family. One at a time the two gangsters brought the twin sisters into their mother's room and tied each to the bed. Still in their nightclothes the twin daughters were permitted to join their mother on her bed. At the request of Mrs. Van Hovenbergh, young Freddie was brought from the clothespress and tied to the bed with his sisters. Without specific instruction, one of the two upstairs gang members patrolled the center hall occasionally peering out the front window. The second sentinel remained in the room with the family. This guard would prove to be both a total rogue and a perfect gentleman.

Mrs. Van Hovenbergh had been tied in a sitting position on the bed. The guard inquired, "Can I do anything to make you more comfortable?" Without awaiting a reply, he provided all those in his charge with both additional pillows and a comforter. With a brashness that was rarely seen in any crime, the guard calmly took a seat on the lounge, which was across from the bed. He calmly placed a pillow behind his own head. In what was later described by the three women in captivity to be a sign of good breeding, the sentinel entered into a conversation with the three ladies in the room.

As her confidence grew, Mrs. Van Hovenbergh asked, "What are the intentions of your confederates?"

"Well, you know our object: we're after the money and we shall have it." There was an air of conceit in his voice.

Mrs. Van Hovenbergh then accused the man of complicity in one of the other major robberies in the area. "You are one of the scoundrels from the Ballston Bank."

His only response was, "I was on the canals and don't know anything of the affair."

Boredom

After a time the guard assigned to the room appeared to be bored. He got up from the lounge and began circling the chamber in what appeared to the family to be a search for bounty. He picked up the framed pictures examining each in turn. Finding Mr. Van Hovenbergh's watch on a dresser, he picked it up to examine its quality.

Seeing what he was doing, Mrs. Van Hovenbergh asked the time. "One o'clock," she was told.

"Are you going to take the watch?" she asked.

"This is a nice watch you have here, but don't be alarmed I won't take it. Nor will I touch your jewelry."

He then asked her where she kept her diamonds. Mrs. Van Hovenbergh advised the man they were a poor family and could not afford diamonds.

"Oh you're not poor!" He told her. The robber felt she was lying, but did not press the issue. Thus confined to the bed, the family spent the next hour conversing with the gentleman rapscallion.

At one point Mrs. Van Hovenbergh inquired as to, "how came you to be in the house?"

The gentleman responded, "It makes no difference to you."

As the night dragged on, the man moved from the lounge to the doorway placing his pillow against the door jam. He asked, "What time does your milkman come along?"

Mrs. Van Hovenbergh responded, "'bout half past 7 in the morning."

In evidence of the lengthy surveillance that had been performed by the group he responded, "I know you're lying to me. Now what time does your butcher arrive?"

"We don't have a butcher; we have to go to the market" the bound woman responded.

There had been comprehensive surveillance and planning of the crime. Each man wore a white hood with eyeholes and some members had mouth openings. They were described later as the types of mask worn by members of the Ku Klux Klan. The men in the band called each other by number. The number ran up to nine. A true sign of the gang's discipline was that at no time during the robbery was a single name used.

Courtesy Returned

With time the gentleman guard became thirsty. He took up the water pitcher on the nightstand to take a drink. The boy, noting what was about to transpire, told the man, "Say Mister, don't drink that water, t'aint good. It's been in there all day." Looking casually at the boy the robber returned the pitcher to its place on the stand.

The Cashier Holds His Own

The men in the bank area were faced with a braver man than they had expected. David Van Hovenbergh was sure that if he delayed long enough someone would walk by the bank and send out an alarm. For almost an hour David, through his inactions, refused to open the safe. At first, he asserted that they had recently changed the combination and he did not have the new sequence. Later, he was forced to alter his excuse, claiming that under the pressure he had forgotten the combination. He used over a dozen excuses to stop from opening the safe. One of the seven gang members in the bank was apparently assigned, or took it upon himself, to keep looking out the window. This man was the most impatient and would often walk over and ask of the one who appeared to be the leader, "Why not shoot him and blow the safe?" Luckily, for the cashier, the leader ignored the request.

After hearing the forgetfulness excuse for some time one of the confederates, known only as number five, took it upon himself to leave the banking room. Patiently number five waited for a several minutes in the hall on the first floor. When robber number five felt enough time had elapsed, he came back into the bank announcing that he had checked with the wife and that David Van Hovenbergh did, in fact, know the combination. (The factualness of the visit with the wife was later denied by all those present in the second floor chamber.) At this point the leader became concerned and told the cashier that he must open the vault or they would kill him and blow the safe. With two guns at his head and his hands still tied behind his back, David struggled for some time before he was actually able to open the combinations for each of the two sets of doors.

And the Take Was?

When the vault was finally opened the gang immediately took the cash, which was reported to be $8,500. Just one short week before a remittance of $50,000 in cash had been deposited. It was fortuitous, for the owners of the bank, that the money had been moved to a bank in Albany during the intervening week.

After removing the cash, 30 to 40 tin boxes, which belonged to depositors, were also removed from the vault. These light boxes were taken into the counting room. The boxes, which were not cumbersome, were placed on the floor and forced open with the same iron bars that had been used to open the family's bedchambers an hour before. The tin boxes contained almost exclusively stock certificates and bonds. These light paper documents were extracted from the metal boxes and placed in softer cloth bags. Several cast iron boxes were so strong they proved impossible to open with just a bar. Each of the unopened boxes weighed between 50 and 150 pounds. Despite their bulk, the gang took the sealed iron boxes with them when they escaped. A theory persisted for several days that because the boxes were heavy they were not taken far. Most in the community expected those boxes would be found with their contents still safe inside.

The Family is Reunited

As the bank boxes were being opened, the gentleman sentinel left the women in the care of the second upstairs men in the band called each other by number. The number ran up to nine. A true sign of the gang's discipline was that at no time during the robbery was a single name used.

Courtesy Returned

With time the gentleman guard became thirsty. He took up the water pitcher on the nightstand to take a drink. The boy, noting what was about to transpire, told the man, "Say Mister, don't drink that water, t'aint good. It's been in there all day." Looking casually at the boy the robber returned the pitcher to its place on the stand.

The Cashier Holds His Own

The men in the bank area were faced with a braver man than they had expected. David Van Hovenbergh was sure that if he delayed long enough someone would walk by the bank and send out an alarm. For almost an hour David, through his inactions, refused to open the safe. At first, he asserted that they had recently changed the combination and he did not have the new sequence. Later, he was forced to alter his excuse, claiming that under the pressure he had forgotten the combination. He used over a dozen excuses to stop from opening the safe. One of the seven gang members in the bank was apparently assigned, or took it upon himself, to keep looking out the window. This man was the most impatient and would often walk over and ask of the one who appeared to be the leader, "Why not shoot him and blow the safe?" Luckily, for the cashier, the leader ignored the request.

After hearing the forgetfulness excuse for some time one of the confederates, known only as number five, took it upon himself to leave the banking room. Patiently number five waited for a several minutes in the hall on the first floor. When robber number five felt enough time had elapsed, he came back into the bank announcing that he had checked with the wife and that David Van Hovenbergh did, in fact, know the combination. (The factualness of the visit with the wife was later denied by all those present in the second floor chamber.) At this point the leader became concerned and told the cashier that he must open the vault or they would kill him and blow the safe. With two guns at his head and his hands still tied behind his back, David struggled for some time before he was actually able to open the combinations for each of the two sets of doors.

And the Take Was?

When the vault was finally opened the gang immediately took the cash, which was reported to be $8,500. Just one short week before a remittance of $50,000 in cash had been deposited. It was fortuitous, for the owners of the bank, that the money had been moved to a bank in Albany during the intervening week.

After removing the cash, 30 to 40 tin boxes, which belonged to depositors, were also removed from the vault. These light boxes were taken into the counting room. The boxes, which were not cumbersome, were placed on the floor and forced open with the same iron bars that had been used to open the family's bedchambers an hour before. The tin boxes contained almost exclusively stock certificates and bonds. These light paper documents were extracted from the metal boxes and placed in softer cloth bags. Several cast iron boxes were so strong they proved impossible to open with just a bar. Each of the unopened boxes weighed between 50 and 150 pounds. Despite their bulk, the gang took the sealed iron boxes with them when they escaped. A theory persisted for several days that because the boxes were heavy they were not taken far. Most in the community expected those boxes would be found with their contents still safe inside.

The Family is Reunited

As the bank boxes were being opened, the gentleman sentinel left the women in the care of the second upstairs highwayman. The gentleman thief proceeded to the basement where he untied Ann's legs. He brought her upstairs to join the other ladies. The gentleman robber then proceeded to tear the sheets on the crowded bed the ladies occupied into long strips. The feisty daughter, Sarah, reprimanded him, "Look here, what are you tearing up my mother's good sheets for? If you want old rags I can get some."

"We usually help ourselves to what we want," he responded coldly. He then used the strips of sheet to tie the women's legs. Assured he had placed sufficient padding against their skin, the robber tied the tarred rope over the strips of cloth. Tied in this manor the women's skin was not hurt. Before using the remaining strips of cloth to gag the women, the gentleman thief dipped the cloth in water so it would not be too dry in his victims' mouths. Before Mrs. Van Hovenbergh was gagged the bigger of the two men lifted her son and took him from the room. "Why are you tying us up and what do you intend doing with my son?" exclaimed the frightened mother.

"We are doing what is necessary for our own protection. Nobody will be hurt."

As the gang finished smashing the boxes in the counting room; Mr. Van Hovenbergh was forced to unlock the front door. Cursing the rain that had proved their ally, the thieves immediately started loading their bounty onto a waiting wagon.

Satisfied that he was no longer needed, Mr. Van Hovenbergh was taken upstairs and placed in his son's room in the back corner of the house. Several of the men tied the cashier to the bed and told the entire family not to move or try to get free or they would be forced to hurt the boy. Silently, the burglars checked the counting room for a final time. Two then drove a buckboard away from the scene. Six more either rode in a wagon south toward Cohoes or walked across the railroad bridge to Peebles Island. Any paper that the burglars did not feel worthy of taking was scattered on the floor. The gang was so confident in their leader's plan that they were comfortable being in the bank building for over four hours!

No one in the family, nor any of the neighbors, heard the gang leave the scene. One of the neighbors was Isaac Ormsby, the district attorney of Saratoga County. Ormsby lived three houses south of the bank.

Sounding the Alarm

The gag that was used on Mrs. Van Hovenbergh was not tied well. It came lose almost as soon at the men left the room. Fearing for her family, and uncertain as to the condition of her husband, she did not utter a sound for several minutes. Eventually Mrs. Van Hovenbergh heard her husband's movements in the next room. She implored him to stop for fear of retaliations against Freddie. Mrs. Van Hovenbergh would have been better served talking to Sarah who was in the same bed as she. Less than 10 minutes after the men had left the room, thin Sarah slipped the handcuffs off her wrist and, still tied with the ropes, struggled from the bed. Finding a knife in her father's dresser, she set about cutting her own and the other women's bonds. She then went looking for her father. Finding him still tied to the bed, she cut his ropes. With his hands still in the cuffs, the brave cashier found his pistol and went into the street firing five shots as an alarm. The distress signal woke several neighbors who, despite the heavy weather, came into the street.

As more of their neighbors joined them David Van Hovenbergh and Sarah were both in the street dressed only in their bedclothes and still bound. The three women who remained in the house soon found the boy. Freddie had been placed back in the clothes press where he had been stuffed previously by the gang. The boy was frightened and tired but otherwise unhurt.

The Pursuit

Within minutes of Van Hovenbergh's gun shots, most in the neighborhood were outside in the cold rain trying to ascertain what had happened. One neighbor, J. B. Enos, who was also an officer in the bank, was sent to Troy to get the police. Other neighbors were sent to their homes to find files needed to free the cuffs from the victims' wrists.

When the Central Police Office in Troy was notified of the robbery the impact was immediately realized. Superintendent McKenna was awakened in his home by one of the officers. McKenna personally went to the scene along with some of his best men. With the superintendent was Chief of Detectives English, Captain Murphy, and Special Officer Squire. The Troy *Times* was obviously a supporter of the police. In the first article the *Times* assured its readers that it was "almost confident that they (the police) will place the shackles on them (the robbers) with a better grasp than they placed them on their victims."

The Amount Taken

Since the crime was not reported to the police until after 4:00 o'clock in the morning, the newspaper reports on the 14th were limited to the afternoon papers, which generally went to press by 11:00 o'clock in the morning. Just like today, reporters were urged by their editors to get the first story. Those few reporters, who did get articles out on the 14th, were only able to gather information from interviews with a few members of the family and neighbors. Even without an audit and with very limited sources, the reporters were able to report that $8,500 in cash and between $350,000 and $500,000 in bonds had been stolen.

How Was It Accomplished

The first day there were three prevalent theories as to how the robbery had occurred. It was assumed that one man had been hidden in the house during the day. This theory went on to say how the man had let his confederates in through the back door. A second theory was that the servant girl, Ann, who had only been with the family a week, was in some way connected to the robbers. There was even one report that a member of the gang had snuck into the house the evening before while the family was in church. All these options were disclaimed in the second day's reports.

To comprehend the enormity of this crime, it is important to understand the current value of the money. All money is reported in 1872 dollars. The magnitude of this crime, in today's dollars, is difficult to imagine. The supervisors of the Town of Halfmoon had just rejected a raise in salary for the superintendent of the waterworks. The raise would have given him an annual salary of $500. It is safe to assume that at the very least every dollar reported should be multiplied by 100. The first day the amount of cash taken was reported to be $8,500. In today's dollars that would be $850,000. In a week it would be established that $443,000 in cash, bonds and stocks was taken. That total would have been equivalent to over 40 million in today's dollars.

Containing the losses

In an effort to limit the loss, the serial numbers on the bonds and stocks were immediately published in many newspapers. The same numbers were immediately telegraphed to the trading houses in New York City and Boston. Depositing bonds in the bank's vault did not make them the property of the bank; therefore, any loss would fall directly to the depositor. At the same time, the person to whom the ownership could be established had every right to reclaim the bonds from whoever had them, so trading houses did not want to be stuck holding the bonds. A bigger problem than the serial bonds was the coupon bonds and bearer bonds. Under the law these bonds were to be paid to whoever held them. They were virtually the same as cash.

Under the banking laws in 1872, the cash stolen would be the only loss to the bank and its owners.

Suspects

By the second day, the newspapers were reporting two dramatically different positions regarding the solution of the crime. The general feeling of all the police involved in the case was that it was a well-planned and executed robbery. Virtually no evidence had been left that connected the crime to any suspects. In stark contrast to the lack of any hard evidence, the name of one desperado was being linked to the robbery. Almost immediately the name of Peter Curley, a former resident of Troy, was being bantered around as the leader of this daring robbery. Curley had recently moved to New York City but had had a long and nefarious life in Troy.

Peter Curley and his friend McCormack were considered notorious men capable of "working the 'big jobs' without detection." The two had become the local police scapegoats. In the late 1860s and early 1870s, these two were considered suspects in every major crime in the region. Curley was considered a suspect in the bank robberies a few years before in Glens Falls, North Adams, and Castleton, Vermont. Although his name was associated with these acts, Curley had never even been arrested for any of these crimes. There were parallels to the methods of these crimes and the one in Waterford. Curley was also accused in two robberies of silk at the Quackenbush Silks Factory in Troy. Curley was even picked up, but released prior to the filing of charges, in connection with the robbery of the Roy's Shawl Factory in Troy, where a gang used dynamite to blow open the safe. Despite his reputation, Curley had never been convicted of a felony.

Curley's confederate, McCormick, also found his name in the paper as a possible suspect. Unlike Curley, McCormick had been convicted in the shooting of John Casey in New York City. It was understood, by the police, that Curley led a gang but that the group was very loosely structured and the men never socialized with each other. The alleged members of the Curley gang were all formerly from Troy but now lived in different places coming together only to plan or commit a crime.

Everyone Wants 15 Minutes of Fame

Mrs. Dowd, of Waterford, was a regular customer of the Saratoga County Bank. The Friday before the robbery she had gone to the bank on personal business. When she went to the counter she noticed that two men were in the bank near the windows. The two were quietly carrying on a conversation. The nature of her transaction required that Mr. Van Hovenbergh open the vault. She told anyone who would listen that she remembered the men stopping their conversation and watching the cashier intently. Mrs. Dowd had not thought much of the incident at the time, but on reflection, she was sure the men were two of the robbers. She told the reporter from one of the Troy newspapers that she was sure she could identify the men if she were to see them again.

The Morgan House

The Morgan House, a tavern and hotel, was found in a brick building, that still stands today, kiddy corner across the street from the former Saratoga County Bank. On August 29, a foppish looking man, believed to be in his mid-twenties and weighing 180 pounds, registered as John Thompson of Syracuse. From the moment he took up quarters at the establishment, his presence was noticed. He spent the next day sitting on the stoop, watching the bank. A couple of times he left the stoop to go for a walk of an hour or so in duration. The owner of the tavern never detected the nature of his business. The second day after his arrival a medium-built man of 24 walked in front of the building and called Mr. Thompson from his post. The two talked for several minutes then Mr. Thompson went into the hotel and checked out paying his bill in full.

On Sunday evening, October 13th, at about 7 o'clock that evening, two men, in their mid-twenties, entered the Morgan House barroom. One of the men ordered a dozen clams and a glass of lemonade. The bartender noted in his mind the fact that the two only made one order. The two took the food and sat behind a screen, invisible to any person who might enter the bar. Around 8 o'clock, the two left in the rain. The truly unusual part was that despite the rain neither took a cab nor stage.

The Politicians

In 1872, as now, it was as important to local politicians, such as top police officers, to be seen in the place where the crime occurred, as it was to actually help. Detective Farley of the New York City Police Department went to Waterford in the company of Chief Maloy and Captain Johnson of Albany. These experts were quoted in the newspapers as adding that in their opinion the "job was well done." Since this crime, these quotes have been studied by the spin-doctors in each police force in this country. This type of unrevealing statement can be seen each night on the local news.

The Escape

It appears that in making their escape the robbers went in several directions. A local teamster, who was hitching his horse to begin drawing sand, remembered seeing a wagon loaded with men going toward Cohoes at about 4 o'clock in the morning. A second man said he saw men walking over the Troy Bridge at about the same time. Two other wagons were reported to have headed northwest toward Crescent. Other reports had up to six men escaping over the Railroad Bridge onto Peebles Island then onto Van Schaick Island.

One report of how the men got away was almost definitely true. The story begins on Friday afternoon, October 11th, 1872. A man and woman, "said to be his wife," checked into the Delavan House in Albany. The first clue of assumed guilt in the Victorian Era was the implication that the woman was not his wife - something just not done by "proper people." On Sunday afternoon, the man hired a livery from Thomas Wilson's stable in Albany. The horse and livery showed up around 7 o'clock in the morning, Monday October 14th, at the house of Mr. Hilton, a farmer living on the Troy Road about four miles from Schenectady. Mr. Hilton was working in his barn at the time he saw two men turn into his drive. The men stopped at the house and got out of the wagon. They yelled to Hilton to unharness the horse and let the poor animal rest. The two men then left afoot on the road to Schenectady. The men were never close enough to Mr. Hilton for him to positively identify them, but he did note that they were probably under 35 and one was rather shorter than the other. According to the farmer, the horse was completely "used up" and unable to go any further. It was later learned that an hour earlier the same two men had stopped at the farm of John Carpenter further out of Schenectady on the Troy Road. The two had pulled up to his barn and asked if they could leave the horse and might he give them a ride with his team into Schenectady? Mr. Carpenter told the men that he had not finished his chores nor had he had his breakfast, so he could not oblige their request. Mr. Carpenter reasoned that the horse was very sweaty and if they were to drive it into the city this early in the morning it would have attracted attention. Carpenter told reporters that if the two had been able to secure a ride with him they would only have been considered his friends and no unwanted attention would have followed.

Left Behind

When the story of the exhausted horse reached Cohoes, Mr. Boughton, the vice president of the bank and a detective, went to the Delavan House to investigate the man who engaged the poor animal. The man had disappeared leaving behind a silk hat, expensive overcoat, and a valise containing dirty shirts.

Supporters

Even without eyewitness news, CNN or radio, by Tuesday afternoon virtually everyone in the Capital District knew of the crime. Those who worked for a living and had no savings to put in a bank did not have the same feeling of remorse as those who had the potential for personal loss. In one local tavern in high-spirited Saratoga, a toast was made: "Well, the boys worked it well, and I hope that they get off with the swag; here's to them and may they never have worse luck."

The New York *World* took the high road in examining the crime. The newspaper, in what would really be considered an editorial and not a report on the investigation, questioned the wisdom of the owners of any commercial enterprise in placing an underpaid man (the bank cashier), who knew the combination to the safe, in the same building as the unguarded deposits. They suggested that a guard having either "four legs or two" would have better served the patrons of the bank.

Get Away, Capture, and Escape

It appears Curley and McCormick, if they were involved, deliberately decided the best course of action was not to hide, but rather to draw attention to themselves. This may have been in an effort to let the others transport the bounty to a safe place. Curley and McCormick hired a hack in Troy, which they took through Albany and then on to Castleton, New York. About a mile out of Castleton they asked the driver to let them out of the cab. The two then set off on foot for the train station in hopes of catching the next train south. Arriving at the station at 10:45 in the morning they asked Ira Van Hoesen, the stationmaster at Castleton, what time the next "down train" would arrive. They were told it would not be until 1:25 that afternoon. The two men then went outside to inquire as to where they could hire a team to take them to Stuyvesant, a train stop further south. The teamster they engaged went into the railroad station and talked to Van Hoesen, while they went to change some bills. It was later discovered that one of the men had gone into the bank and changed two twenties for smaller bills. The second stranger had gone into the store next to the bank where he also had success in changing two twenties. The two men paid the teamster the princely sum of $10 for a ride to Stuyvesant. The stationmaster at Castleton, who had not heard about the robbery in Waterford, told several people that were around the station that he believed the two to be thieves.

Right on schedule the early afternoon train from Albany arrived at Castleton carrying among its passengers the stationmaster's daughter. The daughter immediately told her father the exciting news of the Waterford bank robbery. Remembering the two men who tried to purchase tickets that morning, Van Hoesen stepped into his telegraph office and sent a message to have the men arrested when they arrived in Stuyvesant. Unfortunately, the telegraph connection was not good, so the message was not clear until after the men had left Stuyvesant on a train bound for Hudson.

At least one of the two men in question received special attention when he tried to pay for his 20-cent train-ride with a $20 bill. When the pair arrived at the Hudson Train Station there were officers of the law there to make the arrest.

Arrest

It is at this point that the case gets even more complex. There are two distinctly different stories as to what happened in Hudson. These accounts come from the two newspapers in Hudson. The first was from the *Star* and the second account is from the *Gazette*. In either case the outcome is the same.

According to the *Star*, the stationmaster at Hudson, James Bump, received a telegram informing him that two of the suspects in the Waterford bank robbery had boarded conductor Alexander Hughes's train bound for Poughkeepsie. The telegram advised that the suspects could be expected to arrive at Hudson at 2:50 that afternoon. When the train pulled in Stationmaster Bump asked Conductor Hughes if any men had gotten on together at Stuyvesant. It took Hughes a couple of seconds to recall the incident but then he remembered two men had gotten on but not together. One had paid and was seated without notice. The second man tried to pay his fair with a $20 bill. Hughes said he had no change so the man said it didn't matter he would borrow the twenty cents from his friend. It was at this time that Hughes realized the two men were together. It took the conductor and stationmaster a few minutes to determine who the two were. Bump and Hughes approached the men in the crowded depot. It appeared the suspects had noticed the railroad employees talking.

Like trapped animals the two men in question were backing slowly toward an exit. Before the pair in question was able to reach the door, Bump and Hughes placed them under arrest. Minutes later, William Best and Officer James Dyer arrived at the station. Bump and Hughes turned the suspects over to the officer and his associate. Interviewed later by reporters several spectators in the depot said they were sure the men were on their way to jail.

Escape

Instead of going directly to the City of Hudson's jail, Best and Dyer accepted an offer from their captives to stop at Marcus Curtis's saloon on the corner of Allen and South Front Street. Immediately after getting their drinks, the four entered one of the private rooms in the back, where they remained isolated for five minutes. When the peculiar group came out of the chamber they seemed to Curtis to be acting like old friends. They walked to the bar together and bought a second round of drinks, which they drank in the barroom. Curtis remembered Dyer saying he forgot his "darbies" (a slang reference to shackles) at home. In what the paper called a scandalous and preposterous transaction, Dyer left the two suspected bank robbers in the charge of a citizen, William Best, and went home to get his cuffs. Within seconds of Dyer's leaving, Best decided to take the two outside for an "airing." The two suspects and Best started walking up Allen Street. According to Best, the men pulled a pistol and threatened to shoot him if he were to pursue them. The two then took their leave running down the hill toward the Bay Road.

A second version of the story was told in the *Gazette*. This newspaper's account of the afternoon's events is different in several ways. According to the *Gazette* the Hudson Police had received a telegraph notifying them of the bank robbery. A short time later, Officer Dyer received a second telegram telling him of the two men's arrival at the station on the southbound train due in at 2:50 that afternoon. Not wanting to share any potential reward or credit with his cohorts, Dyer took it upon himself to go to the train station and seek an arrest. It was widely held that Dyer, although slight in body, was "immense in 'pluck.'" While walking to the station, Dyer happened upon William Best. Best was the brother of a fellow police officer. Dyer shared with Best his potential good fortune. Thinking some help, may be needed Dyer had Best join him. The two went together to the rail station to make the arrest. Dyer surveyed the people in the station and immediately surmised who, in the crowd, were the desperadoes. Dyer claimed to the reporter to have moved to confront the brawnier of the pair. According to the egomaniacal Dyer, the suspect could sense his authority and immediately chose to succumb. Dyer knew the situation was strained, as he did not have his shackles or a gun. In fact, he was armed only with the power of his office. Despite his limited resources, Dyer and Best took the men, at a walk, off to jail.

As they came upon the tavern at Allen and Second the burly prisoner suggested that they "take a drink." Dyer had a well-earned reputation of not slighting an offer of this nature. He, along with Best, accepted the magnanimous invitation of the men in their custody. The story of what happened after the group shared a couple of drinks in the bar differs between Best and Dyer. Dyer claims he told Best to wait in the saloon while he went home to get shackles. Best claims that he had not heard Dyer say to wait but rather that he should take the two off to jail. In either event, Dyer left the other three in the bar. Minutes later, Best departed Curtis's bar walking up the Allen Street Hill with the two prisoners. Best claimed to the *Gazette* reporter that near the corner of Third Street the two drew guns and threatened to "blow his brain out!" The last he saw of them they were either near the Catholic Church or running down the revine.

Rather than sound the alarm immediately, Best walked three blocks to the police court looking for assistance. By this time, court was closed so no assistance was available. Best, knowing he would have to do something, went into the street in front of the court and started telling his story to those on the street.

Help Was Available

It was understood that several workmen were in the vicinity of Third and Allen Streets. The assumption was that these workmen would have assisted, thus preventing the escape. In his own account Best admitted he did not ask for their aid when the escape occurred.

The next day Detective Squires of the Troy police and Cashier Van Hovenbergh took a train to Hudson. While they were in the city, Officer Dyer was arrested. He had in his possession $105 in cash and a revolver. It was determined that the bills Dyer had in his custody at the time of his arrest were not from the Waterford bank; however, Van Hovenbergh did identify the pistol as one of those used in the bank robbery. Dyer began his confession by admitting that the gun was taken from the men he had arrested the day before. In his confession, Dyer said another pistol had been given to his partner, Best. Based on Dyer's statement, Best was arrested. At the time of his arrest, Best had in his possession only five dollars but no gun.

Preliminary Hearing

The preliminary hearing in the escape case was quick. Judge Van Deusen heard the evidence presented by Van Hovenbergh, Frank Shaler, the bar boy at the saloon, Detective Charles Squires of Troy and three men from Hudson: stationmaster James Bump, Samuel Edwards, and Benjamin Edwards. Helping with the prosecution was I. C. Ormsby, the district attorney from Saratoga County. Ormsby volunteered, because he knew he would be involved again later in the trial of those arrested for the robbery. After hearing the testimony, Judge Van Deusen ruled that the two would be assigned bail. Dyer had to put up $1,000 and Best $500. Both were able to post bond and were released. Dyer was facing additional charges before the Common Council of Hudson for malpractice of office. In addition to charges in the escape of the two men the day before, Dyer was also accused of having taken a bribe from one Thomas Dyson on the eighth of October.

Since in all likelihood neither narrative is totally true or false, it is most important to note that two of the robbers were in all probability captured. They were, however, able to make their escape through the assistance of some "upstanding" residents of the city of Hudson.

Recovery and Arrest

After the escape in Hudson, the actions of those involved in resolving the crime were bifurcated. Police from the various jurisdictions including Troy, Hudson, Albany and New York City assembled to investigate the robbery. The police's efforts were directed to trying to determine: the perpetrators, the location of the money, stocks, and bonds, with sufficient proof to get a conviction in court. At the same time, the officers of the bank were consumed with trying to recover the plunder.

Following a Lead

The day after the robbery a broken wagon was found abandoned east of Ballston Spa. Ballston Spa, the county seat, was a train hub and natural place to use for an escape. The immediate assumption was that the broken wagon was used in the robbery. The police were using sound logic assuming that an overloaded wagon being driven fast over the muddy roads would have easily broken under the pressure. For several days, the detectives worked under the supposition that the two men who left for New York City were a planned distraction. Many of the detectives were convinced that some or all of the money had never left Saratoga County. The police kept the information about the wagon a secret for several days hoping it would lead to the recovery of the money.

It took a week to learn that the wagon had been rented in Saratoga by a couple who, for illicit reasons, did not want its identity or destination known. When the wagon broke they had unhitched the horse and walked it the seven miles back to a stable in Saratoga. The couple had chosen the proprietor of the livery because he was known for his discretion. To others in Saratoga, he was known for the lack of care for his processions. The livery owner, having his horse back, had taken his time claiming the broken wagon. This series of events, in no way directly related to the robbery, held up the investigation.

The Boxes are Found

A broken metal covered box was found in Albany in early November. A man passing the corner of Broadway and Westerlo Street found a metal covered walnut box. The lock had been smashed and the box damaged beyond repair. The man gave the box to a patrol officer who took it to the precinct house. The empty box was twelve inches long seven wide and four deep. Suspecting that the box was one of those taken from the vault in Waterford, that same night the box was taken to police headquarters where it was placed in the hands of the property clerk.

The next day Stewart and Pruyn, directors of the Waterford bank, along with C. A. Waldron, attorney for the bank, went to Albany where they identified the box as one of those taken in the robbery. At the time of the robbery, three identical boxes had been stolen. The box, found in Albany, had originally contained $34,000 in bonds belonging to a Mr. Mitchell.

Honest Citizens

Two days before the metal box was found, a canvas bag had been discovered in Albany under a stoop on Lodge Street. Like the box, an honest citizen had found it and turned it in to the police. It was soon learned that the bag was also from the robbery. When it was retrieved the bag still contained 20 gold rings that had been in the owner's family from the period of the Revolution.

The same day the canvas bag was found in Albany, the post office delivered to the Saratoga County Bank a land warrant and other documents taken in the robbery. The envelope that the documents arrived in was postmarked from Albany. The envelope provided no additional clues as to the perpetrators.

The Amount of the Take Grows

Since so much of the plunder was from safe deposit boxes, it was difficult to determine the exact amount of the loss. By November 14th the total take was believed to be around $440,000. Even though a month had passed, people were still coming forward asserting loses. N. V. Fort of Clifton Park was the most recent claimant, asserting that he had lost $8,000 in government bonds.

The depositors, who had been robbed, expressed both hope and exasperation. The relief was based on the fact that the serial numbers on the bonds had been widely circulated, restricting the ability of those who held them to sell their booty. Most of those who had lost stocks or bonds had already requested duplicate bonds be issued. The frustration was with the level of loss for the bank. In Waterford, there was a constant discussion as to why that week alone the bank had quietly deposited over $50,000 of its own money in other banks. There was an underlying feeling the directors knew something about exposure to theft that they had not shared with the depositors.

Slowly it was coming out that some of the claims made by depositors had been exaggerated. In many cases people were embarrassed when they found their names in an article in the newspaper stating the amount of the loss and what had been previously reported.

The Escape Vehicle

During third week in November, the police and the bank officers were perplexed by their inability to determine the ownership of the hack that had taken the two men from Troy to Castleton early in the morning of the robbery. It was well established that a hack had waited most of the night in Waterford in the vicinity of the bank. As an incentive the bank offered a reward of $1,800 for positive information as to the ownership of the hack and the men it took to Castleton. The bank offered a lesser reward of $300 for positive information as to the identity of any person in the hack.

A Near Clue

As Thanksgiving approached, the search for either the booty or the perpetrators was progressing at a snail's pace. One reporter, searching for something to report, stumbled onto an interesting coincident. In 1870, the Williams' Jewelry Store in Albany was robbed in what was one of the biggest robberies in the area prior to the Saratoga County Bank. Like almost every significant theft in the Capital District, the jewelry heist had been linked to Peter Curley and James Monkeetrick. On the evening of October 14th, the same night that the two men escaped in Hudson, a Troy detective saw Mrs. Monkeetrick, James's wife, getting off a north bound express train in Troy. The train in question had come from Hudson. The detective went to the precinct and met with Chief English who agreed the woman should be questioned. The next morning the two police officers went to the place she had stayed the night. Mrs. Monkeetrick told the officers she had returned from New York City where she had been with her husband and her mother. The officers did not trust her story and asked about any cash she might have on her person. She told them $110 but in searching her bags they found $160 and 10 gold coins. She was placed under surveillance while a messenger was sent for officers of the bank. The bank sent Van Hovenbergh and a clerk to see if the money she was carrying belonged to the bank. After a careful examination, the men were certain that the money belonged to the bank; however, there were no marks on the money so it had to be returned to Mrs. Monkeetrick. Reluctantly, she was released with all the money.

The real discovery was that the woman's husband, James Monkeetrick, was the cousin of William Best one of the men who had permitted the escape in Hudson. In fact, it was claimed that prior to the robbery, Monkeetrick had relocated to Hudson with his wife and mother.

Trying for a Return of the Money

As November ended, it was determined that the amount taken exceeded $500,000. To make the situation more untenable, the people who had suffered the greatest actual loss were the working class. In an effort to make the crime seem even more heinous and perhaps to stimulate empathy for those who had experienced the real fiscal loss, the newspapers were characterizing them as women and older people who "have no energy or ability to regain their loses." It should be noted that the robbery was only eight years after the Civil War and there were many war widows in the Waterford region.

William Augustus Beach

W. A. Beach, an attorney who had been born and brought up in the Capital District, was now practicing law in New York City. Born in Ballston Spa, Beach practiced law there for several years. In time the demand for his top quality services expanded beyond the limits of a mere county seat, so Beach moved his practice to metropolitan Troy where he became the mayor. Ultimately, Troy proved too small for a man of his stature and Beach moved once more, this time to New York City.

Beach, a true legal celebrity in his day, notified the newspapers and District Attorney Ormsby that they could telegraph him at any time and within a matter of two days he would have Peter Curley appear in Saratoga Court for questioning. This offer plagued the police who had claimed that Curley could not be found. District Attorney Ormsby was too wise to yield to this bait. Ormsby knew that, although suspicion and speculation were waist deep, there was not sufficient evidence linking Curley to the robbery. If Curley was brought back without proof he would be released and charges at a later date would be more difficult to present. Despite the public outcry for Curley to be placed on the stand, the district attorney allowed him to remain at large.

Negotiations

Quietly, the bank officers had begun negotiations with an unnamed attorney in New York City who claimed to have contact with a man who was an agent capable of having the bonds returned. The attorney's offer was especially appealing to the bank, because the officers were constantly being second-guessed by their neighbors as to their motives and effort.

Having received some assurance that the bonds might be ransomed for a percent on the dollar, the bank's officers called a meeting of those who had lost bonds in the robbery. If the decorum of this meeting of the victims had been improved 200% it would have been considered an impossible situation. Most members wanted to hold out for the return of the bonds without any payment. Others felt that a premium of five, ten or even 15% would be acceptable. These depositors felt that having a portion of something was better than one hundred percent of nothing. There was only one opinion constantly put forward that everyone agreed upon. They all understood that once the bonds were returned the chances of actually being able to prosecute the criminals would decline considerably. Ultimately, the bank's officers Dr. Boughton, James Enos and John House were selected to go to New York and see just what would be the best possible terms that could be reached with the "bond custodians."

An Unreasonable Offer

The meeting of the committee (from the bank) and the custodians of the bonds was a journey into the bizarre. It began with the exchange of the polite greetings and the usual compliments required in Victorian Society. The persons who were robbed treated the men who claimed to have possession of the bonds as gentlemen and equals. During the negotiations, the bank's committee suggested that it might be possible to pay the "custodians" as if they were trustees of the bonds. This would mean they would pay six percent on the dollar. The custodians felt that their efforts were worth more than the law allowed. During the time they had held the bonds a premium had become due of 10 to 14%. Being of good faith, however, the custodians felt that they could consider accepting a mere 90% for their services. Since interest of 10% or more was already due on the bonds this would mean that the original owners would be out only 80%. The members of the bank's committee seemed outraged at the gall of the custodians. The custodians tried unsuccessfully to convince the representatives of the bank that at 90% they were very liberal in their financial request.

Assurances

The bank's committee then changed the direction of the meeting. They also needed assurance that the custodians were in fact capable of returning the bonds. To prove they had "struck oil," the custodians suggested that the members select the serial number from one of the bonds or the exact denomination from a stock and they would secure it within minutes. The serial number of a $500 dollar bond was picked and one of the custodians left the room disappearing into the busy streets of Manhattan. Twenty minutes later the agent returned with the bond. The meeting ended with the members of the committee telling the custodians that they would return to Waterford with the terms and try to get clear directions as to the acceptable limits for payment. The bond returned for free belonged to David Brewster.

A Previous Meeting

It was later learned that this was actually the second meeting held with the agents holding the bonds. In the first meeting, a single bank officer had gone to New York. In the same attorney's, office the officer had asked proof of the agent's ability to return the bonds. As in the second meeting this officer was asked to give a number so that he could be provided with the designated bond. In this case, it turns out, the bond chosen was not at random but rather one belonging to his own daughter. The officer had taken care of his family and missed the opportunity to help one of the poor widows.

When the three agents who attended the second meeting returned to Waterford, the rumor mill was working on overtime. The entire village was alive with tales of what had happened in the big city. Among the stories being promogated was one that said the bonds were being returned with no premium being paid. Among the victims there was a human desire that the tales were true. Optimism prevailed with those affected. So ready to believe the rumors, one man, who had offered 10% for his bonds, withdrew his offer.

Meeting of Depositors

To curtail the rumors, a second meeting of the depositors impacted by the robbery was convened. The crowd was anxious and spiteful as they awaited the report of the committee. Some of those gathered so believed the rumors to be true that they arrived at the meeting with secure boxes in which they planned to place their returned bonds. Others, few in number, were actually patiently awaiting the committee's report. Before the meeting began one elderly lady said she couldn't wait and wanted her bonds right away. A fellow in the audience tried to calm her by calling out, "don't be impatient; trust in the Lord."

She responded, " I trusted in the Lord and the Saratoga Bank long enough now I'd rather have the bonds in my own hands."

In due course, the three members of the committee took their seats in the front of the bustling room. Dr. Boughton seemed sorrowful as he told those gathered that the custodians would only give the bonds back if a 90% trustee's fee was paid. The report fell like a wet blanket upon those gathered in the packed room. Slowly those in the room regained their breath. Some wanted to have their names taken off the contract they had signed at the previous meeting. Other disenfranchised individuals said that they were going to file a civil suit against the bank. The nature of the civil suit was twofold. Apparently, Ann Driscoll had been hired only days before the robbery and the required comprehensive background check had not been completed. Additionally, it had been learned that the bank had $150,000 deposited in other banks implying the officers knew their own security was lacking. This argument was arrested when one of those present with a calm head said, "Would you have considered it better if the $150,000 was in the vault the, night of the robbery?" The implication was clear. The community would have been out that money also.

As time went on the mood in the room seemed to quiet to a tolerable murmur. One person from the audience suggested that an offer of 90% showed that the custodians were gentlemen and hopefully not trying to overburden them with an oppressive settlement. Based on the opening from the man in the audience, the meeting ended on the premise that this was only the first offer from the gentlemen thieves and that the committee should be allowed to return to New York to see if better terms might be arranged.

The Troy *Times* reported that the temperament in the room was anything but "turn the other cheek." In fact, it was the reporter's belief that if Curley and his band had been in the room the ladies in attendance would have swallowed them whole, in less than five minutes. There would not have been enough left of the band "to wad a gun."

Along with the charges and threats against Curley and his band there was a second set circulating against the officers of the bank. Murmurs were heard throughout the room that the whole thing "looked queer." Many felt the officers of the bank were in some way profiting from the purposed transactions.

Exactly how the meeting ended was unclear. The Troy newspapers stated that the meeting ended with the majority passing a resolution that the committee be charged with going back and getting the best terms possible from the "gentlemen robbers." The Saratoga paper said that the meeting ended with those present rejecting the terms offered. The fact is that it is doubtful that in the mass confusion even those present would have agreed as to the outcome of the deliberations.

The meeting had allowed the spiteful side in those who had suffered financial losses to be expressed. Many in the audience were vocal in their feelings that cashier Van Hovenbergh had not adequately resisted. The Troy *Times* felt it was time to set the record straight. Their reporter closed the article which was a factual report of the meeting with a editorial expressing their belief that Van Hovenbergh had done all that could be expected of a reasonable man. They pointed out that Van Hovenbergh's family was bound and held by men with guns. The newspaper even went so far as to almost place the blame on the safe deposit holders. Near the close, the article said, "cast no bitter reflections upon him because he would not make all that sacrifice (death or loss of family) for people who had, at their own risk, imposed upon the kindness of the bank by taking the liberty to use, free of rent, a large part of the bank safe…to accommodate the bond owners." The article concluded with total support for the Van Hovenbergh family.

A Break in the Case

The first real break in the case came in mid-December. William C. Brandon, a man with a history of questionable business practices, maintained a loan office at 700 Broadway in New York City. The first week in December, Brandon had sold two bonds taken from the Waterford Bank to Shipsey & Mathews, a brokerage firm on Bowery Street, Manhattan. Brandon had redeemed these bonds at their full value. Two weeks later Brandon returned with two more bonds with a face value of $500 each. With interest the bonds actually carried a slightly higher value. The broker Shipsey purchased the bonds giving Brandon a check drawn on a local bank. After Mr. Brandon left with the check in hand, the clerk noticed that the numbers on the bonds appeared to have been altered. The broker immediately sent a messenger to the bank on which the check was drawn to stop payment. The messenger was well known by the bank manager, so he was given immediate access, even as Brandon waited in line for payment. When Brandon finally reached a teller, he was informed that the bank refused to honor the check stating that payment had been stopped.

Unable to receive his money, Brandon immediately went back to Shipsey's office to find out the nature of the problem. The clerk at Shipsey's told Brandon of his discovery relating to the serial numbers. It was the broker's belief that the true owners of the bonds resided in Waterford. Brandon offered to give back the check if they would give him back the bonds. The clerk refused and Brandon left the broker's office with the worthless check in hand.

Brandon Arrested

Simultaneously to sending the messenger, Shipsey's office telegraphed the New York City Police and the officers from the Saratoga County Bank. Later that evening, after what the officers claimed was a tedious search of the neighborhood, two detectives arrested Brandon. Unfortunately for the depositors in Waterford, during a search of Brandon's office, the detectives were unable to locate any more of the bonds.

By December 16, 1872, William Brandon was a resident of the Saratoga County Jail in Ballston Spa. Brandon's temporary home was a plain cell typical of the day. The furnishings included one window, two wooden chairs, some mattresses piled up to make a bed and a wood stove for heat. Since a preliminary examination had not occurred Brandon was not allowed visitors. Luckily for history, one reporter figured a way around the no visitors provision. Instead of asking for a private interview he suggested the jailer be present during the discussions. Whether out of vanity at the chance to have his name in the paper or the opportunity to solicit additional information from Brandon, Fred Powell, the jailer, permitted an interview.

Brandon Interviewed

Brandon was used to living on the edge making spontaneous decisions that could affect his life. Naturally enough his wit and demeanor proved to be the match of any reporter. Brandon admitted freely that he had taken bearer bonds for redemption. He went on to remind the reporter that the bonds could have been legally cashed by anyone. Brandon then asked why the reporter was given access to him after he had been told that he would not be allowed to see his own brother. Jailer Powell explained the interpretation of the rule of a private interview verses having a guard present. After Brandon was assured his brother would also be allowed to visit under the same terms the interview continued.

The interview added only a few facts to what was known. Brandon told the reporter that after he left Shipsey's office he went to visit his attorney. Brandon wanted the attorney to compel Shipsey to either return the bonds or make good on the check. According to Brandon's story when he returned to his own offices on Broadway, two officers were waiting to arrest him. This version is different from earlier reports that said a "tedious search" was required. Brandon went on to say he was a married man with one child.

Brandon went on to describe his train ride up from New York. According to him, Dr. Boughton, an officer of the bank, had taken the opportunity to tell almost everyone on the train Brandon's identity. The attention received was so constant that Brandon felt eyes were on him the entire trip. Brandon's physical appearance would have caused many to suspect he was a successful businessman. He was in his early thirties with light brown hair, a slight build, a long flowing mustache, and short beard. Brandon dressed in the style of the day. His appearance gave no indication that he was the caricature of a robber.

Brandon told the reporter he was also unsure of his personal safety were he to be taken to Waterford during daylight hours. Saratoga County District Attorney Ormsby resided in Waterford where he also maintained an office for his private legal practice. When Brandon had been brought in to Waterford at 10 o'clock the previous evening the building that housed Ormsby's office was in turmoil. Brandon described the scene as in so much pandemonium one would have thought they had "an elephant or a murderer."

Taking Care of Our Own

It was at this time in the interview that a negative situation was learned. It was determined that it was Dr. Boughton, the officer of the bank, who had attended the first meeting with the attorney representing the bonds' custodians. Dr. Boughton had acted in his own best interest buying back from the agent (at 10%) $5,000 worth of bonds belonging to his own daughter.

Trading Bonds

Brandon showed his knowledge of the brokerage business as he went on to explain the difference between bearer bonds and registered bonds. In Brandon's mind, bearer bonds were no different than cash. Brandon told the reporter that he could not remember from whom the two bonds in question had been purchased.

The focus of the questions then went to whether Brandon had knowledge that the bonds had been stolen. Brandon said that he never saw a list of serial numbers on the bonds supposedly stolen from the Saratoga County Bank. Asked if he could identify the bonds that he had possessed that were missing from Waterford, Brandon answered in a callous but probably honest way. He merely responded that he could not tell one bond from another. Brandon then tried to redirect the inquiry to the accuracy and intent of his accuser. He noted that Shipsey had a list of the stolen bonds, yet still purchased some from him - not noticing they were among those listed until after the purchase.

Hearing

When asked if he was ready for examination the next day regarding the bonds, Brandon responded he was definitely not ready. Brandon told the reporter that the bank's officer, Boughton, and the police had taken him from New York City "hurriedly". According to Brandon, they had left the cashier (Van Hovenbergh) in the City to try to get Shipsey to come for the examination. Brandon had been told that Shipsey could not come until Sunday night. Brandon's first reaction was if they could wait for Shipsey, why couldn't they have waited until Sunday to bring him north? Brandon also remarked more generally about Shipsey's trip which would be paid for by the people of the county, "I do not see what they need him for."

Brandon's Rumor

From the first word of Brandon's arrest there was a question as to whether the numbers on the bonds had been altered. Brandon insisted that the numbers on the bonds he redeemed were not modified in any way. He suspected this report was just "newspaper rumor gotten up for excitement." Brandon went on to say, "If I had known the bonds were stolen it does not seem likely that I would go right in daylight to sell them? Would I give my own name? Is it likely that I would have the check drawn for me personally when every one with whom I was dealing knew me?"

Waterford

When Brandon first arrived in Waterford the night before this interview he was taken to a local hotel named the Howard House. While he was at the hotel awaiting his examination by Ormsby, Brandon had written some letters to friends and counsel. He told the reporter that he expected at that time that he would have had his examination the next day (the day the interview was occurring). Brandon pointed out that the hearing was postponed because of the excitement and threats by the people of Waterford. Apparently, many in the village were calling for him to be buried right there (the threat being a lynching).

With the threat of death hanging over his head, Brandon was naturally asked if he had asked for his examination to be held someplace outside of Waterford. He told the reporter that was just newspaper talk. In fact while he was in Waterford he had been treated "very gentlemanly."

The interview then turned to Brandon's involvement with the commission of the robbery. Brandon assured the reporter that if necessary he could prove he was in New York City on the night of the robbery. When asked, Brandon denied any knowledge of a man named Peter Curley.

The reporter noted Brandon was wearing a Masonic pin upon his vest. Brandon acknowledged he was a Mason and that many of the people he had met with so far were also members of the fraternal order including his accuser Dr. Boughton.

William Brandon

When the interview ended Brandon showed his gentlemanly traits, extending his hand to the reporter and thanking him for the few pleasant moments. The reporter was taken by Brandon's intelligence and language. It was also noted that Brandon frequently called local communities by the wrong name and had no knowledge about the distances between places. The combination of intelligence and a lack of familiarity with the local area were implied as signs that Brandon was not involved in the robbery.

In reality, Brandon was the quintessential rogue. Born in Ireland, Brandon's family came to this country, along with thousands of others, during the potato famine. His family settled in the Hudson Valley in the small community of Salisbury Mills, nine miles from Newburgh, New York. At the time of his arrest, Brandon had one sister and three brothers. One of his brothers was living in Albany.

By the age of 15 William Brandon was already in trouble with the local police.

To avoid further problems he went to New York City seeking a trade. His natural good looks, ambition, and keen mind facilitated his place as a broker. There were few regulations regarding traders at the time and Brandon did nothing to enhance people's view of this often less than reputable profession. Among those who wanted to know, Brandon had a reputation as a fence disposing of bounty collected by others.

Brandon's parents died about three years before his arrest. In the intervening years, he had moved his wife and child from New York City to the family farm. His place in the country gave none of the appearance that he projected as a person. He had a hired man and a fine stable of horses but the house was minus any amenities. After his arrest the Newburgh newspaper said that there were rumors that Brandon had been using the old farm as a safe station for his plunder. This rumor was supported by the number of trunks that had been shipped to and from the farm. To avoid watchful eyes, the ever cleaver Brandon had used several different train stations in the area as shipping points. The various baggage masters told the reporter that the trunks were always heavy.

Con Man

Brandon's reputation was that of the ultimate con man. He was considered the "most daring and artistic in the profession." In an article in the New York *Galaxy* the author called Brandon "an artist in evil." Brandon would take property stolen from both sides of the law. He had once accepted a taro check and another time gambling implements stolen from those with business practices outside that allowed by the law. Literally he was dealing with thieves who stole from other criminals. Although arrested on several occasions including once for possession of a stolen diamond and a second time for having $3,000 in stolen goods, Brandon had never been convicted of any felony.

Although considered to be a con man surviving on his wit, Brandon's crimes were not all without violence. Unsatisfied with a worker's attitude, Brandon was arrested for the beating of an old man who had been doing work for him in his office.

Primarily, Brandon's source of income was the fact he was a broker par excellence. Bold as a lion, brassy as the cock of the yard, Brandon made no secret of his business dealings regarding the Waterford bonds. In point of fact he admitted the sale and said it was well within his legal right to trade in bearer bonds.

Brandon Gets a Hearing

On Monday morning, the first train from Ballston Spa brought Brandon to Waterford for his examination. A large crowd had gathered at the station and along the three-block route Brandon would follow to get to the Howard House. It was in the Howard House ballroom that he was to be examined by District Attorney Ormsby. The anxious throng on the street wanted little more than to get a glance of the notorious agent who was arrested for making money off the hard-earned savings of the local community. On the walk from the station to Howard House, Brandon walked between two officers, never looking to his side. The group of three proceeded to the post office where Brandon mailed some letters. Under guard he stopped at a store to purchase some new linens for his cell.

By eleven in the morning, a large crowd had gathered in the hall at the Howard House to watch the examination. This was to be the match of the local favorite, Ormsby against the upstart, Brandon. Ormsby read the charge then turned to Brandon telling him in simple language he was charged with larceny. "Are you ready for an examination?"

"I am not. I have had no chance to communicate with my counsel or anyone since my arrest," was the calm reply of the prisoner. He went on to explain that while in the Ballston jail he had asked the jailer if he could see friends. Brandon had been told that a dispatch had been sent from Ormsby stating that no one could visit.

"That would not prevent you from seeing counsel."

"I understood that it did."

Brandon went on to admit he did not telegraph for an attorney, but rather had sent a letter on Saturday. Ormsby agreed to postpone the examination until three that afternoon so that defense counsel could be present. Brandon composed a telegram to be sent to his lawyer and the court recessed until mid-afternoon.

Not surprising Brandon's counsel never arrived from New York City that day. After some serious deliberations, the examination was postponed until the next morning.

The examination was now causing problems. Brandon's attorney had sent a telegraph stating that because of illness he could not leave until the 2 o'clock train. Brandon refused to give his consent for the people to go on with the case before he had the benefit of counsel. Ormsby tried to impress upon the justice that in the note from Brandon's attorney it was not even clear who was sick. Ormsby attempted to influence Justice Shepard with the cost of the hearing on the citizens of Saratoga County. The People had been compelled to bring brokers in from New York City who needed to return to their businesses. Brandon countered Ormsby's cost claim noting that if they let the people from Shipsey testify before his attorneys arrived, by the time they got to the city there would probably be a subpoena from his attorney waiting, requiring they return to Waterford anyway. The judge finally decided Shipsey could testify.

Shipsey

Shipsey testified to the sequence of events connected with his purchase of the stolen bonds from Brandon. Shipsey acknowledged he purchased the bonds with a check drawn on a local bank. After Brandon left his office, he noticed the numbers matched the list of bonds stolen from Waterford. Realizing the oversight Shipsey had immediately stopped payment on the check. Shipsey went on to testify as to Brandon's bold behavior when he returned to his office after learning the check could not be cashed. (At this point Brandon received a telegraph from his counsel stating he could not leave until 4 o'clock). Shipsey testified to going to Brandon's office with the police to arrest Brandon. It is uncertain why Shipsey stayed so involved, although it may have been to help the police identify Brandon. Shipsey even walked with the police and Brandon to the courthouse that same night as Brandon was arraigned.

The evening of the hearing, Brandon was returned to Ballston Spa where his wife and brother attempted to visit him. The two were denied permission to see him alone. They were told this restriction would stay in effect until he had been arraigned. A milestone that would take some time to be reached.

Everyone Wants a Piece of the Action

There were those throughout the country who wanted to make money off this crime. At the time of Brandon's hearing it came out that a letter had been received by the chief of the Albany police from a man in Illinois with an offer to solve the case. The letter is as it appeared in the paper:

> Sir,-If you send me a good man here immediately, that will work square, "up and up," give me an even whack, or a one-third stand in, yourself getting your part, I will

go with your man and inside of ten days show up the Waterford Bank mob, and turn up all the bonds and money, excepting about $16,000, on conditions which I will explain to your man when he comes. The mob has not been square with me, and I mean business. Keep this mum and come to me by first train; stop at this hotel, register A. J. Baker and I will see you; make no inquiries of me. On receipt of this letter if you accept of these terms, answer by telegraph as follows; "All is well; will be there by first train," stating train and time you will arrive. Etc. signed A. J. Baker. Pay charges on telegram, for I am not fixed, but know the whole business above referred to and where the bonds and money is; one in the mob is my pal.

Trust this to no living man except the one you send, and one man is enough. Come fixed and prepared for a mob of eight. Answer immediately,

Robt. Demay

Brandon's Lawyer Feels the Heat

That same day, Edward McKinley, the New York City attorney for William Brandon, learned of the depth of local animosity toward anyone involved with the Waterford heist. He also got a taste of justice served Saratoga County style. McKinley served a writ upon District Attorney Ormsby requiring that he show cause for the detention of Brandon, or at the very least that the bail be reduced from the required $50,000. To the city attorney the issue was simple. There was not sufficient evidence shown to hold Brandon. On January 4, 1873, the case involving the writ was heard by Judge Bockes. Not only did McKinley fail to get Brandon released on bail, McKinley was personally brought deeper into the case when he was served with a court order demanding that he provide any information as to the whereabouts of the check issued to Brandon by Shipsey for the stolen bonds.

A Lover of Justice

In early January, the news about the robbery took a twist with further allegations of incompetence arising against the bank's officers. The source of the public concern was a letter that appeared in the Troy *Times* signed "A Lover of Justice." The author accused the bank of wrongdoing perhaps even gross misconduct. The letter relayed facts involved in the finding of six thousand dollars in government bonds in the vault over a month after the robbery. The implications were clear. The bank had not adequately checked for what was missing at the time of the robbery, so other bonds and money that were reported stolen may not have been – at least not in the robbery. The "Lover of Justice" implied that the officers might have helped themselves to some of the assets the robbers missed.

Like all lore attributed to this case, the "Lover of Justice" story had some merit. The basis of the concern was the bonds of John Conaughty. Before he moved west (Buffalo), Conaughty had personally deposited the bonds on a shelf in the vault area. He had wrapped the bonds in old newspaper and placed them on a shelf in the vault area, not in the safe itself. Conaughty's brother, Hugh, still resided on a farm in Clifton Park. As was the custom of the day, Hugh, in trying to tell his brother of the news in the area, mailed John a copy of a newspaper article related to the crime. At the time he wrote the letter, Hugh had no idea that there was any family money in the bank. When he got his brother's letter, John wired Hugh instructions as to where he had place the bonds. Over time, John Conaughty's bonds had been covered by other pieces of old paper. On November 24th, Hugh went to the bank and looked for his brother's bonds.

They were not found. Some time later, Mr. Emrigh one of the bank's tellers, in searching for some waste paper to start a fire, stumbled onto Conaughty's bonds. At the same time, Emrigh founds bonds belonging to the Masonic Order of Waterford. Emrigh stuck both sets of bonds in a small cubby in the vault area, again not in the safe. When a teller finally found the bonds, Hugh Conaughty was immediately notified of the discovery. Not surprisingly, Hugh came to the bank and took possession on behalf of his brother.

The point of the Lover of Justice letter was that prudence dictated that a thorough search of the bank was required immediately after the robbery. By not making a complete search who knew what other missing assets were in fact missing but perhaps not as a result of the robbery. The editor of the Troy *Times* felt the accusations of the letter against the bank's officers were not warranted.

Brandon's Hearing Resumes

It was January 14, 1873, before Brandon's examination resumed. The first person called was the bank's cashier, David Van Hovenbergh. For the first time publicly, David testified to the events of the night of the burglary. The most important thing he added to what was already known was when he said that (because of the masks they had worn) he could not positively identify any of the men who had held him that night.

The real twist in this day's testimony came in the cross-examination of the bond broker, Shipsey. It appears that Shipsey did not follow the time line he reported in his direct testimony given a month before. Shipsey did not simply leave his office after Brandon came back for his bonds or the money to go to the police station. Instead, Shipsey went with Brandon to the entrance of a hotel in the neighborhood of Brandon's office. Shipsey waited by the hotel as Brandon went on to his office building alone. Minutes later the police arrested Brandon outside his office. The police said they had been notified that Brandon would be coming. Was it Shipsey who told them where to find Brandon?

One can only imagine Shipsey's feelings when he had to admit he was carrying the bonds in a folder as he walked along with Brandon. Having learned through the order against McKinley, the effect of having a "big city attorney" for representation, Henry Smith of Albany was now Brandon's lead defense attorney at the hearing. He relished making Shipsey divulge that he had told Brandon he could have the bonds back in exchange for the check. Shipsey said his real reason for having the bonds with him that evening was to give them to his partner for safekeeping. Under cross-examination, Shipsey was obliged to acknowledge he had a safe in his office. Shipsey then said he was giving them to his partner because his partner would give up his life before the bonds. Smith closed this part of the discussion with a rhetorical sarcastic question, "Then you would rather have his life taken than yours?"

Saving the Citizen's Money

As the defense closed its examination, Shipsey assured all those who attended the session that he was certain that Brandon was not one of the burglars. Brandon's New York City attorney, McKinley, was also present and said if forced to go to trial his client would be exonerated. McKinley also said that in the event Brandon were to be held overnight he would rather stay at the Howard House at his own expense than to stay in the jail at a cost to the taxpayers.

At first the court adjourned until Friday morning then, as if correcting an oversight, came back in session to hear the testimony of the arresting police officer, Wooldridge. He testified that at the time of the arrest he had searched Brandon's office looking for more bonds. He admitted that he had seen numerous watches but could not say how many as he was only looking for government bonds. The watches implied that there might have been other booty present that was not related to the Waterford robbery.

The Problems with Brokers

Trying to locate the missing bonds was causing a major stir in the financial community. Brokers complained about the additional cost associated with employing people to check the numbers on all bonds against a list of stolen bonds before they could be redeemed.

In January, it was learned that $18,000 worth of bearer bonds had been cashed back in mid-October. These bonds had been cashed almost immediately after the robbery. It was noted that $3,500 worth of these bonds had passed through three brokerage houses before being detected by the treasury department of Jay Cooke & Co. Naturally, the local newspapers were supporting its constituents, calling for the brokers to stop complaining about the cost, which if not incurred would serve as a shield to the criminals. The local patrons and the Troy *Times* called on the brokers to remain diligent in detecting those who had committed the crime.

By the last week in January, formal charges were finally filed against Brandon. The charge, when it finally came, was not for trying to sell the stolen bonds, but for being part of the robbery of the Saratoga County Bank in Waterford. Brandon pleaded not guilty to the charges and was held for trial.

On February 5, 1873, William Brandon was charged a second time - this time in connection with trying to sell the bonds.

Curley's Arrest

On Thursday night, January 30th, detectives from Troy secretly boarded a train bound for New York City. Their purpose was to arrest Peter Curley. Early Friday morning the detectives met Curley on the street and promptly took him into custody. Since the Troy officers were out of their jurisdiction, Curley was taken to New York City police headquarters. Superintendent Kelso listened to what each side had to say regarding the robbery. Hearing the evidence, which was all circumstantial, Kelso favored Curley's side in the case. Fortunately, it was not up to Kelso to make the final decision, but rather a judge who accepted the warrant issued in Troy and allowed the detectives to take Curley out of the city.

There were allegations in the Troy newspapers that some effort had been made to release Curley while in New York City. The exact quote was "Before leaving the city the officers had considerable difficulty as efforts were made to release Curley, but which proved unsuccessful." This is one of the few times the newspaper played down a story relating to the robbery.

The coverage of the Troy *Times* was, at the very least, colorful. At a time when there was no fear of liability for slander or misrepresentation newspapers, as a group, took editorial license. Even in this bountiful atmosphere the *Times* stood out. It often put more assertion in a story then fact.

The *Times* carried a detailed description of the events involved in the arrest of Peter Curley. Even in trying to screen the information some fiction may have slipped through. It should be noted that the reporter did not accompany the police to New York City and Peter Curley never provided a statement. What was reported in the newspaper article was from the perspective of the police officers involved in the arrest. To provide the reader with a true feeling of the text several quotes are included.

Curley's Arrest Version II

It was on Thursday night, January 29th, that three Troy detectives Squire,

Markham and Murphy left for New York with a warrant for the arrest of two suspects. The warrants were listed in the newspaper with the fictional names "John Doe" and "Richard Doe." Upon arrival in the City, the detectives checked into the Occidental Hotel on the corner of Broome and The Bowery. It was widely suspected that the real names on the warrants were Peter Curley and a man who went by the handle "Omaha Dick," or "Omaha Bill."

Friday was spent in a fruitless search for the individuals in the neighborhoods they were known to frequent. While in the vicinity the detectives asked numerous persons if they knew the whereabouts of the two men. "Their usual haunts did not behold the light of their countenances, and their usual cronies knew nothing of their movements." The fact that the detectives were less than clandestine may very well have backfired a day later. On Saturday morning, the detectives chose to contact Superintendent McKenna of the Troy Police Department and ask that he and John Enos, the bank director, join them. The three detectives already in the City changed their tactics and began to watch one house on Broadway near Eighth Street.

In the early afternoon, the detectives were sitting in a watering hole when they spotted Big Mike Murray driving a carriage up Broadway in the direction of Central Park. Big Mike was known to be a friend of Curley's. Big Mike was known for running a keno game in New York. Big Mike was reported to be worth over half a million dollars. With no better leads to follow, the detectives decided to pursue the carriage in the hopes that Big Mike was going to meet Curley. As they were gathering the few things they were going to take with them, one of the detectives noticed Peter Curley passing the Broadway Theater. Since they were already getting ready to follow Murray, it only took the officers seconds to be on the street. In minutes, a surprised Curley was the prisoner of the Troy police. Curley calmly and in total control asked permission "to enter a fancy goods store to procure some new shirts." It is not clear if this part of the story was included to show how at ease Curley was, or that he might have had a plan to escape, or that he anticipated a lengthy stay and knew he would need clothes. In any event, the detectives turned down his request.

Prisoner in hand the detectives signaled for a hack to take them to police headquarters. When a hack stopped Curley refused to enter. At this point, a large throng started to gather around the four men. In the 1870s there were several notorious gangs in New York, each having a better name than the other. According to the Troy police, among the crowd that was gathering were several members of the "swell mob." Noticing the crowd forming, a New York City police officer went straight to the Troy officers. The City police officer suggested they come with him to the Mulberry Street Station. Fearing that if they did not accompany the officer the crowd might rescue Curley, the detectives accepted the young officer's invitation.

Police Headquarters

By the time they arrived on Mulberry Street, a crowd had gathered at the stairs leading to the door to the police station. This crowd may very well have been the result of the Troy police asking Curley's whereabouts the previous day. Curley, after all, was a popular local personality. In any event, Curley, without prompting, motioned to the crowd to stand back and let them pass. Like Moses at the Red Sea the mob split and Curley led the small band through the potential attackers. The *Times* showed their contempt for the New York City police saying, "It may be remarked that the men who intended to rescue Curley gathered at the spot where they had the most chances of success." (Police headquarters?)

The Troy police were less than enthusiastically greeted when they met the local Superintendent Kelso. The Troy officers had not exhibited common police courtesy, telling the New York Office of their arrival or purpose. "Not to put too fine a point upon it, Detective Squire, who did the largest share of the work, says that Kelso's sympathies were all on the side with Curley." Even the New York *Times* said Kelso "roundly berated the Troy officers for having arrested [a man] without getting his warrant endorsed by a New York Justice." According to the Troy newspaper Detective Squire gave the "punctilious" Kelso a lesson in New York State law - focusing on an officer of the law's ability to arrest a criminal on a warrant even in a different municipality. The issue was resolved when the officers from both jurisdictions agreed to appear before a New York City justice to procure an inducement on the warrant.

At 3:30 o'clock in the afternoon all parties were in the Tombs Police Court. Included with the large crowd were numerous Curley supporters. Attorney William Beach, the former mayor of Troy, was in court representing Curley. Beach argued that Curley should not be sent back to Saratoga County since the witnesses needed to prove that Curley was not involved in the robbery still resided in New York City. Beach argued that it would be an undue hardship on all the witnesses to have to go to Saratoga just to prove his client innocent. The judge listened professionally then ordered that the warrant was genuine and Curley was remanded into the custody of the Troy detectives.

Curley's Supporters

A crowd of Curley supporters was waiting for the three Troy detectives and Curley when they reached the sidewalk outside the Tombs. One man, thought to be Omaha Bill, reached forward to strike Detective Markham. Before he could swing his punch, Detective Squire caught the man's arm and bent the arm behind the potential assailant's back. The detectives believed the captured attacker to be "Richard Doe", the man named in the second warrant they had brought to the City. Detective Squire started to pull the new prisoner back into the courtroom he had just left, when it became apparent that the crowd meant to free Curley. Reluctantly, Squire released his hold on Omaha Bill and joined his fellow officers in surrounding Curley. According to the newspaper account the officers were "willing to take any risk to get away from the spot." The detectives flagged down a horse car and stepped aboard with Curley still firmly in their grasp.

The group got off the horse car at the Occidental Hotel where they met Troy Police Superintendent McKenna and the bank director, Mr. John Enos. Although the hour was getting late, the men felt it better to leave as soon as possible rather than to spend a night in the hotel. They took a cab to the 42nd Street Depot (today Grand Central). It was not until the train actually pulled out of the station that the Troy Police detectives felt they were going to be able to get their prisoner home safely.

The Ride Home

While they were on the train the officers tried to engage Curley in a discussion of the robbery. Curley was too wise for this simple approach and only declared his innocence. On the train ride back to Troy the detectives, having seen the support Curley had among the populace in New York, would give him no slack. When the train stopped in Poughkeepsie, Curley politely asked permission to be allowed to purchase food. The detectives refused Curley's request, arguing that if they could fast so could Curley. After the officers refused his simple request Curley informed

Detective Squire, "If I had given the word, you would have been killed by the crowd. It is only out of friendship I did not do it."

Arriving back in Troy, Curley was immediately taken to the Second Street Precinct House. Curley was given special treatment even in Troy when he was housed in the cell usually reserved for "women lodgers."

Sporting Men

The next day all of the "sporting men" of Troy came by to visit with their long time friend Curley. Curley was very natural, casual and affable as he greeted all his associates. In an over dramatic gesture meant to show dedication, Detective Squire was with Curley at all times except when his attorneys Levi Smith and E.L. Fursman called on him twice that Sunday afternoon. Each visit of the attorneys lasted about an hour. The police told the press that Squire was present to assure that Curley would not escape. The attorneys gave Curley very specific directions not to make any statements. Prior to their directive Curley had told Squire he would be proven innocent by the testimony of witnesses of "undoubted probity."

At 10:30 o'clock Monday morning Curley was taken to the Howard House in Waterford for a hearing before Justice Shepard. The room was not a courtroom, but rather the hall of the hotel. The attorneys, Judge Shepard and Curley were on the stage as if taking part in a Shakespearean drama. As Curley stood in the courtroom, his sporting friends worked their way through the throng to be as close to him as possible. Curley's attorney E. L. Fursman asked that the hearing be moved to Troy as the sentiment in Waterford was too emotionally strong against his client. The judge listened patiently then informed the counsel that there was a concern that Curley might try to escape. The potential for an escape made it imperative that Curley not leave Saratoga County again until the matter was resolved. The reporter described Curley as "looking very pale and somewhat uneasy." Typical of the reporting of the day Curley's condition was attributed to the assumption that he "evidently thinks he had got in a bad scrape."

Ormsby informed the court that he had no intention of producing all his witnesses only enough to warrant Curley being held for trial. Ormsby told the court that his Troy witnesses did not want to be sworn, as they were afraid that if their identity were known they would "be killed by Curley's friends." Ormsby also did not want to put forward his out of town witnesses because he was afraid the same friends would "buy up these witnesses, damn it, with our money, too."

Other Reports

There were two other reports floating around at the time. One held that Brandon the fence was saying, "If I go to prison I won't go alone." The implication being that he would testify against Curley. The second was far more political. The Troy police were going to have a hearing on a new police bill the Wednesday following Curley's arrest and the Waterford hearing. Curley's friends were reminding reporters that Curley would have come to Troy at any time, but the police staged the arrest to gain support of the need for a new bill. Curley's supporters were even saying that charges were imminent against a certain unnamed police officer for trying to blackmail Curley.

Rumors

With the arrest of Curley the gates to the Waterford rumor mill again were open and the stream of falsehoods ran wild. One rumor held that a prominent New York City banker was going to join Curley in the cell. A second was that a deal had been made and the money and bonds were going to be returned. It was even reported in one newspaper that the detectives who had arrested

Curley were going to return New York City on another secret mission. A final story circulated that there had been several arrests of Curley's confederates in the crime and the Ballston jail was now full. Each of these rumors was found to be without merit.

The Hearing

A second man, Jeremiah Flood, was indicted and pleaded not guilty to charges of aiding and abetting Curley. Flood was alleged to be the hack driver that had taken two men from the Delavan Hotel to Castleton the day after the robbery. Flood would prove to be an interesting witness when he testified in the upcoming trials.

The grand jury in Waterford heard the Curley case on Monday, February 5, 1873. There was one very interesting moment during the questioning. John Goodwin, the man who in the previous October gave two men a ride from Castleton to Stuyvesant, at first swore that Curley was one of the men. Under cross-examination, Goodwin was asked again about Curley being the man who rode in his wagon. This time Goodwin hesitated before he answered and stated he could not be sure the prisoner was the man. Miles Beach, son of William Beach, stood before the witness and asked, "Am I not about the size of the man?"

How Tall?

Goodwin, trying to be the jester, gave a smart answer, "You are not the man." Those in attendance broke out laughing.

Beach was fixed and so was Goodwin about to be. "I know that, but am I not about the size of the man?"

Goodwin shifted uncomfortably in his seat. Feeling trapped he answered, "You are not as tall as the man I saw."

Beach asked Curley to stand. Beach was a full head taller than Curley. The room roared with laughter followed by minutes of applause. The judge had all he could do to restore order in the room.

No Witnesses

After the prosecution had called all of its witnesses, Miles Beach spoke first for the defense. He assured the court that if required his client would be able to prove his whereabouts on the night of the robbery. The younger Beach then returned to the offer that his father had made the last day of October. William Beach had written that Curley would have come North at any time. Beach read District Attorney Ormsby's response. The portion in question being "I see no occasion to require Curley's attendance here at this time. Should such an exigency occur in respect to any one, I hope to do things decently."

Beach surprised, or at the very least disappointed, everyone when he told the justice that he had no witnesses present nor was he planning to call any witnesses on behalf of his client. As the room calmed from this theatrically disappointing news, Fursman stood and stated that the charges should be dropped as the man who claimed to drive the two men from Castleton to Stuyvesant could not identify Curley. Even more important not one witness had been put on the stand that said Curley was ever at the Waterford Bank.

Justice Served

Justice Shepard's statement regarding the court's finding was confusing. He told those gathered in his court that he had a "sincere desire to do right." The justice said that putting aside the outrage to the peoples' pocket he had an obligation to Curley. Shepard recognized that America is founded on the idea that a man was innocent until proven guilty. Having said the right thing the eminent judge then acted very differently. Shepard told the throng gathered that, although he had "feelings ever so much in Curley's favor, public opinion does a great deal." He ordered Curley held, stating "there is something due to public opinion." In his verdict, Shepard went on to say for a third time, "something must be done to allay public feeling." On a charge that any lawyer today would have had overturned easily, Curley was ordered held for a trial.

Bail

With formal charges out of the way, at nine o'clock the next morning the bail hearing began. Judge Bockes listened to Miles Beach's arguments that the bail should be minimal. Miles reminded the judge that no evidence had been given that even warranted a charge. Young Beach even read from Judge Shepard's holding, stating that there was little evidence against Curley. Beach reminded the judge that, for three months, Curley had stayed in New York. During that time Curley was available to the People and knew he was under investigation. Beach said, "if he (Curley) had chosen, he could have taken a steamer any day and gone out of the country." Beach's conclusion was that bail needed to be only nominal.

Bockes took a very different attitude. The judge was concerned that no witnesses had been put forward by the defense. The judge felt an alibi should have been provided for Curley. Bockes was also troubled by the fact that if indeed Curley was one of the robbers he had already demonstrated, in Hudson, that he would escape if necessary.

General Bullard, who was representing the bank, asked for bail in the amount of $250,000. Ormsby, the district attorney, asked that it be even higher. Beach again reminded the court that bail should only be enough to insure that his client would appear; therefore a minimal amount was all that was needed.

Judge Bockes told Beach that if he could get two freeholders (landowners) living in the county each able to furnish $50,000 then he would consider the question of bail. He gave the counsel till noon to raise the money.

The politics of this case were evident when the parties reconvened at noon. Beach opened the meeting by saying he had only half the money but the rest was forthcoming and would probably be there by the end of the meeting. The judge refused to wait and in fact radically changed his former commitment. Bockes now held that he would not accept bail for any amount less than the $400,000 taken from the bank. The judge held that his decision was based on Curley's not having put forward witnesses on his behalf. One can only imagine the pressures put on the honorable Judge Bockes to make him go back on his word that morning.

Unable to raise that amount, Curley was committed to the care and company of Jailer Powers in Ballston Spa.

William Beach's Commitment

Two days after the denial of Curley's bail, William Beach (the father of Miles) was interviewed in one of the newspapers. The question in everyone's mind was why a locally born man would defend someone guilty of stealing from his former neighbors. The question was all the more resolute as many felt that the real losers were incapable of restoring their assets. Beach told a story that in his mind cleared Curley of any wrongdoing. In late October, Beach had written to District Attorney Ormsby saying that Curley could be produced upon a letter requesting his appearance. A few days later Beach had received a letter from an elderly woman who had lost all her bonds in the Waterford robbery. The lady implored Beach to do all in his power to help her get her money back. The next time Beach saw Curley he read the letter aloud and said to Curley "if you know anything of the robbery, if you were engaged in it or know anyone who was, I want you to get this woman's bonds and bring them to my office."

According to Beach, Curley responded, "Upon my honor, I was not concerned in the burglary and do not know anyone who was." Beach had looked Curley straight in the eyes as he answered and was sure he was not involved in the robbery.

What Curley Looked Like

It was a well know fact that Curley, like many of the rapscallions of the time, liked to spend his summers in Saratoga Springs, taking of the water and enjoying the sporting life. In 1872, the sporting life included not only the afternoon horse races but also the gaming tables at the various casinos in the evening.

At the time of his arrest Curley was 30 years old and always dressed in the most fashionable of styles. Curley frequented taverns almost as if they were a place of business. He was wise enough to avoid alcohol and would only drink cider. Curley had the rare gift of personal presence. Although he was only medium size with a strong build, when he entered a room everyone could feel he was present. Those who had seen him at the various hearings all felt he was the picture of a man who enjoyed a fast life style. To find out more about Curley, as a man, reporters visited South Troy. These were the neighborhoods Curley considered home until shortly before the robbery. Through interviews with the neighbors, it was learned the south-side locals felt Curley could sit down among "any of the boys" and he was considered "a right clever fellow."

A Prisoner is Moved

In February 1873, Edward Kendricks' residence was the infamous Tombs in New York City. This residence had been chosen for him by the mere fact that he had been selected to sell some Virginia Bonds. The problem was that these bonds had been stolen in the fall of 1872, from a bank in Connecticut. To make matters worse Kendricks had defaulted on his bail, which was $25,000.

Like Curley, Kendricks, was a native of Troy. Kendricks had married the lovely daughter of one of the collar city's Baptist ministers. His youth had been promising. Kendricks had begun a legitimate career climbing the lower rungs of a career ladder in banking. This was while he stilled lived in Troy. Kendricks had such promise he was able to get a position as a cashier at the Bank of Albany. The ready access to cash proved to be too much of a temptation for Kendricks, and one night he felt forced to disappear. It was later learned that he had gone to Canada to avoid detection for embezzlement. The bank was so badly hit by Kendricks that it had to assess funds from its stockholders to avoid defaulting.

A Break for Kendricks

Fortunately for Kendricks, the investigation was compromised and he was eventually able to return to the United States without the fear of prosecution. Unfortunately for many people, Kendricks's return was to Wall Street where he became an unscrupulous broker. Several times he was prosecuted for selling forged bonds and for serving as a fence for stolen bonds. Kendricks' reputation among those in his "business" rivaled the prominence of Brandon.

Employees at Jay Cooke & Co. recognized a picture of Kendricks, saying he was the man who, in mid-October, had cashed in the $18,000 worth of bonds stolen from the Waterford bank. As a result of his identification as the one who had redeemed the bonds, Kendricks had been secretly brought from the Tombs to Ballston Spa to testify against Brandon and Curley. Kendricks' testimony was in a closed courtroom, but it was widely speculated that Kendricks had provided a link between himself and Brandon.

Best and Dyer

In mid-February, stories started to appear that projected a riff between the two men from Hudson, Officer Dyer and William Best. The first was in the form of a letter published in a Hudson newspaper allegedly signed by Best. The article called on the Troy newspapers to assure everyone in its region's circulation that neither Dyer nor Best had ever said, even to Beach, that they could not identify Curley as one of the men who had escaped. On February 17, 1873, Best paid for the following notice to be placed in the Hudson *Register*.

> In Saturday's *Star*, I saw that I was accused of "squealing" on Dyer to save myself. Now the facts of the case is this, we never have had any falling out as "the dirty up-town sheet" claims, nor have I "squealed" on Dyer. I am not so much on the give away as many may think, - time will tell all. You can say to the Poughkeepsie *Eagle*, that justice to us in this matter is all I or Dyer have to ask, until the whole matter may be disposed of.

The most newsworthy portion was when Best said, *"time will tell all."* This expression was widely held to mean that at the trials for Brandon and Curley, Best and/or Dyer would produce some startling revelations.

By mid-March, Curley and Brandon were sharing a cell in the Ballston Spa jail. Each evening Curley would play his violin to his audience of one (Brandon). Jailer Powell reassured all that were worried about a potential escape, when he was quoted in the newspaper as saying that he had the two men under constant surveillance. Powell told the reporter that he was certain Brandon would never try to escape, but was almost equally certain that Curley would if the opportunity arose.

Trial

Peter Curley's trial for grand larceny began at 10 o'clock on the morning of March 5th, 1873. The prosecution's team was comprised of five members. Foremost was Lyman Tremaine the former judge of Albany County whose salary was being paid by the bank. He was joined by three attorneys paid by the people of the county: Saratoga County's District Attorney Isaac C. Ormsby, Jesse L'Amoreaux and his partner Dake of Ballston Spa. Gen. E. F. Bullard of Troy, who also represented the bank, completed the cast for the prosecution.

The defense had a field of egos equal to the challenge. Probably as much for show as need Miles Beach and his father, William, both of New York City were the principal defense attorneys. One partnership that of Levi Smith with Edgar L. Fursman and Esek Cowen all of Troy led the local portion of the defense team. William T. Odell of Ballston Spa, who had served as district attorney for Saratoga County from 1851-1857, completed the defense team.

There were two different attorneys both named Smith involved the defense – Levi Smith of Troy represented Curley and Henry Smith of Albany represented Brandon.

Motions to Dismiss

The trial opened with a series of motions by the defense to postpone the trial. The reasons were the fact that William Beach, the senior attorney, was unavailable along with the defense's inability to secure material witnesses were cited as some of the reasons necessitating a postponement. After hearing arguments from both sides, the court ruled the trial would begin at one that afternoon.

Jury

It took just over an hour for a jury to be seated. This was an unusually short period of time for a case of this magnitude.

Ormsby Opens

In his opening, Ormsby took an hour to outline the prosecution's perception of the facts to the jury. The prosecution's case hinged heavily on the questionable testimony of Officer Dyer and William Best of Hudson. Ormsby assured the jury that these men would testify that they had received $60 apiece to allow two men to escape from their custody in Hudson. Ormsby told the jury that the prosecution would prove that one of these escapees was Curley. Further, Best and Dyer would testify that they had gone to New York City several times to get the rest of the money promised to them at the time of the escape. The two had been "bluffed off" by Peter Curley. As a result of their treatment, the two would now tell the whole truth in the matter.

Witnesses

Putting the events in sequence for the jury, the first witness called by Ormsby was the bank's cashier, David Van Hovenbergh. David took over an hour to testify to what happened the night of the robbery. No new information came out in his testimony.

Moving next to the getaway from Waterford, the conductor on the train from Stuyvesant to Hudson, Alexander Hughes, was the second witness called. On direct, he assured the jury that Peter Curley was a passenger on the train the day after the robbery. Hughes said he witnessed Curley being arrested in the Hudson Station. Even the strong cross-examination by Henry Smith did not rock Hughes. He continued to hold Curley was the man on the train.

Dyer

Shifting to the initial arrest and escape, Officer Dyer was the third and final witness of the day. Dyer testified to his recollection of that fateful day in his life. Dyer told the court he had arrested the bigger of the two men and that Best had arrested the smaller. Under direct examination, Dyer told the court, "I think the man arrested by Best is Curley." Realizing that "thinking" was not strong enough, General Bullard pushed Dyer into saying, "I have no doubt about it." As Dyer reached the point of telling how the group had decided to stop at Curtis's saloon, the judge ended the trial for the day. The judge gave the jury and the deputy sheriffs a strong injunction that members of the jury were not to be conversed with nor were they to converse with anyone.

In his testimony the following morning, Dyer said that when the men stopped for a drink they asked why they were under arrest. Dyer said it was for robbing the Waterford Bank. The two men he had placed under arrest put three $20 bills on the table and said they "didn't want to be bothered." Dyer admitted he and Best took the money in exchange for allowing the two to escape. On three occasions Dyer and Best had gone to New York to collect more money from Curley. They only saw Curley on two of the junkets. The first time they met with Curley was shortly after they had given a statement to his attorney William Beach. This time they talked about how the sale of the bonds had not gone well. Despite Curley's purported problems, Dyer and Best had each walked away with $20. The final visit was the day before Christmas. On this trip Curley had allegedly said there was nothing more for them to receive. The prosecution turned the witness over to the defense apprehensively because Dyer's ability to sustain a rigorous cross-examination was questionable.

Smith wasted no time in attacking the thirty-nine-year-old police officer. Smith's opening volley made Dyer confess he had been dismissed from the Hudson City Police for malfeasance. Dyer also admitted he had lied to the grand jury during its investigation. The witness told the court that he saw nothing wrong with the fact he had taken money from an attorney involved in the prosecution and money from officers in the bank. To Dyer the logic was simple; the money was, after all, only to offset his cost of travel and lost work. Making his testimony even less credible, Dyer acknowledged he was promised a percent of the reward if Curley was convicted. On cross-examination, Dyer had to disclose he had received a letter from the district attorney that he would not be prosecuted for anything he confessed to while on the stand. Smith continued to make the witness burn as he listed a sizable number of people Dyer had told that Curley was not the man arrested in Hudson. Perhaps the most damaging blow to whatever credibility Dyer brought to the stand was when he affirmed he was under indictment at the time of this testimony for robbing a safe.

Dramatic Effect

To intensify the human aspect of the case, the trauma of the robbery on those in the house/bank was to be retold each day of the prosecution's portion of the trial. Ann Driscoll, the Van Hovenburgh's servant, had a much easier time of it on the stand than Dyer. Ann related her treatment by the robbers the night of the burglary. Like her employer David Van Hovenbergh, Ann admitted that because they wore masks it was impossible to identify the men who had been in the bank.

John Gladding, a resident of West Troy, and Frances Lansing, the tollbooth collector on the road to Albany, added nothing to the trial when they testified that a covered carriage passed through the gate between 5 o'clock and 6 o'clock in the morning on October 14th. Both said that they could not see the passengers through the leather window covers.

Five residents of Castleton were brought to testify regarding Curley's identity. The best any of the five could do was to say that Curley resembled one of the men in Castleton the day after the robbery. Mary Harder, the lady whose house a carriage had stopped in front of, testified to nothing more than that Curley was about the same height as one of the two men who got out of the wagon and walked to the station. Fredrick Hill worked in the local tavern. He added only that the two men offered to pay for their drinks with a $20 bill. William Bignall, a local resident, saw two men that morning and told the court that Curley looked like one of them. The cashier at the Castleton Bank told the court that a man who looked like Curley had come in to break a $20 bill. William Clapp, owner of the tavern, said Curley resembled one of the two strangers who took dinner in his hotel the day following the robbery.

A Positive Identification

A sixth witness from Castleton did make a positive identification of Curley. John Goodwin, who had previously testified at the grand jury, was the man who drove the two strangers to Stuyvesant. As their driver, he was with the two men longer than any of the earlier witnesses. Goodwin told the court he had no doubt that Curley was one of the men he drove that day. It should be noted that Goodwin was the same man that, at the grand jury, was unsure of whether the man he drove was Curley. Goodwin was the first to testify that he positively recognized Curley as one of his passengers, yet he was also the man who misjudged Curley's height by a full head.

The Wife

Mrs. Van Hovenbergh was called to reinforce her husband testimony of the previous day. Like the maid Ann, she told of her treatment while in the clutches of the robbers. She added that the men's masks did not cover their ears. She claimed to be able to recognize Curley because his ears were unusually large.

More Witnesses

The next two witnesses were in the Hudson Station at the time of the arrest. Edward Malloy witnessed the arrest but was unable to swear that Curley was one of the men involved. Malloy at first said the man in question had a four-inch scar on his left cheek. When recalled, he swore it was on the man's right cheek. James Bump, the stationmaster at Hudson, testified that he was the man who had sent for police support. There was no doubt in Bump's mind that Curley was one of the men arrested that day.

Constable James Cook of Waterford stated that on the morning of October 14th all the bridges out of Waterford were open. Cook's statement only meant that the robbers, whoever they were, had access to all possible escape routes. Cook was put on the stand to assure the jury that all escape routes were open after the hard rain the night of the robbery.

The Best of Best

The prosecution called the second man implicated in the escape of the two men in Hudson, William Best. Best testified that he and Dyer had arrested Curley in the City of Hudson. On the way to the police station, it was Curley who had suggested that "all hands have a drink." While in Curtis's tavern Curley had said, "you've got hold of the wrong two men." Best, along with Dyer, was drinking gin while the two men in custody only "moistened their clay with a little sherry." Best said Curley told the officers he had been working a job in Castleton but had nothing to do with the Waterford robbery. According to Best, he and Dyer split a bribe that consisted of $120 and two pistols. Best went on to say Curley assured him that there was to be more money later. Before releasing the two suspected robbers, Best had given the two men directions on the route to follow as they ran away. Several weeks after helping with the escape, Best had gone to New York City on three occasions to have Curley make good on his promise to pay additional money for allowing the escape. In time, Best realized that there would be no more money and Curley meant to give him a "cold shake."

The prosecution closed Best's testimony by having him tell the jury he had lied in the statement he had provided in Beach's office back in November. Best also said he lied to the grand jury and he had lied when he said that Curley had pulled a revolver on him in Hudson (at the time of the escape). In fact, Best told the jury that at the time of the initial arrest he had told a series of lies. Best, always someone to try the impossible, said that after he heard Dyer's pistol had been taken by the police during his arrest, he pawned his revolver to Sheriff Ham of Columbia County, rather than have it confiscated.

On the stand, Sheriff Ham of Columbia County confirmed Best's story that he had pawned the pistol to him.

Henry Smith attacked Best just as he had Dyer. On cross-examination, Best told Smith he worked for the railroads. He almost immediately told Smith it was true he had not worked since October but that was because he had "no inclination" to work. Best claimed to be living off the $175 he had saved. There were a series of questions designed to pursue Best's ability to have some income. Eventually, Best was compelled to affirm he was also receiving money from the officers in the Waterford Bank and the attorneys for the prosecution. Best told Smith and the jury he was not sure why those people kept giving him money. Best closed his questionable testimony, conceding he had been arrested several times and jailed for "various offences."

And Yet More Witnesses

Captain Philip Knickerbocker ran a steamship between Stuyvesant and New York City. On the day of the infamous flight of the suspected robbers, he had been in the train station in Stuyvesant. The captain said that he noticed two men who appeared nervous hanging around the station. Knickerbocker told how the two men waited until the train had actually begun to move before they boarded. The implication was clear. The men wanted to be absolutely certain they were not being followed before they boarded. Knickerbocker said Curley resembled one of the men in size and appearance but was smaller probably because the men had been wearing heavy coats. The boat captain said the coats appeared to be filled with something. Again the hypothesis was that the men had part of the booty under their coats. Under cross-examination, the captain said he could not identify Curley by his face, only his size and shape.

The baggage master at the station, Charles Palmer, testified almost identically to the captain. Palmer, like the captain, could not positively identify Curley.

The Sisters

To keep the issue personal the two Van Hovenbergh sisters, Sarah and Mary, were the next witnesses. The prosecution wanted to keep reminding the jury what it was like at the time of the robbery, so they staggered the Van Hovenbergh's testimony over the various days of the trial. Like their mother, father and the maid, their testimony was as to the events on the night of the robbery.

Closing

The final witness for the prosecution was Sheriff May of Saratoga County. He tried to settle the issue of the beard Curley now sported. May said Curley had only a mustache when arrested, but had grown the full beard in jail. The sheriff and his deputies would not let Curley shave, as they were concerned about how he might use the straight razor. The purpose of the beard by the time of the trial, however, was potentially different. First, it would have covered any scar that could have been on Curley's cheek. Second, it could have modified his appearance enough so that witnesses would not be positive in their identification. It is interesting that the sheriff may have provided Curley with the ultimate reasonable doubt. With the testimony of the sheriff over, the prosecution rested.

The Defense

Miles Beach asked for an adjournment until Friday morning, so that the defense team might have time for a consultation. Court was recessed until Friday at 9 o'clock.

Ladies in Court

The number of ladies in attendance grew each day of the trial. It was as if they were coming to realize that attending a criminal trial did not infringe on their proper Victorian Image. The women would sit in the courtroom doing their crochet and embroidery while the lawyers argued the case. The compulsion to do handiwork probably fell under the value "idle hands are the devil's playground." The crowd was so large by the time the defense opened on Friday that when the court had its morning, afternoon, and lunch breaks, the sidewalk and courtyard outside were jammed to capacity.

Special Seating

This trial was at a time when the belief persisted that women should be treated special, like delicate flowers. On Thursday and Friday, the crowd was so large that the clerk let the ladies in through the jailer's apartment. After the women were seated, the doors were opened to the men. Even though the county had the sheriffs' deputies at full force, they could not hold back the mass of men who wanted to see part of this contest of lawyers.

A Second Chance

Before the defense began, District Attorney Ormsby asked permission to recall Edward Malloy, one of the witnesses from the Hudson Station. Without much discussion, permission was granted. Malloy said he had seen Curley before the grand jury. According to Malloy, at that time Curley had a scar on his cheek (prior to the beard). On cross-examination, Smith caused Malloy to make so many conflicting statements that it is probable Malloy had the sympathy of the jury, but most likely not its trust.

Impeach Witnesses

With the string of prosecution witnesses at an end, the trial took one of its many turns. Smith called for the prosecution to have two of its own witnesses impeached. Smith was referring to Best and Dyer, who had each given sworn statements on both sides of the facts. Tremaine, speaking for the prosecution, said that early on the defense had corrupted these two witnesses. To prove the men were liars, Smith showed the sworn statements of Best and Dyer taken in Beach's office. In these signed statements they swore that they had not arrested Curley. Smith asked how the prosecution could put witnesses before the court and then not stand by their own previously sworn statements (the ones made in Beach's office).

For What They Are Worth

The court allowed in to the record the sworn statements made by Best and Dyer in Beach's office. The judge pointed out that, "if a witness had made a false statement out of court, the witness had a chance to correct himself in court." Judge Bockes ruled that the testimony the two men had already given would be allowed to stand and was to be taken by the jury for "whatever it is worth."

To defend Best's statements in the courtroom, the prosecution was given permission to bring him back to the stand. Under direct examination, Tremaine asked, "Why did you make the false statement that you did in New York (in Beach's office) as to the identity of the defendant, as you have testified?"

A series of objections followed with the ultimate decision to let the question stand along with the answer. "I was promised $250 for it and got it."

Under cross-examination, Best told the court he was in the area at the time of the grand jury investigation. Best was not in Waterford, however, as Enos, an officer of the bank, had him stay in Schuylerville. Best admitted that while he stayed in Schuylerville, as a guest of the bank, he spent most of the time drunk. Several names were given to Best. To each name Best was asked if he had told the person that he had not arrested Curley. Best admitted telling each person named that it was not Curley whom he arrested. On re-direct Best told the court he had lied in each case except this day in court.

Dyer was called to the stand by the prosecution. Long before videotapes it appeared in this 1873 court that an instant replay of testimony was in progress. Dyer's statements and those of Best were virtually identical. To all present, there was a genuine concern as to when to believe either Best or Dyer, let alone both of them in the same case.

At this time the prosecution rested formally.

The Defense

Fursman was the attorney selected to make the opening statement for the defense. The lawyer's statement was brief and to the point. Fursman told the jury that had Curley been born to better circumstances his name would never have been suggested in this case. Fursman assured the court that there were stories that Curley's life was not the best for the last 10 years but that is all they were - stories. In fact, this was the first time Curley had ever been brought into court. Fursman attacked Best and Dyer as the "most consummate of scoundrels and liars ever to enter a court." Fursman closed by assuring the court that Curley was not even in the area the night of the Waterford Bank robbery.

Edward Flynn was the man who drove the mysterious hack the night of the robbery. Flynn said he had seen Curley several times at the grand jury. He assured the court it was true he had picked up two men at the Delavan House in Albany and for eight dollars taken them to Castleton. Flynn swore that Curley was not one of the men he picked up that night. To make matters worse for the prosecution, Flynn said that one of the officers of the bank (Pruyn) had offered him $300 and part of the reward for saying it was Curley he had picked up.

Flynn's cross-examination was as difficult as any would be for the prosecution. Press as hard as the prosecution could, Flynn never faltered or hesitated. His memory was so clear he even described the house in Castleton where he had left off the two passengers. Flynn told Ormsby he was not suspicious of the two men, as he did not hear of the robbery until he got back to Albany.

Frank Shaler, an employee at Curtis's Saloon in Hudson, was called to describe the four men's behavior the day they stopped in the tavern. Shaler told the court that as soon as the four men entered the bar they immediately adjourned to a private room where they stayed for five or six minutes. While they were there Shaler had served them drinks. Shaler told the jury he did not recognize Curley as being one of the two men in custody.

Trying to establish just how accurate his memory was, Ormsby asked if Shaler would recognize either of the two men in custody. Shaler hesitated then stated he did not know if he would have recognized either of the men.

James Bannon of Green Island gave a very different testimony when he said it was not Curley who was arrested in Hudson. Green Island is a small community that is a neighbor of Waterford, the place of the robbery. Green Island also borders Troy, the former home of Curley. Bannon was working in Hudson at the time the two men were arrested in the railroad station. Bannon happened to be in the railroad station at the time of the arrest. What separates Bannon from the rest of the witnesses is that Bannon knew Curley before the arrest. In fact, Bannon told the court he had known Curley for over 20 years. The prosecution's witnesses were asked to recognize a relative stranger, Bannon was asked if the person he saw was someone he knew.

Cross-examination added nothing. Bannon would not budge from the point that it was definitely not Curley who was arrested while he was in the station. Bannon held he could see clearly the two men arrested, even though the station was crowded. Pushed by Ormsby, Bannon refused to concede that he told anyone that the men were too far off for him identify Curley.

Henry Fales, a conductor on the Hudson River Line, lived in Troy and worked on the train to New York City. Like Bannon, Fales had known Curley for years. He told the court that on the day of the robbery he had worked the morning train to New York. While spending the night, he had seen Curley in the St. Clair House (NYC) the day of the robbery between 6 and 7 o'clock in the evening. The prosecution tried to show it had been too long between the day of the robbery and the trial for Fales to remember that it was on that specific day that he saw Curley. Ormsby wanted to know how anyone could remember seeing someone that long ago. Fales would not yield - insisting it was the day of the robbery.

Best and Dyer

The defense then made a blatant attack on the character of Best and Dyer. To embarrass the men, the defense called Mr. Powers, the former mayor of Hudson, to the stand. Powers told the court that both Best and Dyer "bore hard characters" in Hudson. Under cross-examination Powers did have to admit that the two men's reputations had been worse since the escape.

The former police magistrate of Hudson, Myron Van Deusen, was put on the stand to support Powers's testimony that Dyer and Best were not to be trusted as men, let alone as witnesses. As is all too often the case in those who condemn the behavior of others, Van Deusen proved to have his own integrity issues to deal with. Under cross-examination, Van Deusen had to admit that he too had been arrested and placed in New York City's infamous Tombs. Van Deusen said that prior to the City arrest, he had been arrested in his home city of Hudson. On redirect, Van Deusen dismissed the charges as irrelevant since the New York City charge was for a patent violation and the one in Hudson for forgery on a "real estate deal." With a straight face, Van Deusen tried to correct any ill-feelings, saying he had never been arrested in Albany. Character assassination aside Van Deusen did help the prosecution when he told the jury that no one had spoken badly of Dyer prior to his arrest in October.

Other Witnesses

John Fitzgerald was a liquor salesman who had known both Curley and Best for years. He testified that, in November, Best had told him that Curley was not one of the men who escaped. Press as hard as they wanted, the prosecution was not able to get Fitzgerald to yield on cross-examination.

A tavern owner in New York City was the second person that established Curley was out of Waterford on the night of the robbery. Twenty-seven-year-old William Flynn was part owner of a tavern that Curley frequented in New York. William Flynn was not related to Edward Flynn the hack driver. William Flynn remembered that on Sunday night, October 13th, Curley had been a customer. Curley had arrived about 10 o'clock, staying to closing at midnight. Flynn always remembered Curley since he never drank anything but cider.

One of the customers in Flynn's saloon the night of October 13th, was James Lewis. Lewis also testified to seeing Curley in the tavern. The reason Lewis Flynn was sure of the date was he remembered reading the newspaper the next day with its account of the robbery. Pushed on his memory, Lewis named several other customers who were in the bar that night. One of the most significant points about Lewis was that he had never spoken to Curley, thus had no reason to lie on the stand.

With Lewis's testimony over, the defense closed its case. The herd of defense attorneys felt that they had proved, at the very least, a reasonable doubt as to Curley's being one of the men arrested in Hudson. Further, they had also shown that Curley was not even in the area at the time of the crime.

Without mercy, the defense had used Dyer and Best as targets on the character assassination range. It was now time for the prosecution to have some payback. The first two arrows were from Clarke Carpenter of Lansingburgh and a Mr. Filley of Troy. Both men told the court that they had heard Bannon say that the rail station at Hudson was so crowded at the time of the capture, that he could not see who was arrested. The next arrow was for the carriage driver, Edward Flynn. John Enos, an officer at the Waterford bank, said that Flynn had told him he would not recognize either of his passengers that fateful night. It should be remembered that Enos is the man Flynn previously testified had offered him $300 to testify it was Curley in the hack.

Rebuttal

The prosecution now tried to mend the wounds inflicted on Dyer and Best. Three men, Columbia County Sheriff Ham, J. W. Holsapple and Edward Roarback, all testified that they had known both Dyer and Best for years. These three witnesses all said they would absolutely believe Dyer if he were under oath. They were all less sure about Best. A fourth prosecution witness, Edward Winans, added levity to a long day in court. After being sworn in and telling how long he had known Best and Dyer, he answered the next question having to do with if they could be trusted to tell the truth differently from his predecessors. Winans said he could "hardly judge the reputation of either." End of testimony.

Closing Arguments

Although it was 4:30 in the afternoon when the testimony ended, Judge Bockes insisted that closing arguments be held that evening. A dinner break interrupted the defense attorney Henry Smith's remarks. It appears Henry Smith had a very good sense of humor. During his closing he pointed out to the jury (and anyone else in the court) that the prosecution's witnesses had condemned Curley based on his big ears. Smith reminded the court that they were no ears bigger than General Bullard's (a reference to one of the prosecutors). Smith really got in trouble when he pointed out that the mutton chop whiskers that some witnesses said Curley were sporting the day of the robbery matched Lemuel Pikes' (a reference to a second prosecutor). Judge Bockes had had enough and told both sides that no future humor would be tolerated.

General Bullard closed for the prosecution. He didn't begin his statement until 8 o'clock, and concluding at 10 o'clock that evening.

Bockes Charges the Jury

The court opened on March 8th, with Judge Bockes's charge to the jury. The judge's charge was actually carried in its entirety in one of Troy's newspapers. Most of those present felt that Bockes's charge was fair. He did elaborate on two points beyond just what was in the testimony. As if to congratulate the robbers, he noted at length how the robbery had been "studied and perfected." He felt that the captain, whoever he was, "had studied the whole enterprise as a student would study a problem in algebra." The judge then went on to discuss the selection of the bank. Bockes told the jury that the bank was "in a locality from which escape was easy; for perhaps no other village could there be found the same opportunity for flight." For at least a few moments the judge seemed to play to the jury's emotional side. The judge said the bank had lost little but "the larger portion of the property taken was owned by persons who could ill bear the loss. Little sums gathered from day to day."

Bockes reviewed for the jury whether each witness actually testified that they saw, Curley with any certainty. He almost seemed to dismiss Dyer and Best reminding the jurors that "more trustworthy witnesses" had also stated that Curley was the man involved in the carriage ride to Castleton, then onto Stuyvesant, concluding on the train ride to Hudson.

As the judge ended his prepared closing statement, the defense wanted him to add two major points. First, that it was possible to believe that Curley was in flight, but not involved in the robbery in Waterford. The judge said they must be confident that the man, whoever he was, could be traced back to Waterford. Smith also wanted to be sure the judge instructed the jury that if a reasonable doubt existed they must find the defendant not guilty. The judge did say that Curley needed to be proven guilty.

The Verdict

The jury stayed out until 8:30 that evening. At half past eight Judge Bockes called the jury into the courtroom. The judge pooled the jury finding it was six to six and no change in position had taken place in hours. Realizing the situation was hopeless, Bockes discharged the jury. Curley was remanded to jail to await another trial.

Earlier that same day, a trial had been set for early May in the criminal trial for Brandon. Brandon's issues were now criminal for possession of the bonds and civil seeking the money received for the bonds.

Court Notes

In 1873, there was a new portion to trial reporting. It was called court notes. During Curley's trial, several notes appeared - one of which stated that he was considered by the women in attendance, (there were many) to be the best looking man in the courtroom. Another note mentioned that Judge Tremaine, who had represented the prosecution, was in ill health throughout the trial.

By Monday, the *Daily Saratogian* had conducted its own unscientific poll of the people who had lost savings in Waterford. The newspaper reported that most felt a second trial would probably not bring a more successful result than had the first. There was $200,000 in registered bonds that were useless to the thieves. If a reasonable rate could be established most in the community would rather have most of their money back than spend more money housing the likes of Best and Dyer, while they waited to be witnesses for a second time.

Curley's Retrial

This investigation had from its opening looked like a two-dimensional maze with more twists, turns, and corners than a street map of Washington, D.C. On Thursday, May 22, 1873, the second trial of Peter Curley was about to begin. Suddenly, a set of circumstances became public that made that maze turn into a complex three-dimensional labyrinth.

Since the arrest of Curley and Brandon, Saratoga County's District Attorney Ormsby had worked closely with the former Judge Tremaine of Albany. For the first trial, the officers of the bank in Waterford had agreed to compensate Tremaine. On Monday May 19th, three days before the second trial was supposed to begin, Officers Boughton, Enos, and House told Ormsby the bank was no longer going to pay for Tremaine's services. Ormsby was given the news while making a routine deposit at the bank. Ormsby had immediately gone to Tremaine to tell him the news and to personally solicit his support in the upcoming trial. Tremaine assured Ormsby he would like to help but because the bank's decision was so close to the trial date it would be necessary for Ormsby to get a stay from the court. Tremaine explained to Ormsby that he was already scheduled to appear on Monday, May 26th, before the New York Court of Appeals (New York State's highest court) in the Stokes case. Stokes had been convicted of the murder James Fisk. Further, since he was not sure of being retained in the Curley trial, Tremaine would have to accept a retainer from Boss Tweed whose trial was to begin on the following Tuesday, May 27th. Ormsby left knowing he needed Tremaine and he needed a postponement.

What Goes Around Comes Around

When William Beach heard Ormsby's plea in court he almost smiled. In March, when the defense had asked for a postponement because William Beach was not available, Ormsby had personally argued against it saying that Curley had many other fine lawyers present. Happy his worthy advisory, Tremaine, would not be available, Beach now challenged the court to hold to its own precedent and begin the trial as scheduled.

Ormsby reminded the court that he, as district attorney, could not be forced to put forward a case. Beach reminded the court of a legal technicality, which held that if two sessions went by without a successful trial a prisoner could sue to be released. Judge Bockes looked down from his bench into the faces of the clashing verbal titans. The judge repeated the arguments to the sets of lawyers assuring each side the other was correct. Bockes then asked the two sides to take a few minutes to consult with each other to see if a resolution was possible.

The flock of lawyers was called into the judge's chambers. A half-hour later the two teams returned to the courtroom. By mutual agreement Tremaine and William Beach would both withdraw from the case and the trial would go on as scheduled. The superstars were officially out of the game and now it was up to the remaining players to win the venture. The lawyers had just days to get ready.

And Now for Brandon

Coincidentally, a civil suit against Brandon had been placed on the court docket for the same day as Curley's criminal triai. As the attorneys left the room to gather their thoughts for the Curley trial, they were replaced in the same courtroom by attorneys representing Brandon.

The civil suit was put forward by David Brewster. Brewster had owned one of the thousand dollar bonds that Brandon was accused of having successfully sold on his first visit to Shipsey's brokerage house. Brewster had filed a civil suit demanding the money Brandon had received for the bond.

General Bullard, who had represented the bank's interest since the inception of the civil trial, represented Brewster. In his opening argument, Bullard took an extensive amount of time telling the jurors they were not involved in determining if Brandon was involved in the burglary, but rather whether Mr. Brandon had obtained and sold one of the bonds. Bullard only put two witnesses on the stand. The first was David Van Hovenbergh who testified that there was a robbery and that Brewster's bonds were among the items stolen. The second witness was Jacob Shipsey, the man who had cashed the bond for Brandon. Shipsey said little more than that he had cashed the bond in question for Brandon.

Henry Smith, who had so ably represented Curley in the first trial, was now representing Brandon. Smith moved for a non-suit, holding that the plaintiffs had not shown a cause of action. Judge Bockes disagreed saying that by showing the bonds were stolen it was now up to Brandon to tell how they came into his possession.

Henry Smith's defense of Brandon was simple. According to Smith's theory, Brandon had purchased the bonds on the open market taking only the precautions required by the law. Having followed the precautions of the law, Brandon was not in any way liable to Brewster.

Brandon on the Stand

Now that the judge had ruled that the suit had merit, with no one else who could establish where the bonds came from, Brandon was forced to take the stand. To no one's surprise, Brandon testified that he bought the bonds for $3,500 from a stranger. Brandon assured the court he did not know the person. Like everyone else in the trials relating to the robbery, Brandon's memory was called into question. Brandon was able to relate quite clearly the remainder of the events of the day in question.

Not surprisingly, Bullard went after Brandon when it came time for cross-examination. Brandon admitted to having been charged, but not tried with regards to some stolen Kentucky bonds. He denied being charged with ever having in his possession stolen Missouri or South Carolina bonds. Brandon told the court that to his knowledge he was never even investigated regarding any Pittsburgh bonds. To a humble jury it was most important for Brandon to clarify his standard of living. Questioned on his spending practices, Brandon denied he owed his shoemaker $210.

As defense attorney, Smith made the first summation. Smith reminded the jury that, "it is the intention of the government to have these securities circulated as free as water. A man who buys them therefore takes his chances on having them stolen."

Smith pointed out that Brandon, like Shipsey, had purchased the bonds in his line of business. The only difference between the two men was not their actions, but rather that Brandon did not know the bonds were stolen.

The Prosecution

Bullard's case hinged on whether Brandon had ever paid for the bonds. Bullard told the jury, "if you believe that Brandon paid $3,500 for the bonds find for him." The implication was clear, if Brandon was a duped player he was innocent. If instead Brandon was cashing the bonds to pay a portion of the money to another, knowing the bonds were not legitimately obtained, he was guilty and owed Brewster the money.

The jury took only 25 minutes to rule in favor of Brewster.

Bail

Interestingly, although he was found responsible in the civil suit, Brandon was given a bail hearing on the criminal charges the next day. At the hearing, Judge Bockes, reversed many of his previous stands in this case and allowed bail for a mere $5,000. Brandon's brother who lived in Albany provided half with the remainder coming from an associate in New York City.

The newspapers attributed the knowledge the plaintiff (Brewster) had in the civil suit as to the sequence of events to the mysterious Kendrick who was safely back in the Tombs.

Curley's Second Trial

The agreement to have both Judge Tremaine and William Beach out of the Curley case was the first clue that this trial was not going to take on the importance of the March trial. The prosecution now rested in the hands of District Attorney Ormsby and General Bullard of Troy. E. L. Fursman of Troy, Miles Beach of New York City, L. B. Pike of Saratoga, and Col. William Odell of Ballston Spa represented the defense.

The Good Old Days

There were many interesting laws in the 1870s that have, unfortunately, disappeared from the books. One of those laws held that in the event not enough freemen were present to form a jury, the sheriff would go into the street and literally pull people in to serve. An event recorded in this trial shows how this law probably had a chilling effect on commercial business in the county seats at the beginning of trials. A local teamster, John O'Riley, learned first-hand that he should keep better track of the events at the courthouse. As the second Curley trial was about to begin there were not 55 persons from whom to draw a jury. At the direction of the court, the sheriff went into the street and brought O'Riley from his wagon to the courtroom. After a quick interview, both sides accepted O'Riley as a juror. The poor teamster asked the judge to please excuse him as he had a load of lumber on his wagon and a group of carpenters were awaiting delivery on the other side of town. The judge told both sides he didn't think it fair to detain O'Riley and asked that they not object to his excusing the man. Knowing this was not the type of issue to upset the judge over, both sides relented and O'Riley was given his leave. One can only imagine the alternative route planning that went through O'Riley's mind as he drove the wagon to the construction site.

Waterford is in the southeast corner of Saratoga County. This was a case where the economic impact on those from whom the money was stolen could impact the impartial nature of a jury. Perhaps to insure a fair trial no jurors were selected from the southern portion of the county. Five of the 12 were from the town of Galway, which is in the extreme western part of the county. This trial was almost a 100 years before the concept of political correctness. The *Daily Saratogian* looked at the men who were selected to be on the jury and went out on a limb pronouncing they were "seemingly intelligent."

Interest

The energy level of this trial was nothing like the first. It was as if the two sides knew this trial was a formality. Either because the public was weary of the case, or because the superstar lawyers were out, the two sides agreed to place into evidence testimony from the first trial rather than calling the same witnesses for a second time. The first four witnesses to benefit from this were the Van Hovenbergh family. Their testimony was simply read into the record.

The morning of the trial, as if by some magic, the train failed to stop in Castleton. Four witnesses to the two strangers having been in town on the morning of October 14th were suppose to board the train that didn't stop. These four were also to tell the court how the men were eager to catch a train and exchange $20 bills. Both sides agreed to have their testimony from the first trial read into the record. The final testimony read into the record that morning was that of James Cook the Waterford teamster who had helped raise the alarm.

Witnesses

The first two witnesses called had added nothing to the first trial and were just as valuable to this trial. James Gladding told of a carriage passing his house. Again because of the curtains on the carriage, he said he did not see the passengers. The toll keeper, Lansing, saw a carriage pass early in the morning after the robbery. Like Gladding, Lansing could not see the passengers.

The next two witnesses said they had seen the two men in Castleton. The men were anxious to change $20 bills and catch a train from Castleton to Stuyvesant. These two witnesses were Hill, the clerk at the hotel in Castleton, and Hughes, the conductor on the train. Hill could not positively identify Curley. Hughes was slightly more decisive, raising the bar to "it looks to be him." Hughes said under cross-examination that he would not swear the man he saw was Curley.

The first witness to positively identify Curley was the Castleton's stationmaster, James Bump. To Ormsby's question he answered, "I have not doubt that Curley was the man." When young Miles Beach took on the cross-examination, Bump changed his tune. Now Bump would only swear, "I have not much doubt in my own mind but I would not swear positively to it [being Curley]."

Because one of the defense's witnesses had to catch a train to New York City he was allowed to testify out of order. Henry Fales was a conductor on the train from Troy to New York City. On the 14th of October he had taken the 6 o'clock train, arriving in New York at 11:30 that morning. Fales, who knew Curley, swore he saw him in the St. Clair House at 6:00 o'clock that evening. If Curley were one of the men who at 4:00 o'clock that afternoon had escaped in Hudson it would have been impossible for him to have been in New York by 6 o'clock that evening.

Hard on Wood

The prosecution then resumed by calling Ira Wood. Wood was the first witness who appeared in this trial and not the first. Ira Wood had known Curley as a child having come from the same neighborhood in Troy. Wood was also the first witness to hold both in direct and cross that he had seen Curley arrested at the Hudson Station. Under cross-examination, how well Wood still knew Curley was brought into question. Wood said he had seen Curley in Troy several times in December 1872, and at least one other time before October 14th. He was even so specific that he said the sightings were at the American Hotel. At one point, Curley had owned the American Hotel. The defense asked if Wood, could remember any conversation he had in which he had said that he could not tell if it was Curley as he

(Wood) "didn't have me glasses on." They were referring to a conversation with John Scully.

Witnesses Resume

Four of Castleton's citizens, Clapp, William Brandon, Jacob Lewis, and Charles. Downer all testified as they did that first time. They all said that on the day after the robbery they saw the two mystery men walking around their community. They all agreed that one of the men resembled Curley.

George Goodwin, who had been tricked into judging Curley's height at the grand jury, was still not a strong witness. Goodwin was the man who drove the two mystery men to Stuyvesant. Probably in his heart he felt one of the men was Curley, but under the professional cross-examination of Fursman he began to doubt his own feelings. Ultimately he would join the cadre of witnesses who would only say the man in question resembled Curley.

The baggage man from Stuyvesant was the last witness for the day. Charles Palmer said he could not recognize either of the men who had gotten on the moving train that day.

The prosecution was planning to finish the day with Best. The problem was Best was ill. Judge Bockes told Best to go lay down and the trial would resume on Monday.

Although it was understood that the prosecution would soon close, they had only put one person on the stand who held categorically that the person he saw during the mystery flight was Curley. Several had said that the man looked like Curley but only one was positive he was the person.

The Weekend Break

It was Saturday night, and unlike during the Billings Trial that happened several years later, (and is reported in the book <u>To Spend Eternity Alone</u>,) everyone vacated Ballston Spa. The town that had bustled all week fizzled for the weekend.

One of the interesting members of the audience during Curley's trial was Brandon. Brandon, accompanied by his wife, attended all of Curley's second trial. A second mystery audience member was Henrietta De Conde. Henrietta, if that was her real name, was using letters to the newspaper as a way of expressing her belief that the bank committee was out to railroad Curley. De Conde continuously maintained that representatives of the bank were bribing witnesses to recount their position, not necessarily the truth. According to De Conde, she owned a business in Syracuse and just before the trial had taken a train out to experience the atmosphere of the courtroom. She reported that Detective Bradford had shadowed her. It was a well-established fact that Bradford was working for the bank committee. It should be noted that whoever the couple was who stayed in the Delavan House the weekend before the robbery they had claimed they were from Syracuse.

Finding a Story

With the lawyers and witnesses putting on such a pathetic performance, the real battle was between the Troy *Press* and Troy *Times*. On the Saturday the court was on break, the *Press* wrote, "The *Times* takes great delight in throwing petty contemptible slurs at any and every man to whom it may owe a spite." The *Times* was holding that Ormsby was in possession of an affidavit from a Mrs. George Paxton that would play heavily in the trial. To make matters worse the *Times* claimed to have a copy. The *Press* challenged the reporter to tell the truth and publish the affidavit. The article ended, "We mean the reporter who will not only lie, but will glory in it. Everybody will instinctively recognize the description." It is great that we live in a time when reporters would never have any information that had been taken illegally on would they attempt to publish anything that was not fully true.

The Jury and the Sabbath

The jury spent Sunday in the care of the sheriff and his deputies. Two of the deputies, May and Gilbert, took all 12 to the Baptist Church in Ballston Spa for Sunday morning services. As an exhibition of how ecumenical Ballston Spa and probably all Saratoga County was, the 12 went to Sabbath School at the Methodist Church in the afternoon.

Curley's Trial Resumes

The first witness called on Monday was David Van Hovenbergh. The prosecution wanted to get a second witness who could unequivocally identify Curley. They asked the bank's cashier if the prisoner's voice was the same as any of the men who held him captive the night of the robbery. Van Hovenbergh said he could not answer, as he had not had an occasion to hear the prisoner speak. Before the witness could finish his thought, the defense objected. It was obvious the prosecution was hoping the judge would order Curley to take the stand. The judge agreed with the defense and Curley was allowed to remain silent. Curley's protracted public silence in the courtroom allowed him not to be incriminated. On the stand, Van Hovenbergh did little more than identify the ropes, gags, and lanterns used in the robbery.

Best at his Best

Finally it was time for William Best to be put on the stand. Best was the prosecution's last true chance at a conviction. In the period between Curley's first trial and this trial, Best's reputation had gone down hill. He was now making his income as a shad fisherman. Over the course of the time from the robbery to the trial, Best had repeatedly changed his story as to whether Curley was one of the men he allowed to escape on October 14th. Best's courtroom statement had to startle the prosecution. On direct examination Best testified, "I have some doubts that about one of them (the men he and Dyer arrested) being Curley." The courtroom rumbled from the turn of events.

General Bullard was in a corner. He asked how long Best had had these feelings. Bullard was looking for a connection that could link a bribe or a threat to Best's change in testimony. The witness answered, "About six weeks ago I seen a man at Hudson that looked so much like him (Curley) I thought it were him."

Bullard asked, "Where was this man?"

"At the depot. Dyer says to me 'look at that man he be the picture of Curley." The witness took a breath as if thinking about what had happened in the train station. Best continued, "I thought maybe Curley was out on bail."

"Exactly how much did this man look like Curley?" Bullard was scrambling.

"I was going to speak to the man and ask him if he was out on bail."

"Why didn't you engage the man?"

"I supposed if it was Curley he might give me a short answer." A short answer was slang for being cut off.

Best went on to tell the story of the arrest and stopping at Curtis's tavern. He said that at first he and Dyer had been offered $10 to let the men escape. Dyer had forced the rate up first to $40 then to $120. He stopped there because the men said, "It were all the money they had on 'em." Best went on to show what a sharp negotiator he was when he added, "I would have let 'em go for the $10." On cross-examination, Best said he realized that, as Dyer was negotiating, "the price of Hudson Constables had gone up."

Best went on to retell of going to New York in anticipation of getting more money from Curley. Best told the court that he and Dyer had each gotten $250 for giving the deposition in Beach's office.

Under cross-examination, Best admitted that, at 17, he had been in prison for larceny. Best assured the jury that this arrest was nothing. Best said he was convicted of merely steeling an ax in order to cut wood for money. Best maintained that he, along with some cohorts, had broken in to a store taking some items. Although he was with those who took the tools, Best had personally only taken tobacco products. As if to put those in the courtroom at ease, Best said that other than that one time he had never been arrested except for drunkenness and assault. Clearly he felt drunkenness and assault didn't count. Best had his own standards, which had to be in conflict with the fine gentlemen of the jury who had spent the previous day in Protestant services.

No Dyer

Without calling Officer Dyer, the prosecution rested. One had to wonder if Ormsby felt he had any chance for a conviction. There had been only one witness who would say he was positive he had seen Curley. There were no witnesses that held Curley was in the bank. To add to the frustration, the prosecution had not directly linked the two men who engaged in the mysterious flight to the robbery. A link between the flight and the robbery was a logical deduction but not a given.

The Defense

Several defense witnesses testified virtually the same as they did in the first trial. Frank Shaler, the bartender at Curtis's Saloon; John Flynn, the owner of the tavern where Curley allegedly had drinks the evening of October 13th, and James Lewis, a patron Flynn's tavern all defended Curley. James Bannon, the Green Island man who was in the Hudson Train Station, said that Curley was not one of the men arrested in Hudson.

New Witnesses

The defense put on the stand several new witnesses. Unlike the prosecution, whose witnesses became unsure in their identification, the defense witnesses remained positive in their identification of Curley. These witnesses all placed Curley away from the scene of the crime. Since under cross-examination these defense witnesses would not weaken in their identification, Bullard and Ormsby were forced to use character assassination.

One of the new defense witnesses was John Birke, an Albany bartender. Birke said he was on a visit to New York City on October 13th (the day of the robbery). While he was in the City, Birke had talked to Curley in a tavern. Birke went on to say he had known Curley for several years. Birke was supposed to add credibility to the defense witnesses as he had been a correction officer at Sing Sing, but had to give up the position for health reasons.

A second new witness was Andrew Forest, a liquor salesman. In November, Forest had had a conversation with Best about the escape. Best was tending bar at his brother's place in Hudson when the conversation took place. Best told Forest that Curley was not the man who escaped.

A witness switches sides.

In the first trial, Edward Malloy had testified for the prosecution. In the second trial, Malloy was called by the defense. Malloy was the man who had testified that one of the men arrested in Hudson had a large scar on one of his cheeks. At the first trial Malloy had trouble remembering which cheek, but was sure there was a scar. At this trial, Malloy said the scar was on the left cheek starting just below the eye. Curley had no such scar. Exasperated, Ormsby asked the witness if he had not told him he could identify Curley? Malloy was up to the question. Malloy's response was destructive to the prosecution. Malloy answered

Ormsby, "I don't remember saying that I could identify Curley, I said I could identify the man if I should see him again."

Whether it was necessary or not the defense wanted to offset the testimony of new prosecution witness, Ira Wood. Wood was the prosecution witness who said he saw Curley arrested in Hudson. The defense called three Troy police officers and Wood's local grocer. Wood had testified that he had seen Curley in the vicinity of the American Hotel before October and several times the previous December. The three officers, Fay, O'Neil, and Dunn all had known Curley for years. These three officers were assigned to patrol in the vicinity of the American Hotel. All three told the court they had not seen Curley in years. John Scully, a grocer and wheat-buyer, was considered by both sides to be a truthful and sincere man. Scully had talked to Ira Wood several times about the arrest in Hudson. Wood had told him that he had no idea if the man arrested in Hudson was Curley because, "he (Wood) had not 'ad his glasses on."

Feeble Attempt

It was as if the prosecution had given up when the attorneys announced they had no rebuttal witnesses. They were able to get the court to allow them to read into the record the testimony of two witnesses from the first trial (Filley and Carpenter). These two men had told the first court that in private conversation Bannon had told them that the station was so crowded he could not see if it was Curley who was arrested.

The defense actually had rebuttal testimony. They closed with Best's character being questioned. The defense put on three more witnesses, each telling how Best did not have a positive reputation in Hudson. The prosecution put into the record the testimony of Columbia County Sheriff Ham, the man who thought more highly of Best and the man who Best had gone to when he hocked the pistol.

Closing

Fursman had to feel confident as he approached the jury to make the defenses closing remarks. Point by point Fursman picked apart the prosecution's case. First there was no direct link proven between the two men who had apparently fled south and the robbery. Virtually no prosecution witness had held that Curley was the man they saw in the flight south. Fursman conceded that it was true witnesses had said one of the men was about the same size as Curley. Fursman's concession on size was only a ploy. Boldly he pointed out to the jury the size comparison between Curley and one of the men in the audience saying size isn't a good measure by itself. Fursman went to say he was also the same size as Curley. To Fursman, a comparison based only on size was of no value. He spent a major portion of his closing making the jury see the lack of relevance in all the comparisons. Fursman went even further asking a member of the audience to come forward and sit next to Curley. All present were struck by the resemblance. One needs to wonder if the man just happened to be there or was planted by the defense. [At this point there was a major disruption in the court as deputies had to take an intoxicated man from the room.]

Fursman went after the prosecution's only major new witness, Ira Wood. Wood had told the court he had seen Curley in Troy in the December preceding the robbery. Fursman pointed out the conflict between Wood's testimony and the three constables all of whom were assigned to the same area and none of whom had seen Curley during the time period. Fursman stressed that Wood's identification was based on a childhood memory of Curley. Fursman's remarks relating to the issue of recognition deserve to be quoted directly: Wood came from faraway Texas to swear away the liberty of Curley. I will assume he is an honest man. He is human liable to err, he is not infallible. He says, 'I knew Peter Curley, I have known him from childhood.' How many boys have I known in childhood that I would not know now? How many of you, as men, knew men [you] would not know now?

The final portion of the defense's summary was reserved for an attack on Best. Best had done enough damage to himself while on the stand that Fursman probably did not need to spend much time on him. Fursman reviewed for the jurors the number of times Best had changed his identification of Curley as one of those who escaped in Hudson. He reminded the court that Best was a man for sale. Fursman could not resist reminding the jury that while Best was on the stand he had testified that he had been willing to let the prisoners, whoever they were, go for $10. Fursman asked the jury to question, if Best was the better witness of the two who made the arrest in Hudson, what did that make Dyer? After all the People were not willing to put Dyer on the stand.

Fursman knew that because of the extreme economic impact of the crime, there was at least as much emotional pressure as a real basis for conviction. For justice's sake, Fursman tried to make the jury aware of its need to separate its feelings from the evidence before them.

"I want to ask you a question, the answer to which may send the prisoner to State Prison for twenty years. Would you send a man to State prison on the evidence of William Best? Would you send me to State prison on his evidence? But if you would not send me why would you send him (Curley) who the law presumes to be as innocent as you or I?"

Fursman closed by reviewing the testimony of the defense witnesses who placed Curley in New York City at the time of the bank robbery.

Prosecution

As Ormsby approached the jury, he had to feel like the defenders of the Alamo: out numbered, out gunned and with no means of escape. Although Ormsby may very well have had right on his side, he had been terribly out preformed and his witnesses were weak at best. The people of Waterford and the press had demanded this trial. They wanted revenge and a story. Ormsby had been forced to prosecute a feeble case. His true crutch, Tremaine, had been pulled away at the last possible minute. Ormsby knew that his only chance was to appeal to the jury's heart and feelings of guilt. Ormsby needed to make the jurors realize they would feel guilty around their neighbors in Waterford, if they did not convicted Curley.

Ormsby appealed to the emotions of those gathered in the courtroom and the jury. Ormsby started by saying, "I knew that great attempts would be made to free the good-looking man. He has been attended by some who are among the most eminent in the whole State. But I now stand here addressing men who will be governed by convictions that will come home to minds and hearts."

Ormsby tried a route that he knew would be cut off. "This defendant's claims of mistaken identity have been brought out before. Prisoners have the right to go upon the stand themselves-" Before he could finish the sentence the entire defense team was on its feet arguing the fact that just because a defendant did not take the stand could not be used against him. The judge reminded the jury that Curley's not taking the stand should not influence the deliberations. Ormsby and the defense knew that a judge saying not to consider a point did not erase the impression from the jurors' minds.

Ormsby then reviewed the sequence of events showing the logic connecting the two men in a mad flight south with the robbery in Waterford. Ormsby acknowledged the men who had planned and executed the robbery were intelligent. The district attorney pointed out that, as intelligent men, the thieves would anticipate that detectives would be at every local station. They went south to catch a train because they knew that they would be identified if they went to one in Troy or Albany.

He Did His Best

Ormsby did as well as anyone could as he tried to explain away Best's weak character. "He has been tempted once too often. I believe he would barter away your life and mine for pay."

With Best's character fully shredded, the prosecution's case rested on the testimony of Ira Wood. Ormsby put it squarely before the jury, "If you believe Ira Wood, if you believe in a man's memory, you must place Peter Curley in the position that belongs to him (prison)."

Ormsby reviewed the defense's witnesses, carefully avoiding the three Troy police officers who said Curley was not in Troy in December. Ormsby suggested that perhaps Curley was so cautious he knew how to avoid the watchful eye of the police.

His brief pointed closing over, Ormsby appeared disappointed as he resumed his seat. In fairness to Ormsby and General Bullard, they had given it their all. The prosecution was wise enough to know that the factual aspects of this case were weak. The only true chance the People had for conviction was if the jury acted out of emotion. Ormsby sat wondering whether justice would be served better by an emotional conviction or a factual acquittal.

The Jury's Charge

Judge Bockes charged the jury for almost an hour. There was virtually no difference from this charge and the one he had made to the first jury. Bockes was not surprised when, less than an hour later, the jury returned with its verdict.

During their brief deliberations the jurors had decided that Peter Curley was not guilty. As the verdict was announced, the courtroom, which was filled even at this late hour, first cheered then erupted with thunderous applause.

Judge Bockes took it upon himself to admonish Curley. Although the jury had found him not guilty, as judge he felt Curley was guilty. Bockes then released Curley.

Peter Curley's Wine

The jury had been staying in the beautiful Sans Souci Hotel in Ballston Spa. After the court was closed Peter Curley, the defense attorneys, and the men on the jury went to the hotel to celebrate. As a token of his appreciation, Curley bought several bottles of wine, which were shared freely among the jurors.

There is a story told to this day that at the celebration Peter Curley stood before the jury, raised his glass and asked the jury to join him in a toast. It is claimed he then said, "this on the people of Waterford." This claim, which cannot be found in any newspaper, is probably an exaggeration that is based on a report from a Troy newspaper. One paper said in total: "Before Pete Curley's departure for New York City, he sat down to a sumptuous spread laid out for him at a well know restaurant by members of the fancy fraternity of this city. Wine flowed freely and many quaffed the creamy cup to the health and long life of Pete, the bank smasher."

The Troy *Press* was at this point a supporter of Ormsby. This is evident in its closing paragraph covering the trial:

> Mr. Ormsby is deserving of much praise for the manor he had conducted the case of the People from the start. Few men would have worked against the odds he did. Having suddenly been deprived of the assistance of the bank committee and the able counsel of Lyman Tremaine, he has made a stand that adds all the more to his previous reputation as a lawyer and prosecuting attorney.

There is a question as to the level of support of the bank committee. One could question whether the committee members were out for justice or their own personal interest. Later events and reports probably answered the question.

The blame for an injustice by not convicting Curley would, in one swift motion, shift from the prosecution and bank committee to the jury. Numerous articles appeared in newspapers, both in the region and from as far away as New York City admonishing the jury for its decision. The projection was in part based on the infamous Curley's Wine.

Rumors and Reports

With the jury decision rendered, the rumor mill started grinding out speculation as to the reason for the outcome. The fact that the testimony did not warrant a conviction was not enough of a reason for the local populace to accept an acquital. The perception was that there had to be some other reason why Curley was now on the streets instead of in prison.

Settlement?

The day after the verdict, newspapers started to circulate articles suggesting that the registered stocks and Bonds, taken in the Waterford robbery, were going to be returned. This rumor was predicated on a supposed secret agreement between Curley's representatives and either the district attorney or perhaps even members of the jury. The concept was that, in exchange for Curley being found not guilty, the bonds would be rendered to a third party. If the source was correct the *Daily Saratogian* had it that $350,000 in bonds would be restored. There were even stories in several newspapers that the bonds had already been turned over to the authorities.

Both General Bullard and District Attorney Ormsby were quoted as saying they were unaware of any settlement. The general insisted that the trial had been a hard fought battle in which both sides wanted to win with no expectation of a settlement. Fursman, the leading defense attorney, said, perhaps rather unflatteringly, that he had "never seen Ormsby work harder."

One day after the trial, both Bullard and Ormsby made statements blaming the trial's outcome on the newspapers. According to one article, the prosecuting attorneys maintained that the extensive coverage had so impinged the reputation of Best that the jury considered him unbelievable. Ormsby and Bullard acknowledged that much of their case was based on the connection of the arrest and release/escape of Curley by Best. The prosecution's assessment was that without Best the case was weakened beyond repair. If this explanation was actually from either of the attorneys it shows their lack of understanding of what happened in the courtroom. The fact was that Best, in his final testimony, had said he was not sure it was Curley he had arrested that day. The jury's verdict had nothing to do with newspaper coverage, but rather the reasonable doubt put in the jury's mind by the prosecution's primary witness.

There was yet one more theory being propagated regarding the reason for the jury's verdict. The day after the decision it was speculated that one of the jurors had been compromised. The theory was actually published in a Troy newspaper. The article said that one of the heaviest losers in the robbery had somehow gained access to a juror. The big loser allegedly told this juror of a potential compromise and suggested that by leaving Curley a free man the people of Waterford would be better served. The story continues that this juror in the deliberation room laid "whole matter before the gentlemen." The suggestion was that to punish Curley was to cause many poor people to suffer. The implied outcome was - better to release Curley than to extend the suffering. The compromised juror was reported to the same man who had been quoted prior to the trial as saying, "If they need someone who would send Peter Curley to prison I'm the man." The juror later wrote a letter to the newspaper confirming he had in fact made this statement, but denying he was compromised.

Speculation on the Outcome

The *Daily Saratogian* carried an article claiming it had learned, from unnamed sources, that the bank committee had at first believed that Curley was indeed one of the robbers. But during the period between the first verdict and the second trial, the committee had gathered information that Curley, at the very least, was not at the scene of the robbery. The newspaper was unable to learn if the committee believed he was not involved in the planning. In any event, this information caused the committee to withdraw its support of the prosecution.

Who Gained?

The *Daily Saratogian* tried to ferret out the biggest winners in the trial. Reports ruled out the people of Waterford because even if a compromise had been reached the best they could hope for was the return of their own money. The people of Saratoga County were eliminated, as they had to foot the bill for two long and expensive trials. Assuming the jury was wrong, the *Daily Saratogian* felt that the winner might have been Curley and his band. The newspaper was careful to note that since he had been found not guilty, Curley's guilt was only conjecture. The newspaper acknowledged Saratoga County had definitely proven to be a profitable place for lawyers.

Compromise?

Speculation of a compromise had filled every local newspaper for a week. On May 29th, the Troy *Press* decided to send in its self-appointed "News Commissioner" to determine what was the truth in the affair. According to this person, if there was a compromise in the works no one involved in the trial knew anything about it. Both sets of attorneys had done their "up most" to secure a verdict on behalf of their side. This commissioner was now certain that there never was a compromise involved in the trial. Instead, the commissioner had found that the ban committee was still trying to get the money back through negotiations.

The commissioner noted in his report that it was a fact that no one could legally buy bonds they knew were stolen. With all the press about the trial, the brokers would now be much more careful, since if they were to buy the bonds from someone other than their rightful owner, they (the brokers) would be out the money. Therefore, the value of even the coupon bonds had dropped radically even for those who now held them. The commissioner pointed out that it was in every party's best interest to get the bonds back to their owners at as low a percent as possible.

It is interesting to note that the district attorney of Westchester County was serving as a representative of the parties now holding the bonds.

Reviews of the Jury and the People of Saratoga County

The Rutland *Globe* did an outstanding job of presenting the dilemma that faced the Curley jury. This newspaper had reviewed the evidence and the quality of the witnesses. It took the high road - not casting blame for the outcome on the judge, jury, or prosecution. To the *Globe*, the fault was in the character of Best who had obviously accepted money from both sides in the twisted affair.

The *Globe* envisioned a potential outcome that it felt warranted notice to its subscribers. "It is certain that there is a practice of settling with rogues who have made large hauls, and thereby encouraging them to prey upon other members of the community in consequence of which the most dangerous rascals have the best chance to run at large." In short commit a small crime, go to prison; commit a big crime, go free.

The *New York Express* took quite a different attitude. It projected to its readers that the jury was very wrong in arriving at the not guilty verdict. Here is the relevant portion of their editorial:

> Compounding a felony is, in the spirit of the law and the opinion of the public, quite as bad as committing a felony. The counsel for the people did his utmost to bring the robbers to justice and to render the State's prison it own. But his efforts were thwarted by a 'corrupt jury.' ...The dignity of the law and the public confidence in the honor of man should be shaken by this event. If evidence is forthcoming the jury or some of the jurors should be indicted for, as the matter remains, not only those who lost their money by the robbery suffer, but a stigma hangs over the entire community from the fact that, as above stated, a compromise has been effected between the criminals on the one hand and the respectable (?) citizens on the other.

The Utica *Observer* was without a doubt one of the most opinionated newspapers that covered the trial. It was quick to point to the perceived flaws in the persons involved in the trial. The first attack was leveled at David Van Hovenbergh. After admitting that Van Hovenbergh's family was bound and in the hands of armed men, the newspaper stated its feeling's regardin Van Hovenbergh's and all teller's responsibility to the depositors in the situation.

> His faithlessness and cowardice call for severe condemnation. He was the custodian of the wealth and savings of scores of persons. It was his business to guard that money at all hazards. His life was in no real danger. Thieves are not often murderers and in this case nothing was to be gained making way with the cashier. But he fell an easy victim to his own timidity. He opened the doors and the robbers having secured all the valuables within their reach made their escape.

The attack of Van Hovenbergh was only the appetizer. The *Observer* was serving their main course on the directors of the bank. "It may surprise the directors of the Waterford bank to be told that they are more dangerous characters than Curley and his gang. But it is full time that their guilt is branded on upon their foreheads. It is they who have set up a premium upon robbery; it is they who have taught thieves that it is safe to steal, if they steal enough. It is asserted that there is a great rejoicing among the favored stockholders over the return of their valuables. But there is a greater rejoicing in the slums of New York, and among the criminals everywhere over the result of Curley's Trial and of these negotiations. The robbers chose the ground on which they consented to meet the robbed. All fear of punishment was banished, all question of guilt held in abeyance. The entire transaction was conducted on a purely business basis. The thieves said in substance, 'These securities which were formerly yours are now ours. It is not worth while to inquire how we obtained our title to them. But we possess them and in this case possession is ten points of the law. If we could use them we would we should keep them. As we can't use them we will sell them back to you for thirty-five cents on the dollar.' And the directors responded substantially as follows; 'Gentlemen thieves – we appreciate your high tone and will freely aid you to escape any penalty which may attach to your operations. We have considered your offer and thanking you for your unexampled kindness in not destroying our bonds altogether, we accede to your terms and hereby tender you $100,000. Accept the same with our best wishes and your future prosperity.'

The *Observer* went on to say that robbers had brought themselves to the level of bank presidents.

> Let this sort of thing go on for a few years longer, and all honest men will be absolutely at the mercy of thieves. If the wickedness is to be checked and the safety of property secured, the condemnation of the public must be visited first of all on the capitalist who thwart justice and make terms with thieves in or to secure a percentage of the money which they have lost.

Some Money Returned

The *Observer* may not have been as far off base as it may have appeared at first glance. Since the conclusion of the trial there had been a rumor afoot that the bonds would be returned for 33% of their face value. This would mean that the $300,000 in bonds would cost $100,000. It would take until August before one of the Troy newspapers was able to break the second biggest part of the robbery.

From the beginning, it was understood that the $18,000 in government bonds that were redeemed within days of the robbery and the $8,500 in cash were permanently lost. About $430,000 was stolen - the exact figure was never established. This meant that there was at most $400,000 up for negotiations.

The Troy *Press* was able to learn that the bank committee was indeed trying for the return of the bonds. The report was well researched. "At the conclusion of the second Curley Trial, the bank committee, by an arrangement and solemn covenant with the alleged bank burglars, proceeded quietly to New York City and prowled 'about the metropolis, visiting strange haunts and dealing with hard characters that shunned the light, until at length their purpose was realized and the surrender of the bonds for a certain sum agreed upon.'"

The excursion to the underworld of New York took only days as on May 30, 1873, a rickety New York City hack cab pulled up to the curb outside a popular hotel. A single horse, that looked to be "little more than a skeleton," pulled the antediluvian vehicle. With patched and battered harness the transport looked like something belonging to the poorest of the poor. "The shrewdest auctioneer, if engaged to dispose of the equipage, would have knocked down to the first bidder at any offer." The carriage demonstrated that one should never judge a book by its cover, as inside was the trove of a virtual treasure. This fortune represented the life's work of many of the people of Waterford. There were several members of the gang inside the rickety cab guarding the fortune. "The servants of Justice were as blind as their mistress, and so a big rag-picker's bag was removed from the carriage unmolested to the apartment where the thievery was to be compounded." The thieves were wiser than the bankers were, as they would only accept cash not commercial paper. Looking at the bag on the floor like a starving man does a steak "the head of the bank committee, in the hurry and excitement of the moment," counted out 10% of the supposed contents or $30,000 in bank notes. The thieves even provided a receipt for the money showing it met all their demands.

A Royalty

Those involved in the negotiations now took part in the second and greater larceny inflicted upon the depositors in the Waterford Bank. Through the negotiations the bank committee had paid the bonds's custodians only 10% of the face value of the bonds. Yet before the committee members left for New York they had entered into a contract with the customers. Under the terms of the contract the committee was allowed to settle for as much as 33%. On the way home the members of the committee agreed that their efforts deserved a royalty and applied a five to 23% fee for their services. When the 23% royalty was combined with the 10% paid the custodians the total still came in at the agreed upon 33%. Since even on the highest end (33%) the total paid by the depositor was at the rate allowed under the contract, no one realized for some time that in addition to paying the thieves, they had actually paid the bank committee.

Ormsby, hearing of the issue, said if warranted he would take the matter before a grand jury. The members of the bank committee probably lost little sleep, as they were already aware of Ormsby's success rate with bank theft.

A Paper's Analysis of Security

In November of 1873, the Rochester *Democrat and Chronicle* attributed the Waterford Bank robbery to members of the despicable crowd who visited fine hotels of Saratoga Springs the previous summer. The reporter's hypothesis was based on the number of burglaries that had taken place in the popular resort. The reporter's speculated that whoever had committed the crime had heard about the bank and its assets while in the vicinity. The newspaper felt those involved in the robbery may actually have cased the bank during the summer.

The Rochester newspaper went further, saying that the practice of having a person who knew the vault's combination living so close was neither wise nor the best practice. Although electricity as a tool was relatively new, already electrical alarms had been installed in the door jams of some banks. Unfortunately, it was already known that these early systems were easy to bypass. The newspapers theorized that the best system was numerous windows and constantly lit gas lamps. For security reasons, those who passed by should be encouraged to look in, not discouraged by curtains or shades.

Was Peter Curley Still At Work?

In January 1876, the Northampton National Bank in the village of Northampton, Massachusetts, was robbed of over $720,000. The execution of the crime was almost identical to the Waterford robbery. Around midnight, seven men broke into the house of the bank's cashier, a Mr. Whittlesey. The family was tied, gagged and gathered together in one room. Unlike the Van Hovenberghs, Whittlesey and his family did not actually live in the bank building but in a house just a short distance away.

The crime had intricate planning and was perfectly executed. Prior to the break in, the robbers had constructed gags using children's rubber balls with a wire through them. A ball was placed in each family member's mouth, with the wire tightened behind his or her head. Each member of the gang wore a mask cut from the legs of men's trousers. The masks totally covered their faces except for an eyehole cut out. When members of the gang noticed that Whittlesey appeared to be trying to find identifying marks a blindfold was placed over his eyes. When it became time to gather information, the cashier was separated from his family and taken to a downstairs bedroom. To this point the execution of this crime exactly paralleled the Waterford robbery.

Members of the gang forced Whittlesey, at pistol point, to impart the combination to the safe. Like David Van Hovenbergh, Whittlesey tried three times to prevent a robbery by providing the wrong combination. This group of robbers anticipated problems with Whittlesey, so one member of the gang was writing down his directions. It was easy for the band to determine that he was making up the numbers and directions on the spot. Whittlesey was unable to repeat the directions or numbers a second time thus demonstrating the lie. Finally fearing for the safety of his family, he provided the correct combination.

The crooks were a patient lot. They waited in the cashier's house until they were sure the bank's watchman had left for the night. At 4 o'clock in the morning, four of the robbers went to the bank, where, with considerable effort, they were able to break into the safe. When they left for the bank, the robbers took a key that was needed to open the interior doors of the safe. In total, four keys were needed to open the interior doors. For security reasons, the remaining keys were in the hands of other officers of the bank. [Something had been learned from Waterford] The interior doors proved not to be a problem for the robbers as they removed the locking mechanism with a crow bar. With the security guard home for the night, the gang worked unmolested for the two hours it took them to enter the safe and remove its contents.

Without any notice, somewhere around six o'clock in the morning, the three members who had remained to guard the family silently slipped into the night and headed toward the train station. Five members of the gang had previously bought their tickets, so the station clerk was unable to provide any description. One member did forget to buy his ticket in advance. The description given by the station clerk was very plain and would fit most men in the area. The seventh member left with the bounty probably by wagon. The men were loosely identified as men who had been seen hanging about the town for about a month prior to the robbery.

Before the robbers left the bank they jimmied the lock on the vault making it impossible for the clerks to open it. Without access to the contents of the vault, the enormity of the act was not known for several days. Ultimately an expert at opening safes had to be brought in from New York City to get the vault open.

Isn't it a coincident that Peter Curley was on the streets at the time of the robbery.

Visiting Today

Waterford is one of those rare communities that should become a living museum. Through oscillating financial times, this village has maintained its architectural dignity from the period when it was the economic hub of the Empire State. If, after you read this book, you have the opportunity to visit Waterford you should consider it a requirement to park your car and walk the streets as did, Ormsby, Brandon, Curley, Enos and the Waterford gang. Most of the sites you have read about still exist. You can walk the various getaway routes, although at this time you may not walk across the bridge to Peebles Island as most of the gang did early in the morning of October 13th, 1872, as they were escaping.

The painted brick building that housed the Saratoga County Bank still stands on the northeast corner of Broad and Second Street. The original entry to the bank was through the area where the corner window is today. The bars that "so effectively" protected the money are still on the windows to the basement. The building is now a private home so respect for the privacy of the owners is necessary.

Kitty corner across the street is a brick building that was the home of a tavern; that was the Morgan House mentioned in the book. This is still a restaurant where you are able to get a fine tavern dinner. Show your knowledge of the story and wait for a table near the window. At this site you can actually put yourself in the exact place of the men who sat and planned the robbery you just read about. If you look away from the bank and down toward the river you will see Isaac Ormsby's house. He lived in the third house from the corner on the eastside of the street.

You can walk three blocks north to the former railroad station (now the library) and reenact the daily trek taken by Ormsby as he went to the station to board the train for Ballston Spa and the trial. As you walk back down the street you will be walking the footsteps of Brandon as he went to the Howard House for his hearing.

The hack that was believed to have waited most of the night for two of the men was on First Street one block closer to the river.

Lyman Tremain

Henry Smith

The bank in Waterford as it is today. The corner window was originally a doorway leading directly into the bank. The fence the burglars climbed was to the left of the building.

WHO'S WHO IN THE ZOO

Since ideas and beliefs don't develop in a vacuum, the background of individual attorneys in these cases was considered an important supplement to the text. This section is premised on the concept that a lawyer's training and experience play into how he or she presents a case. The research regarding these lawyers' attainments led to the discovery of an elaborate web, in which these men had trained each other or been partners in practice. Perhaps equally important was who was in the "in group" and who was not.

William Augustus Beach was one of the most highly esteemed lawyers of his time. Beach was born in 1813 in the Village of Ballston Spa. His family moved for a period to Saratoga Springs where Beach attended the Saratoga Academy. He completed his high school education at the military school in Middletown, Vermont.

For generations his family had long been involved in the practice of law. His grandmother on his father's side was the sister of Supreme Court Justice Smith Thompson. He was admitted to the bar in 1833, after studying under his uncle, Judge William Warren – his mother's brother.

Unlike most lawyers he successfully moved his practice to different communities three times in his career. He began his practice in Ballston Spa, the seat of Saratoga County where he had his office for 18 years. While in Ballston Spa, in addition to his general practice, from 1843 through 1847 he was the district attorney of Saratoga County.

He formed two partnerships during his time in Ballston. The first was with Daniel Shepard – the judge in the preliminary hearing for Brandon and Curley in the Waterford Bank Robbery Case. The second partnership was with Augustus Bockes, the judge in the Waterford Case. His reputation was so stalwart that in 1851 he was able to move his practice to the industrial center of Troy without financial ramifications. Later he moved again to New York City, where he was ranked among the premier attorneys in the nation.

In the centennial anniversary of Troy, Roswell Parmenter described Beach as:

> Whatever fame now belongs or shall be hereafter awarded to William A. Beach was acquired by him in his professional capacity, and in the ordinary practice of his professional life, while engaged in establishing and defending the legal rights of others and not of himself. He demonstrated the great truth that man at times makes the circumstances under which he acquires distinction among his fellow-men. He possessed in a large degree quick perception, sound judgement, critical discrimination, and an analytical mind. .... I do sincerely believe, that as an orator in the judicial forum William A. Beach was the peer of Demosthenes or Cicero or both combined.

William was also the father of Miles Beach who was on the defense team in the Waterford trial.

Augustus Bockes was born in the Town of Greenfield, Saratoga County in October 1817. His high school years were spent at Burr Seminary in Manchester VT. He taught school for three terms, one in Greenfield where one of his students was Isaac Ormsby. He completed his law studies under William Beach. He was such a good student that shortly after he was admitted to the bar in 1843 he became a partner of W. A. Beach. In 1847, he left his partnership to become a county judge. He was a judge at different levels for 35 years.

Edward Fitch Bullard was born in Schuylerville in 1821. At 19 he was admitted to the bar in Waterford (1840). Just four years later he was appointed by the governor to the position of examiner of the chancery. This position was abolished in the constitution of 1847. He then began practicing law in Troy and built a large practice. Like Beach, his reputation continued to grow and by the late 1890s he was a lawyer in New York City.

Edgar Luyster Fursman was one of the youngsters in this case, having been born in 1838. He was from Schuylerville where he practiced law for several years after he was admitted to the bar in 1858. He had studied law under Judge Wait of Fort Edward. In 1866, he moved his practice to Troy, in Rensselaer County. He joined a firm with Levi Smith, a former partner of W. A. Beach. By 1882 he was a county court judge - a position he was reelected to in 1888. One year later he went to the Supreme Court (New York).

William Learned was born in 1821 in New London, Connecticut. He was descended from an old New England family with both of his grandfathers having served in Congress. Unlike any of his contemporaries mentioned in this section of the book, Learned graduated from college before studying for the bar. In addition to being a member of the famous society, Skull and Bones, he was also salutatorian of the Yale class of 1841. Learned studied for the law under Gould and Olin in Troy and was accepted to the bar in 1844.

Learned moved to Albany in 1850 where he joined a partnership with two older, more experienced attorneys, Gilbert Wilson and James Cook. By 1867, both of his partners had retired and Learned found himself in private practice, representing some of the biggest clients in Albany. In 1870 he was appointed to the Supreme Court of New York and promoted to the head of the Third Department in 1875. At the time there were only three judges in the Third Department, one was August Bockes.

He was on the faculty of Albany Law School of which he would later be president. He was also president of Albany Female Academy (1880s name), and a trustee of Albany Academy.

He married twice. By his first marriage he had three daughters.

Nathan Moak was a man who was either defined by his birthright or defined himself in such a way as to overcome it. Born in 1833, Moak was one of 11 children. His parents had a small farm near Sharon, New York, where he, like all children born to the same circumstances, was required to help as soon as he was old enough. He attended the district school then attended the Sharon Academy for three terms. Having saved sufficient money, he enrolled in the Cooperstown Academy. In Cooperstown he resided in the home of Dr. Fox. In addition to his academics, he spent as much time as possible learning from Dr. Fox and considered himself well-schooled in physiology. In 1851-52 he was a teacher in the district school. His obituary in the *New York Times* tells much about how he envisioned himself. He "never forgot his early struggles and therefore the student found in him an ever ready listener and a true friend."

In 1852, Moak began the study of law in Cherry Valley, being admitted to the bar at Cortland four years later. From his admission to the bar in 1856 until 1865, Moak was a member of two different firms in Cortland. He then moved to a partnership in Oneonta where he practiced for two years. In 1867 he joined a firm in Albany, headed by Henry Smith, an attorney in the Waterford Case. In 1871, in addition to his private practice, he was district attorney of Albany County, his only elected office. He served as district attorney for only two years. Later in his life he was appointed to serve as a temporary justice to the Second Division of the Court of Appeals. For two years the governor had appointed a second set of judges to clear up a backlog of cases.

To be a judge at this level was the ultimate achievement for someone who saw himself as a student of the law. He prided himself on his law library, and on how his legal advice had been sought in some of the biggest cases in the country. He was even an advisor to James Ramsey when he took on Fisk and Gould in the "Susquehanna War." Unlike any of the other lawyers in this book, Moak continually listed in his credits the convictions he had attained, not his acquittals.

Moak's personality and manner in court eventually cost him his ultimate goal. In the early 1890s Governor Hill considered Moak for one of three vacant positions on The State Supreme Court. When former Albany City Mayor M. N. Nolan heard Moak was in line for one of these high positions he paid Hill a visit. The ex-mayor, who was a wealthy brewer told the governor that if he appointed Moak, he (Nolan) would contribute $20,000 to have the governor and his slate defeated. One report in the *New York Times* even claims that Nolan held his fist under the governor's nose threatening him in every way possible. Moak's offence – a few years before the ex-mayor's daughter was involved in a divorce case. Moak, who represented the other side, took the opportunity of the courtroom to cast aspersion on the mayor. *The New York Times* characterized Moak's attack as "savage and uncalled for." The governor decided to take his second choice and a man supported by Nolan – **Cady Herrick**.

When Moak heard that he was not to be the governor's choice he cut lose with a tirade against the governor that showed his true colors. Moak was brilliant, and his vocabulary excellent, but his manner defiant and bitter. He said the following of the governor in the *New York Times:* "He has rarely met or squarely disposed of any duty imposed upon him…(he) thinks statesmanship consists in evading responsibility."

Moak become ill in 1895 and went to Cooperstown to rest and recover. His obituary shows the depth of his personal friendships as it points out he died there in mid-September among his books.

Isaac Ormsby was born in 1820 in the town of Greenfield, Saratoga County. He was a student at the district school with his last teacher being Augustus Bockes. After teaching for two years he studied law under E. F. Bullard in Schuylerville. He was admitted to the bar in 1846. He practiced for his entire career in Waterford where he lived in the house with colonial pillars just three buildings south of the Saratoga County Bank. For 15 years he was the district attorney of Saratoga County.

He was considered the noblest of men, above a bribe or a threat. Of equal importance to his ethics was his integrity. He completed his task without wanton attacks on his opponents.

Ormsby died in 1892 after suffering a stroke that left him paralyzed. He and his wife, the former Laura Cramer, had one son, Charles, who also was an attorney.

Daniel Shepard, one of the judges in the Waterford case, died at a young age. In Ballston Spa, he had been a partner of William Beach.

Henry Smith, born in 1829, was admitted to the bar when he was only 18 years old. He set up a practice in Cobleskill where in 1854, at the age 25, he was nominated to be county judge. He lost but received the highest number of votes of anyone in his party. This loss may have been a positive event since he then relocated to Albany in 1857. In 1865 he became a partner with Nathan Moak. It was said that he had total recall, "every fact, every rule, every principle remained with him forever." He was involved in three of the biggest cases in the area, the Brandon case in this book and the cases of General Cole and Fredrick Smith that will be found in the subsequent volumes.

Politically he was the district attorney of Albany County, assemblyman from Albany and Speaker of the Assembly. He was a congenial man surrounding himself with many friends socially, politically and professionally.

Lyman Tremain was born in Greene County in June of 1819. On his mother's side he was descended from the Lyman family, an old Connecticut family. He studied at the Kinderhook Academy before going to New York City to study law. Admitted to the bar in 1840 he began his practice in Durham. In 1844, he became the district attorney of Greene County and in 1847 he became a county judge. In the early 1850s he moved to Albany County where he became a partner of Refus Peckham.

Tremain was a giant in both legal and political circles. He defended Edward Stokes for the murder of millionaire James Fisk. After appeals to the highest courts in the state, Stokes was given a second trial and ultimately only served four years in prison. He was also involved in two other major cases that will appear in future volumes in this series - General Cole and Fredrick Smith. Politically Tremain was known Statewide having served as attorney general of New York State just prior to the Civil War and running for lieutenant governor in 1862.

His personal life was much more traumatic. He had three sons and one daughter. His oldest son, Frederick, was at 21, a lieutenant colonel in the New York Calvary. He was killed in the battle of Hatcher's Run Va., in February 1865 just two months before the end of the war. Tremain wrote and published a book documenting Frederick's life. His third son died as the result of a fall over the railing of the family home when seven years old in 1868. His second son, 30- year-old, Grenville was his law partner in 1877. That year Grenville was nominated to be State's Attorney General. Shortly after losing the election Grenville became suddenly ill and died within days. The blow was too much and Lyman became ill himself and died the following fall.

Shaw

A Story of Misguided Love

The Beginning

If it had not been for one tragic event, the life of Charles Shaw would have passed without warranting so much as a footnote in a local history book. Instead of the good fortune of peace, tranquillity, and anonymity, a series of circumstances led to Shaw's name being related to the most monstrous event in the annuals of the rural village of Cambridge, in Washington County, New York. This rough, uncouth, part-time farmer, part-time teamster and part-time pursuer of women was accused of the murder of his wife and three of his children. He was not charged in a fifth death, that of his infant grandchild, though it was attributed to the same events that caused the demise of the other four.

To insure a conviction on at least one of the charges, the prosecution decided to have separate trials for each victim. Ultimately, Shaw was convicted and sentenced to be hanged for the murder of his wife, a crime he may very well have not committed.

The Scene

The incident that changed Shaw's life occurred in a small rustic red house on the west side of the turnpike approximately halfway between the village of Cambridge and the hamlet of Eagle Bridge. The old road near where the house stood is narrow, having followed a streambed slowly north for several miles. The land is rugged with the foothills to the east leading into the Green Mountains of Vermont. So close is the home to Vermont that the first of the low rocky foothill begins just beyond the field across the road from where the house stood. The Shaw house and the others of note in this story have, as a result of entropy, disappeared from the landscape replaced by one modern house.

Even in 1873, the Shaw house was considered ancient. The unassuming dwelling sat on a small knoll. The simple house was described as the type of two-story home typically built for a farm laborer. Despite a history of difficulties between husband and wife, the house was neat, clean, and had decent furniture, reflecting positively on Mrs. Shaw's spirit.

The Shaw homestead was part of the Fowler farm. Blackman Fowler, the owner of the land, was a well-respected man in his late seventies. A portion of his income was derived from renting out sections of his large farm, which were worked as shares. Fowler had attained the status of a semi-retired gentleman farmer.

The relationship between the Shaws and Fowlers could be found throughout the northeast. Working a farm "for shares" was a form of sharecropping. Sharecropping is usually considered a uniquely southern circumstance. In the decades after the Civil War, however, it was also common in New England for a family of limited means to work a farm and share the profits with the owner of the land.

The Incident

On the fateful Monday, January 17, 1873, most of the members of the Shaw family were present when the mid-day meal was served. At this meal, six of the female members were believed to have ingested a "corrosive poison." Whatever the source, within hours the first members of the family were stricken. While the ill-fated could still talk they described the symptoms as having come on violently and suddenly. Over the next several days, three doctors - in some way - attended the afflicted family members. Two of the doctors described their condition as extreme dehydration as a result of purging and vomiting. By the following Thursday, the twentieth, when the story broke in the newspapers, six members of the family were sick including the mother, Julia Shaw. By Friday morning one of the children, fourteen-year-old Elizabeth, was already dead. As the circumstances were slowly revealed by the newspapers, the people of the region immediately determined that the incident was a crime and ascribed the blame to the father, Charles Shaw.

Within a month, five members of the Shaw family lay dead. The five included the baby born to Marrietta, who only lived a few hours.

The Family

At first, the newspapers reported that the Shaws were married 25 years. Today, the problem with that number of years would be that Charles was only 40 at the time of the "illness." By the time of the trial, it would be determined that the couple was married 24 years. Charles and Julia were married when he was barely 16 and she only 15. During the course of their marriage, the couple had 10 children, eight of whom were alive at the time of the murder. The oldest son, Alvanza, was 22 years old, married and no longer living at home. The second born was twenty-year-old Fannie. Fannie, like her older brother, was married and living outside the house. Fannie's one-year-old illegitimate son, Willie, was living in the house the night of the poisoning but was one of those not affected. The six remaining Shaw children all lived home. The third oldest was Marietta, 18, who had married the year before. Marietta was pregnant with a baby due at the time of the onset of the illness. The remaining siblings were Elizabeth age 14; Hattie, age 12; Anna, age eight; Ida, age five; and Emma, age three. Another girl, Betsy, was born between Hattie and Anna. She had died in the two-year period before the incident. The tenth child was probably born between Marietta and Elizabeth, as the family appears to have had a child every two years.

Only the two youngest children living in the house were not stricken. There was some confusion over Emma, the youngest girl. Some reports listed her among those afflicted; however, Emma had a bad cold but never suffered like her siblings from the poison. As mentioned the other child who was never "sick" was Fannie's illegitimate child, Willie.

The Shaws as Neighbors

The Shaw clan arrived in the area of Cambridge about 15 years prior to the murders. Charles had started out as a day laborer and teamster. He owned his own team of horses that he would hire out (thus the derivation of the term). Over the years the family lived in the region, there had been a history of trouble between Shaw and his employers. The root of the problem was Shaw's lack of respect for them and the work they provided. The Shaw family's lot seemed to improve a few years before the deaths when Charles landed the contract to farm for shares. This was the home in which the family was living.

The Shaw children were described in the Troy *Times* as "strong physically but weak morally and mentally." Although by 1873 there was access to a free public education, the children in the family were basically unable to read or write. Today we would describe most of the children as ruffians. Marietta may have been the exception as she was always after her parents to attend church.

To outsiders, the Shaws looked as though they felt the incident was "not much worthy of comment." This reporter may not have understood the severe nature of the symptoms. Whatever struck the family, and by the time of the first death it appeared to be poison, the symptoms rendered those it impacted with maximum force, draining its victims of all their strength. Their fight for survival may have taken all their will, leaving them without the energy needed for compassion.

In the terms of the day, the Shaws

were considered by their community to be "poor white trash." Reports in *The Daily Saratogian* were only slightly more polite when on January 22, 1873, they referred to the family as one whose "society was not much sought by many." There were, however, exceptions made when the men of the community, in sowing their wild oats, savored physical companionship from the opposite gender. In 1871, the eldest daughter, Fannie (age 18 at the time), had, without the "benefit and custom of marriage," given birth to a son. Charles, Fannie's father, was unusually close to both the illegitimate child and Fannie. The relationship between the three was so close that some in the neighborhood had questioned the paternity of the boy. When the poison did not affect the boy, all the neighbors took his escape as confirmation of their worse suspicions, whispering that Charles was the boy's father.

The Eldest Daughters

In the year that followed Willie's birth, Fannie had married Burton Mattison (in some papers the name was reported incorrectly as Madison). Burton was a man that the *Troy Times* described as looking "like an idiot."

Approximately a year before the poisoning, the second daughter, Marietta, married a man named James Hathaway from Warren County. Shortly after the wedding, Hathaway and Marietta's relationship was impaired by the presence of Hathaway's other wife. The court felt serious enough about Hathaway's transgressions that he was sentenced to serve time in the jail in Salem. Hathaway felt incarceration confined his relationship with women and liberated himself. This escape was with force and violence resulting in his conviction on the more severe charges of "breaking jail." On the evening of the murders he was serving time in the Albany Penitentiary.

Charles Shaw

The family's unfavorable reputation was primarily attributable to the behavioral patterns of Charles. He was reported to be a lazy pilferer with a passion for women other than his wife. To his close neighbors, Charles Shaw was considered repulsive and contemptible. Over the years his name had been associated with several minor thefts in the area, a fact he disputed to the reporters. One of Shaw's neighbors, hearing of his denials, related that on one occasion he had hired Shaw and his team to bring the hay in from a field. Checking at the end of the day, the owner of the land found one wagonload of hay missing. He traced the hay droppings to Shaw's barn. The hay was later returned to its rightful owner.

Shaw was universally weighed to be without honor and cruel to his family. To persons of lesser strength, Shaw was maligned as a mean, repulsive bully. Typical of men of his character, when confronted by those who were his physical equal, he was a coward. In short, Charles Shaw was considered one of the meanest, most despicable men in the vicinity. Ascribing the deaths to him was no great leap.

Despite some early reports to the contrary, Charles was either a temperate man or, at worst, a rare binge drinker. As rough as his behavior was, Shaw did not regularly imbibe. Early newspaper reports that he was a heavy drinker may be attributed to the fact that this crime happened at the incubation of the temperance movement. For political reasons, violent crimes, especially those committed against family members, were often attributed to the ingestion of alcohol. To blame alcohol for violence was especially true in Cambridge.

Historical Note

The temperance movement had a real foothold in the area. In 1873, Cambridge was a dry community forbidding the sale of any alcoholic products. It is interesting that society allowed for poison, opium, and ether to be bought without any prescription but the sale of alcohol was illegal.

The economy of the country was weak with a depression in progress. As in all bad times, when people are not getting financially ahead they become religiously dogmatic. Although not the capital of intolerance, in 1873, Cambridge at least had a seat at the table.

Julia Shaw

Mrs. Shaw enjoyed a much better reputation than did her husband. It was the community's perception that she was compelled, by circumstances beyond her control, to constantly struggle to keep the family together. To earn extra money, each Monday she worked for a neighbor, Mrs. Blakesly (or Blakely). Julia Shaw's service to Mrs. Blakesly was in the most humble of occupations, that of a wash woman. Few talked of Julia's personality but some of those who did said she was subject to radical mood swings, fits of anger and emotional withdrawal. One repeated source of her hostility was jealousy of the time her husband spent with other women. Clearly, over the years, Charles had provided her with sufficient reason to be jealous.

The Other Woman

Around 1870, the Briggs family moved to a farm on the plains north of Cambridge. At the time of the murders (1873), LeRoy and Sarah Briggs had been married seven years. The Briggs family consisted of Leroy, Sarah and their two sons. LeRoy, at 28 was a farm laborer, although he had no regular job.

Before the Briggs family came to the Cambridge area they were friends with Hob Shaw, Charles's brother. While living on the plains, LeRoy met Charles. Charles's first visit to the Briggs's was to deliver a dairy cow that LeRoy had purchased from him.

Despite her humble station on the social ladder, Sarah was extremely beautiful and personable. Two reporters, who interviewed her in jail, were both wowed by her appearance and social skills. Similarly, Charles was taken by Sarah's attractiveness. Over the first year he knew the Briggses, Charles contrived a variety of reasons to visit the Briggs's house several times. It was widely reported, but not proven, that on at least one occasion while the Briggs family lived on the plains, Charles spent the night at their house. On this occasion LeRoy was away looking for work. Sarah, 24, did not work outside the home but was distinguishable in a negative way; she was a member of the Fones family of Battenville. Other members of her family had had experiences with the courts in the county. Included in the list of near-do-wells was her sister-in-law who had been charged in an assault on an elderly neighbor. The sister-in-law was drunk at the time.

The Shaws and the Briggs

In the fall of 1871, the Briggs and Shaw families became neighbors. The Briggses moved across Cambridge to a residence less than a quarter of a mile from the Shaws. Charles had enticed LeRoy to move into the "old toll collector's house," a house just north of Shaw's homestead. Shaw had convinced LeRoy that in the new home he would be nearer to possible work. Shaw may have had several ulterior motives in attracting Briggs to his neighborhood. Leroy paid the rent for the family's new abode directly to Shaw. A second motivation for Shaw's interest may have been to be nearer to the fair-skinned Mrs. Briggs. Sarah was, at the very least, quite the flirt - raising her skirt too high as she flitted around the kitchen.

The "tollhouse" came with basic furnishings. To rid the new home of bedbugs, Sarah had used some "stuff" attained from her former neighbor, John McClellan, to clean the beds before they moved. She would later testify that she had thrown the stuff away in the fall. In court it would be contended that the product might have been the corrosive sublimate that resulted in the five deaths.

Despite Shaw's assurances of employment, LeRoy was not able to find work in the new neighborhood. Eventually Briggs went to Williamstown, Massachusetts, in search of employment. Often employment kept Briggs away from home for weeks at a time. Even before Briggs's absences, Shaw had started visiting the Briggs's house each day and eventually every evening.

Although Sarah Briggs and Julia Shaw "did not get on very well," Sarah would often return Charles's visits. Sarah would later claim that she had called at the Shaw house almost every day. Her visits may not have been so much a desire to be in the company of the Shaws as her need to have companionship. Sarah was extremely gregarious, pursuing the company of others like famished people seek food.

While on one of her visits, Sarah suggested to Julia that she use some of her poison to get rid of the bedbugs. Several of the Shaw children later reported that Sarah went so far as to say she had enough poison to kill a regiment. According to these same Shaw children, Sarah had even bragged that if she did poison anyone she would never get caught.

Since the children in both families were not in the habit of regularly attending school, the Briggs children and the youngest of the Shaw children were constant companions who played together daily.

Sarah and Charles and Julia

No later than the spring or early summer of 1872, twenty-three-year-old Sarah and thirty-nine-year-old Charles became paramours. The newspapers, which were not fearful of slander suits, stated that, by her looks and persona, it was doubtful if Charles was Sarah's first extramarital relation. Having established a firm commitment to being a drunk, LeRoy treated the relationship between his wife and Shaw with indifference. Julia was less accepting. She confronted her husband, charging that he was spending his meager earnings for the support and comforts of their depraved neighbor. Julia didn't seem to be troubled by the physical part of the relationship only the use of the family's limited money. To his wife's charges, Charles responded by cursing and threatening her. On at least five separate occasions he beat his wife to a point that she filed charges for criminal assault. Initially some of Shaw's own children claimed that he went beyond just a beating when he threaten their mother's life.

Emotionally weak, LeRoy later told of having been in the Shaw house when Charles went after Julia with an ax. LeRoy claimed to have taken the ax from Charles. Comparing the stature of the two men it is doubtful Briggs could have stopped Shaw from any form of action let alone disarm him. It is far more likely that when Briggs told the story he was purely bragging. Even in his version, after taking the ax from Shaw, Briggs took no action when Charles then struck Julia with a fist. Another version of the same story simply holds that eighteen-year-old Marietta stood in front of her father and he dropped the ax.

On December 4, 1872, there was an incident so serious that Julia went to Justice Leonard Fletcher to have Charles arrested. On this occasion Charles had again hit his wife, leaving severe bruises. On December 16, Shaw was arrested on his wife's warrant. Not surprisingly, Shaw was unable to raise the money for bail. A couple nights in jail resulted in the promise from Shaw that he was repentant. Based on Shaw's penitence, in conjunction with the assurance that the Briggses would move out of the area,

Justice Fletcher released Charles with just a reprimand. A few days later, Julia withdrew the warrants against her husband.

Sarah and LeRoy Move

With the catalyst of Shaw's arrest, the relationship between the two families became so strained that, on Christmas Day 1872, the Briggses moved to Hoosick Corners. The parting, like all forced separation of lovers, was extremely emotional. Despite - or maybe to enhance - the hostility that existed between the two women, on the day of the move Sarah stopped at the Shaw house and reportedly gave Julia a "large" piece of her mind. The argument grew even more critical when Charles joined in, taking the side of Mrs. Briggs. As she left the scene, Sarah assured Julia that she would be the children's stepmother within six months.

Multiple members of both the Shaw family and Julia's family reported that Charles had, on several occasions, offered his wife a cow and fifty dollars for a bill of divorce. Divorce was very rare in the 1870s. It appears that Julia firmly held that Charles had been led astray by the wiles of Sarah. Julia probably felt that with the Briggs move final, her relationship with Charles would again settle at the level it was at before the Briggses had moved next door.

One Possible Source

At some point on Thursday, January 13, Charles went to Cambridge and purchased from the local butcher, Allen Skiff, 40 pounds of sausage. Shaw's purchase was part of a batch Skiff had made up days before. In total, Skiff had made about 100 pounds of sausage. Over the first few days after the sausage was made, Skiff sold about 60 pounds to his neighbors. In fear the sausage was aging, he sold the last 40 pounds to Shaw at a discount. The day after the sale to Shaw, Skiff had some of the sausage for breakfast and noted that it was slightly sour. Two other families who purchased the sausage were interviewed and both said that they had eaten at least a portion of the sausage without any side effects. It was this sausage that the defense would hold was the source of the "illness" in the Shaw home.

The Lovers Meet

On Saturday, January 15, 1873, Charles harnessed his team and went to the Briggs's apartment in Hoosick. Charles spent the night with the Briggses, returning to his own home about four o'clock in the afternoon on Sunday. LeRoy was home with his family during Shaw's entire visit. In front of LeRoy, Charles and Sarah talked of leasing and running a hotel together. Although he knew they only included him out of courtesy, LeRoy could not imagine how they could ever get the money to open the hotel. He, therefore, wrote the conversation off as idle dreaming. There is no official statement as to the sleeping arrangements on this night; however, it is doubtful the LeRoy would have objected to any accommodations.

Charles Comes Home

There were two claims as to Charles's behavior after his return. One, which is probably a rumor, holds that upon his return he went to Wait's Corners were it is claimed that he spent the night with a bottle of whiskey. The reports which hold he was drinking on Sunday night maintain he returned to his home on Tuesday. The other claim, including a statement from his wife, state he returned on Sunday, and didn't leave until early in the evening on Tuesday.

On Monday, January 17, the day after Charles returned from his excursion to the Briggs's, and four days after the butcher noticed a strange taste, Julia cooked the sausage for the family's mid-day meal. There were nine people present at the meal: the six Shaw children, Fannie's illegitimate child, Willie, Charles and Julia. All nine at the table ate from the same platter. Everyone agreed Charles ate at least as much as any other member of the family. By late afternoon the symptoms had begun their agonizing onslaught.

Treatment

On Tuesday, Charles decided that rather than pay a doctor's bill he would go to Wait's Corners and purchase a bottle of whiskey to make the family vomit whatever was making them sick. He came home and fixed a sling - a hot mixture of whiskey, water and sugar. Charles first served his daughters who were sick. He then offered some to his wife, who refused to drink fearing it was poisoned. To alleviate her anxiety, Shaw drank half the tumbler. Shaw later fixed a separate mixture for those who were well, Emma and Willie, and more for himself.

On Wednesday evening, when it became apparent that the illness was not subsiding, Charles harnessed his horses and left for Cambridge seeking the services of a doctor. Charles first called on Dr. Kennedy who refused to come to the home. He then went for Dr. Benjamin Ketchum who also refused to come out. Ultimately, Charles went to Dr. Lyman Clark who, although he refused to come to the house, did give Charles some medication to get the family through the night. Virtually nothing is known of what Dr. Clark prescribed.

Thursday morning Elizabeth was so sick that Charles went again to get the veteran and venerable Dr. Kennedy to aid the family. When Dr. Kennedy visited that morning, he immediately realized the gravity of the situation. Since Dr. Kennedy was also a county coroner, he felt that if he treated the family he could find himself in a conflict of interest. Dr. Kennedy transferred the case to Dr. Ketchum, who had been practicing medicine in the community since his graduation from medical school 13 years before.

Dr. Ketchum went to the house on Friday morning and immediately perceived the problem to be poison. Pursuing his belief that it was foul play, Dr. Ketchum inquired as to what the family had eaten. Shaw noted only the sausage and did not mention the liquor. The failure to mention the liquor may have been because of Dr. Ketchum's deep involvement in the temperance movement. It had been four days since the family had eaten so the doctor believed the poison was already in their systems and did not try to pump their stomachs or give emetics.

Dr. Ketchum's prognosis for Elizabeth was that she would only live a few hours. The doctor was right; Elizabeth died the night of January 19-20th. On Saturday morning, Charles hitched his horses and went into Cambridge to tell the doctor of Elizabeth's death. Upon hearing what happened to the girl, Ketchum consulted with the coroner, Dr. Kennedy. Dr. Kennedy told Dr. Ketchum to get Dr. Henry Gray and go to the Shaw house. Gray and Ketchum were to perform an autopsy on Elizabeth. As part of the autopsy they removed Elizabeth's stomach for further examination. Without a search warrant the doctors examined the house quickly but were unable to observe any containers that may have held a poison.

As the family's physician, Dr. Ketchum examined the remaining family members, telling Mrs. Shaw that another death was probable. He informed all of the afflicted that they should all make statements relating to the nature and onslaught of their symptoms.

The Statements

That morning, Mrs. Shaw made her initial statement to Dr. Ketchum. Mrs. Shaw would later make a second statement. The difference between the two caused issues at the trial. The statements made to Dr. Ketchum were not legally recorded. In Julia's initial statement, which was riddled with inconsistencies, she said she did not believe Charles had poisoned the family. Later, Julia told the doctor that she had feared for a time that Charles intended to poison her. Her fears were based primarily on an incident the week before the poisoning involving her nephew, Christopher Shaw. According to Julia, Christopher claimed Charles had approached him with a request that he poison her with a white substance. She professed that, although Christopher was "a bad boy," he would verify her statement. Julia went on to relate the story of her husband's trip to Hoosick. According to Julia, Shaw went to Wait's Corners, on Tuesday, to purchase some liquor. When he came home, he made up a drink and gave it to her and all six of their children. When Fannie's bastard child asked for some, Charles responded, "Wait until they get through, and I'll fix you up." In this statement, Julia said the little boy and her husband later drank from a different tumbler. Later she says that her husband drank from the same tumbler.

Charles Meets the Doctors

On the Saturday morning following Elizabeth's death, Charles remained in Cambridge for a while probably making the arrangements for the funeral. Charles was not home when the doctors came and performed the autopsy in his home near his sick family. When the autopsy and the treatment of the stricken family members were completed, the two doctors started back to Cambridge. Along the road to the village the doctors came upon Shaw. Charles seemed eager as he asked the doctors what their examination had uncovered. Dr. Gray informed Shaw the entire family was in very bad shape from what was almost certainly a result of poison. Dr. Gray asked, "Shaw, how is this?"

Charles responded, "I don't know what it can be unless it is the sausage."

Along this frozen road, Dr. Gray informed Shaw that they had Libbie's (the families name for Elizabeth) stomach for examination at Albany Medical College. Before they even left for the Shaw house, the doctors had planned that as part of Libbie's autopsy her stomach would be sent to Dr. Stevens of Albany Medical College and Professor Perkins of Union College for analysis.

Dr. Ketchum's Analysis

With what he had learned at the Shaw house, Dr. Ketchum felt strongly that Charles was guilty. Upon his return to Cambridge, Dr. Ketchum went immediately to Justice Fletcher seeking a warrant for Shaw's arrest.

When he arrived home, Shaw saw his daughter's body after the autopsy. He was angry with his sick children for allowing the doctors to perform the postmortem. As he told his wife of the death of Libbie, Shaw assured her that if he had been home they would not have taken their daughter's stomach. This conversation where he said he would have somehow prevented the removal of the stomach was presented by both the newspapers and the prosecution as proof of Shaw's guilt. Since it was said to his dying wife, the statement may have equally been a concern over the separation of his dead child's body and the knowledge that she would not be buried whole.

The doctors wanted to eliminate the possibility of trichinae. Under a powerful microscope, they examined a sample of the pork sausage and a portion of Elizabeth's stomach. Based on this examination the doctors determined that the culprit in this case was not trichinae.

Arrest

After Dr. Ketchum's warrant was issued on Saturday, Deputy Sheriff James Archer went to the Shaw's house and arrested Charles as he was splitting wood for the fire. As the deputy shackled him, Shaw claimed his innocence in what was described as the "most emphatic language." Cambridge did not have a jail, so Shaw was held for the night in the lobby of the Union House.

On Sunday morning, and for the next couple of days, Deputy Archer exhibited what appeared, at first glance, to be remorse for the prisoner. He agreed to accompany Shaw to the house for visits with his family. Archer may have had ulterier motives for allowing the visits. He may have been seeking to witness comments made by the family to Shaw. During the trial he would testify to some of the conversations he heard during the visits to the house.

Shaw Visits His Family

When the deputy and Shaw arrived at the house, the oldest daughter, Fannie, was home ministering to her mother and sisters. Fannie asked Archer if she could have a private conversation with her father. Archer informed Fannie that privacy was not a possibility. For his diligence, Archer was rewarded with proof that the use of vulgarities was a family skill shared equally among the members - regardless of gender.

Two of these visits in which Shaw was allowed to see his family took on strange twists. Once, Shaw went to his wife's bedside and his outpouring of affection for her was so strong Archer was forced to restrain him. On a second visit, as Shaw leaned over his wife, there were comments made between the two that Archer would later testify to in court.

Rumors Persist

As is usually the situation in a case of this magnitude, from the very beginning rumors exceeded the truth. One rumor that was reported at the end of the Saturday held that Ida had also died. The error was corrected by the newspaper on Monday.

A Visit to the Death House

On Monday, the reporter from the Troy *Times* accompanied Justice Fletcher and the coroner's jury on a visit to what was being referred to as "the death house." They found the mother, Julia, prostrate on the bed. By this time, Julia's condition had diminished so greatly that she was blind and had virtually no energy. On the bed with Julia were two of her daughters, Ida and Anna. In the same room were the other stricken children. Fourteen-year-old Hattie lay close to death on a lounge. Pregnant, eighteen-year-old Marietta was on a second couch. Two chairs were pushed together to form a bed on which lay Emma, the youngest girl. Emma was only suffering from a bad cold - not the same symptoms as the rest of the family. The amount of agony in this one room would have weakened even the most hardened person's heart.

The oldest daughter, Fannie, and her husband and the "well" child, Willie, were in a separate room. In a third room was the coffin for Libbie whose funeral was scheduled for later that day. The reporter was emotionally struck by the fact that the sick were indifferent toward their dead sister.

Already the family's accounts, as to what happened that fateful Tuesday, were changing. Comments made the previous Saturday to Dr. Ketchum, most of which were perceived to incriminate Charles, were now being modified. Reporters and the police involved in the investigation believed these alterations were the work of Fannie, who they knew was "close" to her father.

Suspects

The investigators felt that there were three possible candidates responsible for the poisoning. In order of probability it was either: Charles, Sarah or a stranger characterized as the mystery man. The family described the stranger as being a "bad looking cuss." There was even one theory running around the community that the act was committed by a combination of the three. In this rumor Charles and Sarah hired a bad looking cuss to poison the family.

In 1873, as today, the first person to be considered as a suspect was the spouse. To the already established fact that Shaw wanted to be free of his wife was added several other condemning circumstantial actions. Shaw had purchased the sausage giving him potential access to this as one source of the illness. Although virtually no one believed that the sausage was contaminated while in the store, some felt Shaw may have used the heavy flavor of the sausage to mask the taste of the poison. For this theory to be true, Shaw would have had to have placed the poison in the sausage after his return from his weekend visit to Sarah. Second, everyone had heard of Mrs. Shaw's claim that her husband had tried to induce his nephew to poison the family. These two incidents, as well the reports that he used a separate tumbler for his own drink, placed Shaw clearly as the primary suspect in the investigation.

Sarah, the temptress, was considered to be less of a suspect in the actual murder. Rather, she was being perceived as an accomplice perhaps even to the extent of providing the poison. For Mrs. Briggs to be a suspect she would have had to have had an opportunity to administer the poison to the family. There was no evidence that Sarah had been at or near the Shaw house at any time since she had moved the previous Christmas Day. Mrs. Briggs's complicity, and all felt she was in collusion, was theorized as that of an accessory. Most residents of Cambridge felt that, through her notorious feminine wiles, Sarah Briggs had lured Charles into the ghastly deed of poisoning his family. This enticement was the culmination of the weekend of Charles's visit to the Briggs's home.

The third suspect was the phantom stranger. Perhaps under Fannie's guidance, the Shaw children were now telling a story of a mystery man who had come by the house the week before the onslaught of illness, announcing that he was a friend of LeRoy Briggs. At his visit, the stranger had stated his purpose was to do an inspection on behalf of Briggs, who wanted to purchase the farm. Believing Briggs did not have the money, the family was suspicious but let the man tour the house and barn and to drink from the well. The Shaw children now theorized that on his visit this stranger may have poisoned the well. Although most of those close to the investigation believed the story was concocted, water was taken from the well to be tested.

One of the more interesting twists in this braided investigation was the input of Fanny Wolff, Julia, mother and the newspapers' subsequent follow-up. Fanny Wolff had arrived at the house on Saturday just after the arrest of Charles. The children's maternal grandmother had been called in to help Fannie Mattison (Shaw's oldest daughter) with the care of the surviving children. She was quoted as saying, "Charles Shaw is an indifferent sort of man, but I'll never believe that he did this; he thinks too much of his children."

The yellow press was near its apex in the 1870s. Newspapers not only reported the news; they freely intermingled editorials and theory with the facts. This liberty in reporting is demonstrated by this exact quote from the Troy *Times* in response to the mother-in-law's observation. "A man may think a great deal of his children, but when the devil, in the shape of a woman, who controlled him and who hated them bitterly, was directing his movements, his love for them may have been in haste to do her bidding." This quote shows a prevailing political perception as to the source of blame perceived by the general public. A man may be capable of doing an evil deed but he needs the catalyst of a woman's passion to trigger acts against his family. One wonders how much public perception has changed in the last 140 years.

A New Theory Appears

On Monday, the case took on a new shape. One of the few people who would claim to be Shaw's friend was quoted as saying that for the past year Charles had believed that his wife was plotting to poison him. This advocate went to so far as to say that Charles was afraid to "e't at home." Shaw's unnamed friend was spreading a different tale than the one told by the newspapers. The friend was claiming that Mrs. Shaw had poisoned the food intending for her husband to eat it. Somehow there had been a mistake and the poisoned food was eaten by the family. To this line of reasoning the friend offered no evidence.

The Deaths Continue

Before Marrietta's bigamist husband went to prison, James Hathaway had facilitated in his eighteen-year-old bride's becoming pregnant. When the poisoning occurred Marrietta was in her ninth month. Dr. Ketchum, in his visit to do the autopsy of Libbie, declared Marietta was recovering well from the effects of the poison. Although still feeble by nature and weak from the poison, Marietta insisted on going to the funeral of her younger sister. Charles also attended Libbie's funeral escorted by Deputy Archer. While the family was gathered for the funeral at the North White Creek Baptist Church, Marietta was chilled and caught a cold. On January 24, one short, painful week after the fatal meal, Marrietta went into labor. The frail infant died within minutes of her birth. Marietta, already feeble, died two days later.

At the time of Marietta's death, the prognosis for Mrs. Shaw was that she would not survive. On a more positive note, the doctors expected that the remaining daughters affected by the poison, Hattie, Emma, Anna and Ida, would all survive. The doctors were wrong, as the next to die would be poor Hattie.

A new rumor had developed that another local physician, Dr. Niver, had been called to the Shaw house the previous year because it was feared Julia had been poisoned. Mrs. Shaw's speedy recovery prevented any follow-up. There is no record that a Dr. Niver ever gave a statement that he had in fact been to the Shaw house.

There was a certain coldness that prevailed over the community regarding the investigation. Those who knew the Shaws saw them as immoral, brutish animals - almost subhuman. Although they wanted a guilty party punished, there was little true sympathy for the surviving members of the Shaw family.

The Newspaper Slips

The *Washington County Post* was generally neutral in its reporting of the crime. On February 6, in reporting Hattie's funeral, the newspaper noted in a small section that the child had been "buried like dogs," meaning without the benefit of clergy. This editorial note was probably meant to elicit sympathy for the family.

A letter was published the following week from a local minister informing the newspaper of how numerous ministers in the area had been to the house to comfort the dying. The *Post* also reported how the Reverend Mr. Lewis, the pastor of the Center White Creek Baptist Church, had provided the dead a funeral service. Further, at each of the funerals the choir had sung.

Printing the letter from the minister was one of the few times when one of the papers came even close to actually retracting a story concerning the case. The *Post* defended its story explaining that its source was one of the victims, Mrs. Shaw. The newspaper maintained that Mrs. Shaw had told the reporter that only one minister had come to the house. When the *Post*'s reporter was at the house he had bent over Mrs. Shaw as she said through her parched lips, "Pray for me; oh, Pray for me."

Coroner's Jury

Beginning on January 24, Dr. Kennedy held a hearing in Justice Fletcher's office to see if enough evidence existed to warrant holding Charles for a grand jury investigation. Dr. Ketchum was the first person called. The doctor's testimony revealed nothing new with respect to the facts. The cross-examination by the court-appointed defense attorney, Charles W. Stroud, did indicate one possible approach to be taken by the defense. Stroud asked one question that indicates much about the economic status of the Shaw family. The attorney asked if, "a feeble person scantily clothed and fed, should eat a quantity of hard food, be taken sick on a Tuesday and having nothing done until Friday, might not the symptoms be the same as in this case?" Dr. Ketchum assured the court that the symptoms would not be the same. It was obvious that the defense was going to hold there never was a poisoning but rather a malnourished family ate food that was tainted.

Dr. Gray's testimony followed and supported Dr. Ketchum's. In this forum he added nothing to the investigation.

During the illness, Dr. Ketchum visited the house daily. On Wednesday, January 26, Mrs. Shaw was completely prostrate. Her left side was paralyzed and she was totally blind. Fearing that she and others in the family would soon succumb to the poison Dr. Ketchum urged that they give legal statements as to what had happened. At that time a person's statement taken just before death was considered to be always truthful as they were soon to be judged in the ultimate court and therefore would not lie.

On January 26, 1873, Julia gave the following as her *ante-mortem* statement. This statement was recorded by Shaw's attorney, Stroud, who continually objected to Justice Fletcher asking questions of Mrs. Shaw rather than merely having her relate her own story. In reading the text below, the questions asked by Justice Fletcher are obvious.

> I am the wife of Charles Shaw. I think I shall never get well. I have no hope of recovering. We have always lived peaceably together until a certain Mrs. Briggs disturbed our peace - Sarah Briggs. She swore solemn revenge upon us and my family. Said if she could not get it one way she would get it another. She wanted my husband to leave me and go with her. My husband has always been kind except for Mrs. Briggs. If he only had kept from that woman we should all get along well enough. My husband struck me once in the face when Mr. and Mrs. Briggs were present. My husband never threatened me, and I do not think him guilty of putting anything into my food or drink. he has said he would not live with me. My husband has never threatened to poison us. I was taken sick a week ago last Monday, about the middle of the afternoon. My children Harriet, Libbie, Anna and Ida were taken sick on Tuesday, and Marietta was taken sick the next day. We were all taken in the same way with a headache, pain in the bowels and vomiting. I had eaten nothing unusual upon the day I was taken sick nor upon the day before. My husband left home on the Saturday before I got sick and returned on Sunday about 4:00 and remained home until we were taken sick. Tuesday afternoon my husband went and got some whiskey and fixed some of it in a glass and gave it to the children, who were sick. He then fixed some of it in a goblet and offered it to me. I told him I should not drink it until he drank some of it. I told him that this was because he thought so much of Mrs. Briggs and that I was afraid to drink it. Mrs. Briggs had sworn that she would

have my life and take comfort with my husband. I did not know but that there might be something wrong with the liquor. My husband drank most of the whiskey and I drank the rest of it. My husband brought home quite a quantity of sausage the Thursday before I was taken sick, and all ate of the sausage twice a day until we were taken. I gave some of the sausage to my daughter Fannie, who keeps house. There had been no one in the house but our own family for several days before we were taken sick. There had been no stranger in or about the house for a week before we were taken sick that I know of. About a week before Briggs and his wife moved they both swore that they would have revenge upon me; that I need not think I was to have comfort with Charles Shaw the rest of my days. Briggs and his wife moved on Christmas day. I have not seen either of them since. Charles Shaw has threatened my life a great many times. I don't recollect that he ever threatened to poison me. Think Charles Shaw and the Briggses know all about the trouble. About a week before Mrs. Briggs moved away she told me she had two bottles of corrosive sublimate and offered to give me one. I did not take it. She said she had it to kill bedbugs with. Mrs. Briggs often told me she could kill a regiment of folks and not be found out. I did not feel well when I took the liquor, but the children were not sick until after they drank the liquor. Neither the children or I vomited until after we drank the liquor. I had not vomited at all. My husband told me last summer that Mrs. Briggs would be the stepmother of my children. My husband has asked me several times lately if I would give him a bill, and told me he would give me a cow and $50 if I would give him a bill of divorce.

Inconsistency

Within Mrs. Shaw's statement there exists a glaring conflict regarding the health of the children. In the beginning, she states her husband gave the liquor to the children who were sick. Later she said that none of the children were sick until after they took the liquor. This inconsistency is key to the defense. It is also important to note that Julia never implicated the sausage as a possible source, holding to the end that it was the whiskey slings. She fails to give any indication why she was so sick or why she felt the drink made her sick. She also provides no reason why Charles, who drank a great deal from the same glass, was never sick.

Later the same day both LeRoy and Sarah Briggs were arrested and charged in connection with the death of Libbie.

Shaw Gets Moved

Justice Fletcher had heard enough evidence to transfer Shaw's confinement from the lobby of the Union House to the real jail in Salem. After the move, Shaw was characterized by those who came into contact with him as being very quiet. On the few occasions that he talked to his fellow inmates in Salem jail, Shaw repeatedly professed his innocence. The deputies charged with monitoring Shaw felt that the fact that he was in jail seemed to bother him more than the loss of three members of his family.

The day following Mrs. Shaw's death statement, the Coroner hearing reconvened. Dr. Kennedy began the day's testimony by calling Electa Blakesly to the stand. Electa was the woman for whom Julia was employed as a wash woman. On the previous Saturday, hours after Libbie's death, Shaw had gone to visit Electa. Mrs. Blakesly told the court that while Shaw was at her house she asked him the cause of his family's sickness. According to Electa,

Shaw responded, "I am the cause of it; I done it myself, there is no one to blame 'xcept myself." That afternoon Shaw cried in front of Electa. She interpreted his emotional outburst as penitence. Oddly, Mrs. Blakesly took that occasion to lecture Shaw on how he should raise his children. Electa testified that Shaw went on to say that he wished he would be the next to die.

As Mrs. Blakesly removed herself from the witness chair, the spectators, and there were as many as Justice Fletcher's office would hold, were treated to the spectacle of Sarah as a witness. By this time, it was taken for granted throughout the community that Sarah was Shaw's partner in the conspiracy, if not the act. In 1873, just as today, people wanted to see a woman who had the power to entice a man to kill his own children.

Sarah Testifies

Below are the principal points of Sarah's testimony. Each point was refuted by at least one other witness. Through this testimony, she added the perception that she was a habitual liar to her already tarnished reputation. According to the record, Sarah testified to the following:

- She had never heard Charles threaten his wife or say he was going to leave her.
- Shaw with his team had moved her on Christmas Day but that she did not help as she and her two kids were "on a visit."
- She never stayed if the Shaw's started to quarrel, she just walked out.
- Shaw had never complained in her presence about his wife.
- The only "high words" she and Mrs. Shaw had had were when Julia came over and found Charles splitting wood for her.
- She testified that Charles had never given her any gift of clothing or anything else.
- According to Sarah the only reason her family moved in December was her husband's need for work. Sarah asserted the move had nothing to do with Mrs. Shaw.

The Witnesses Continue

The next witness called by Dr. Kennedy was Leonard Fletcher, Justice for the Town of Cambridge. Fletcher testified to the five complaints of assault Mrs. Shaw had filed against her husband. He spoke of the most recent events which had happened the previous December. Fletcher stressed he had released Shaw on the promise the Briggses were moving and that he would have no further contact with Sarah.

Adding to the cast of colorful characters, Julia Ann Mattison was then called. Mrs. Mattison was Fannie Shaw's mother-in-law. Mrs. Mattison told the coroner that she had been to the Shaw house many times but never suspected that Shaw would kill his wife. She went on to say he had "a curious way of speaking." She never really explained what she meant by this phrase. In reading her testimony, it may have meant he used reasonably good English because she did not. Mrs. Mattison said that often Shaw claimed he had a bad life on "'count of his wife's ugliness." In an effort to show that Shaw's problems were with the entire family and not just his wife, Mrs. Mattison testified that she was present when Charles and Fannie had had many quarrels. The most recent argument was when Shaw told Fannie that, within six months, Mrs. Briggs would be her stepmother. On one occasion, when both Mrs. Mattison and her husband were present, Fannie had gotten her father to say that Sarah was a "very bad woman" but he liked her "well 'nough" anyway. According to Mrs. Mattison, before Shaw left that day he insisted that Fannie agree not to tell Mrs. Briggs how he had described her. Mrs. Mattison said that after his arrest Shaw, who was accompanied by the deputy, had come by the house to tell her not to use the well water, as it appeared that it may have been poisoned.

The Mattisons and the Shaws had a relationship in which their contacts rode an emotional roller coaster either high or low but never level. When Marrietta eloped with James Hathaway the year before, the young couple went to the Mattison's house to spend the night. Hearing of their nuptials, Charles Shaw had gone to the Mattison's to get his daughter back. Shortly after Shaw arrived, he and Hathaway were involved in a fistfight. Mrs. Mattison's husband elected to join the fray on Hathaway's side. With the odds at two-to-one Charles was bloodied and returned home without his "beloved" daughter.

The "idiot" Burton Mattison followed his mother on the stand. The crass nature of his testimony, especially where it pertained to Sarah, forced the press to be creative - rewording his statement so that it would be suitable for public consumption. Even then when he described the criminal intimacy he had witnessed between Charles and Sarah the Troy Times declared "the details are unfit for publication." One has to wonder how many red faces there were in the justice's office that day.

Like so many witnesses before and after, Burton told that he was at the Shaw house on several occasions when Charles and Julia were arguing. Burton reported the reason for the quarrels as almost always Charles's habit of going to "bed houses." (bordellos). Burton reported things were so bad that once the previous fall he was forced to physically separate the two Shaws. As he pulled them apart, Burton heard Charles threaten his wife's life. Free of her husband's grasp, Mrs. Shaw had run to a neighbor's house for shelter.

The Source

One of the mysteries that plagued the resolution of this case was the location of the container which held the poison. On this day, Burton tried to shed light on this mystery when he told those gathered that on the Sunday after the poisoning he had found some bottles in Charles's everyday pants. This find was after Shaw was arrested. Burton explained that when Charles had come home with Deputy Archer, he had changed his pants, leaving the bottle in the pocket of the pants he left behind. Burton had immediately turned the bottle over to Dr. Ketchum. Later, during the same day's testimony, it would be found that Dr. Ketchum determined that the bottle contained a harmless product known as sugar lead, which Shaw used regularly. Dr. Ketchum's findings that the bottle was not the missing container nullified Burton's discovery of the bottle.

Without the container, the focus of the inquiry became the nephew, Christopher Shaw. Julia had given a statement that Christopher had been offered $50 to poison her. Newspaper reports indicated that according to a Dr. Niver, Christopher had been out of work so long that he could only be described as extremely poor. The doctor said that, at the time of the hearing, Christopher's wife was literally dying of starvation. The $50 that Shaw allegedly offered his nephew must have been very tempting.

LeRoy Gets Released

The case consumed the village of Cambridge. There was other news regarding the investigation besides just the hearing. Having no evidence against him regarding the poisoning, LeRoy was released from custody. To LeRoy, his release meant the loss of free food and warm lodging.

At the time her husband was set free, Sarah was also released from custody. The deputies asked the two to stay in town until 5:00 o'clock. Late in the afternoon Sarah was formally arrested on the charge of accessory to murder.

Dr Kennedy was informed by Dr.

Ketchum that twelve-year-old Hattie was not expected to live much longer. Earlier it was believed that Hattie would be one of the survivors, now it was apparent that she would soon join her older sisters. Dr. Kennedy moved the coroner's jury to the Shaw house to take the ante mortem statement of the weak young girl. When the jury arrived they saw a frail child incapable of finishing a sentence without pausing to regain her strength. At the time of this murder, very few people could take an official court transcript. Generally the transcripts of the period carried only the answer and not the question. In many cases the statements left out nonessential words. This is the official testament made by Harriet Louisa Shaw:

> I do not think I will get well; about a week before the Briggs family moved out of the old tollhouse, Mrs. Briggs brought two bottles of corrosive sublimate to our house; One was about six inches long the other was half as large; the contents were in a powder form; Mrs. Briggs mixed the powder with water; she asked mother if she wanted some of it; mother said she always killed bedbugs with hot water; mother put some of the powder on her bed; Mrs. Briggs said she could kill a thousand people and not be found out; my mother told her she ought to be ashamed to say it; Mrs. Briggs said she had done nothing with the poison yet; Anna and Ida were at Mrs. Briggs's house playing with her children the day before; the children all went into the pantry to get a drink of water, and finding the bottles brought them out and played with 'em; they were the same bottles Mrs. Briggs brought to our house; I saw the bottles on both occasions; Mrs. Briggs took them away from the children and put 'em on the top shelf of the pantry; the bottle was full at the time; Mrs. Briggs said she got the contents from Henry Ackley's; did not say when she got them, but she had had some before, and used it all up; have heard her threaten to poison all the family; she utter this threat to mother and no one else. Never heard her threaten to poison the well; never heard father threaten to poison the family; but have heard him threaten to kill mother; father frequently brought liquor into the house; the last time he brought liquor was when Libbie was taken sick and he brought some the second day afterward. He made it into a hot sling and gave it to her; all of our family drank of the liquor; father drank of it too; he drank one swallow then fixed up some more and drank that too; he fixed it both times in the pantry; the other children were in the pantry then; did not see him put anything in it; he made a sling with warm water sugar; did not feel any bad effects after drinking it; all drank out of the same tumbler except mother who was not home; my sister Marietta and myself were at the Briggs's house when she mixed the corrosive sublimate powder with some water; there were not labels on the bottles to swear where she got them; she did not leave the bottles with mother; am sure father swallowed some of the liquor.

Inconsistencies

Like her mother's official statement, there are portions of Hatttie's that should be emphasized. First, the Shaw women knew that the poison had been placed on the top shelf of the Briggs's pantry where it apparently was left after the move. Second, according to Hattie the whiskey that was considered to be a potential mask for the taste of the poison was not brought in the house until Thursday. By Thursday, Elizabeth was nearly dead. A major conflict in stories has to do with Julia's presence when the whiskey was consumed. According to Hattie, her mother was not at home when the whiskey was consumed. In Julia's statement she was present when the whiskey was consumed and, even more important, the day was Tuesday. Since she was too weak to be cross-examined, Hattie's statement was accepted as factual.

Fannie on the Stand

The oldest daughter, Fannie, was one of the most complex characters in this case. Many people thought that her illegitimate son was the result of a relationship with her own father. This taboo was supported by early charges that shortly after the incident she was publicly accused of enticing her sisters to change their statements so that their father would not be charged with a crime. To the surprise of most of those following the case, Fannie's testimony at the hearing supported a finding of guilt.

This reversal in attitude may have been the result of the distribution of the family's limited assets. While in custody, her father had a conversation with her brother, Alvanza. Charles told his son that in the event he was not freed that he could have the furniture. In contradiction, her mother, while awaiting death, allegedly gave the furniture to Fannie. Whatever the reason, Fannie's testimony before the coroner came out strongly against her father.

In front of the Dr Kennedy, Fannie supported what had already been ascertained from other witnesses regarding the relationship between her parents. In addition to admitting to having been present when comments had been made regarding a divorce, acts of physical abuse by her father, and the constant quelling over Mrs. Briggs, Fannie added the most condemning comments attributed to her father. According to Fannie, one afternoon while she was visiting her parents her father had told her mother he would have a divorce or her life. Fannie told the court that her father admitted to her mother that he loved Mrs. Briggs and wanted her "to stay the night" in the Shaws's house. Not surprising, Julia Shaw denied her husband's request. Charles told his wife if Sarah could not stay with him he would stay with her. According to Fannie, Mrs. Shaw threatened to follow her husband right into the Briggs woman's house. Charles had responded if she did she "would never come out of the house alive."

Fannie went on to relate a conversation she had with her father the Saturday after Elizabeth's death. The conversation was when the deputy brought her father home to visit the family after his arrest. This was the day when Deputy Archer had denied Fannie a private conversation. Fannie told the coroner's jury that on that occasion her father told her Mrs. Briggs had poisoned the family. Fannie went on to testify that her mother had feared for her life ever since Sarah had moved into the tollhouse.

Cambridge Merchants

Two of Cambridge's merchants were called before the coroner's jury. The butcher, Skiff, told of preparing, selling and later tasting the sausage. Another merchant, Sidney Wright, was called for two reasons. Dr. Kennedy was still trying to assure this jury the source of the illness was poison, not tainted meat. Wright testified that he had purchased and eaten some of Skiff's sausage without any side effects. In an effort to establish that Charles was purchasing gifts for Sarah, Dr. Kennedy asked Wright whether Shaw was a customer. Wright said that the previous fall he had sold Charles a pair of women's shoes. Wright went on to say that later, when he asked Mrs. Shaw about the shoes, Julia told him the shoes never came into her house.

The Jury Rules

The coroner's jury, which worked under far simpler rules than the criminal courts, had heard enough testimony to support a finding that Charles Shaw was responsible for the murder of his child. The finding was as follows:

> We find that Elizabeth Shaw came to her death on the 17th of January, 1873, by poison administered by the hands of Charles Shaw, and that Sarah Briggs was known to the fact and accessory thereto.

The actual date of Libbie's death was three days later. What the jury apparently meant was that the poison was administered on the seventeenth. Later the coroner's jury would add three more murder charges each dated the seventeenth. Charges were added for Julia, Marrietta, and Hattie. There was never a charge for the death of the infant.

In the 1870s, only very significant people were awarded newspaper space for an obituary. Just prior to her death, the Troy *Times* offered a final description of Mrs. Shaw in what had the tone of an eulogy:

> Poor woman; her life has been a sad one. Ignorant and unenlightened, "she has done the best she could." Her life is the sacrifice, which she pays for loyalty to her marriage convenent and devotion to her offspring. Of all connected with this terrible tragedy, this woman, good only by comparison, is the only person of whom the people speak with tenderness. Her hopeless fate commands pity and urges that the veil of charity be thrown over her shortcomings.

The corrosive poison was so strong that it had eaten a hole through the walls of Julia's stomach. Near the end, her immobile, blind shell of a body lay motionless on a bed, awaiting the gentle hand of the angel of death. Early in the morning on February 5, Julia, suffering ended. She had died a slow, painful death, having become weaker each hour.

Incarceration

The Washington County Jail in Salem that housed Shaw and Sarah for nine months still stands. The building is small by comparison to edifices of confinement constructed today. Since there was only a rare need for accommodations for women, Sarah cell was among the men's. The rules that governed the jail in 1873 were very different. Sarah was allowed to have her youngest child, Georgie, stay with her during her confinement.

While in jail, Sarah agreed to an interview with the reporter from the Salem *Press*. The interview provided evidence of her sense of humor as Sarah told the reporter the cell was comfortable and she was "not in any danger of getting lost any way, I find myself right here every time I turn around." She went on to say that she was not concerned about the charges against her, as she was not guilty. Sarah assured the reporter that she had known nothing of the poisoning. When pushed to describe Shaw, Sarah said he was not a "bad man" but rather a "mild man." In one of the few articles that ever described Mrs. Shaw, Sarah told the reporter that Julia was "the most jealous and horrible sharp tempered woman I ever saw."

The reporter tried to break the case by telling Sarah he had heard she was going to turn state's evidence. Sarah responded calmly and with a strong voice, "I don't know anything to tell one way or another. They say Shaw got some corrosive suplimate but it 'taint so."

When asked if there was any truth in the "queer stories" about her and Shaw, Sarah responded emphatically, "No Sir, I should think a woman must be in great want to have anything to do with him."

On the way out the reporter stopped at Shaw's cell. The description of Shaw was anything but glamorous. The reporter told his readers that Shaw had "the same debased and sniveling appearance that he had when first incarcerated."

The Lovers Try to Get Together

Two weeks after her arrest, Sarah

made a hole between her cell and the one occupied by Shaw. Other prisoners overheard her tell Shaw that before her arrest she had visited a fortuneteller. Sarah whispered that she was certain she would be cleared of the charges. She also quoted a common phase of the period when she tried to calm Shaw with "what's been done can't be undone." Over the summer, Sarah had to be moved from the second floor of the jail to the third floor. Apparently she and Shaw had made too many attempts to be "together" to suit the sheriff. Sarah's "first love", her husband, LeRoy, visited the jail on a few occasions that summer.

Early Analysis

The press doubted that much of the evidence allowed in the coroner's investigation would ever be admitted in court. To the press of the area, the prosecution was already over and the case decided. Newspapers went so far as to say Charles Shaw, with the encouragement and support of his harlot, had conspired to put his family "out of this world." The press was sure that, even if a court could not convict Charles, the community already had and was on its way to insuring he would not return to Cambridge. All knew a guilty man, even if not convicted, would leave for the West as soon as possible.

Trial

On October 16, 1873, Acting District Attorney, Grover of Washington County opened the trial of Charles Shaw for the murder of his wife. It was nine months almost to the day since the "alleged" poisoning. The prosecutor's office had decided that trials for the murders of the three children would be postponed pending the outcome of this trial. If the district attorney was unsuccessful, he would be able to reevaluate his presentation and try again on the charges involved in the children's deaths.

The court had appointed two of the best attorneys in the region to defend Shaw. The one who opened for the defense was Daniel Westfall. Although young, Westfall was already respected by his fellow citizens in Cambridge. The second attorney was Charles Hughes. Hughes was in practice with Charles Northrup in Sandy Hill. Hughes, as a defense attorney, was without equal in the area. He was also politically connected, having previously served as congressman, and was soon to be a state senator. He was brilliant and articulate with a truly charismatic personality. His demeanor in court had already resulted in several major acquittals. Hughes would play his best role five years later in the trial of Jesse Billings Jr., featured in the book To Spend Eternity Alone.

Separate Trials

It was reported from the beginning that Sarah and Charles would be tried together. At the last minute, District Attorney Grover decided Sarah's trial as an accessory was to be separate from Shaw's trial for murder. It appears Grover did not want the jury confused as to any of the charges. It is very likely that he evaluated the case against Sarah as weak and did not want the jury to be thinking about innocence in the jury room. In any event, Grover was convinced that a conviction of Charles on the charge of murder was needed before a case for accessory to murder could be proved against Sarah.

The brick building that housed the infamous trial is just off the southern point of the triangular park in the center of Hudson Falls. A large building was necessary to host the massive audience (400 at a time) which attended trial. The building was brand new at the time of Shaw's trial, the construction having been finished the previous summer. This historic edifice is not longer a courthouse but instead serves the community as a theater. There is a taste of irony to the modern use, as during the Shaw trial, and many thereafter, the building entertained a variety of courtroom theatrics.

Most of the witnesses at the trial provided essentially the same testimony they had given at the coroner's inquest. Virtually all the family members and neighbors testified as to the constant quarrels between Julia and Charles. The testimony featured here is where it substantiates or adds to the details previously given.

The first major issue for the prosecution was to determine the cause of death for the members of the Shaw family - primarily Julia - as the trial was for her murder only. The prosecution wanted the jury to believe that Charles deliberately gave poison to his family in the whiskey slings.

Since the defense did not need to prove innocence, only create reasonable doubt, the attorneys maintained several different options. First and foremost, the defense believed the primary cause of the "illness" was the sausage not the whiskey. Of nearly the same importance, the defense team held the root cause was not necessarily a poison in either product but was tainted meat. Leaving no stone unturned, the defense attorneys even tried to imply that the real cause of the deaths could have been the medication prescribed by the various doctors, who prescribed these medications without visiting the family.

By innuendo the defense planned to forward its most comprehensive theory regarding poison. The premise was that the family became sick, and sick only, from eating "tainted" sausage. The defense intended to show that it was through the medication given by the doctors that the poison might have gotten into the systems of those who died. A major piece of the defense's case rested on the lack of sufficient records as to which prescription was given to Charles the night he went for medical help. This defense was bolstered by the fact that on that cold January night three doctors refused to come to the family's aid. Throughout the trial, the doctors were defending their own actions as well as condemning Shaw's.

The Prosecution Opens

The first two witnesses were Drs. Gray and Ketchum of Cambridge. These were the two doctors who had attended the Shaw family in the days following the "poisoning." Their testimonies supported each other. Dr. Gray stated that he suspected from the beginning a corrosive poison had been administered. According to Dr. Gray, the medical signs of a corrosive poison were vomiting, purging, and colic pain - all of which were present in the victims he treated. Both Drs. Gray and Ketchum were present during the post mortems of four members of the family. The doctors told the jury that the stomachs of all the victims showed signs of some form of corrosive poison.

The defense attorneys felt they had won a point when under cross-examination Dr. Gray stated that he was familiar with cases where poison was administered in sausage. The victory was short lived as Dr. Gray added under re-direct that a corrosive poison could have also been administered in a whiskey sling without the taste being discovered.

The Effects of the Poison

Dr. Ketchum rendered a painful description of the effects of a corrosive poison on the human system. His testimony was explicit including details of the immense pain the victims had undergone. Any jury would have to have been moved by the descriptive agony his testimony reported. According to Dr. Ketchum, Elizabeth had died of the primary effects while her mother, Julia, died of secondary effects.

The Witnesses

LeRoy Briggs was the next witness called by the prosecution. He added little to the evidence except that he was present when Mr. and Mrs. Shaw had several battles. Briggs reported that while Charles stayed at his house on the night of January 15-16, Sarah and Charles talked of opening a hotel together. The evening after testifying, while celebrating his ten minutes of fame, LeRoy succeeded in repulsing the reporters and everyone else in the local tavern. He treated the men in the bar to in-depth information of his wife's behavior with other men including Charles Shaw. The blue laws of the mid-Victorian era prevented the details from being printed but LeRoy's tales resulted in his dropping three steps on the social ladder. This collapse is even more significant as LeRoy was barely on the first step of the ladder to start. LeRoy finished the evening sleeping in a livery barn among the animals.

Professor Perkins of Union College, in Schenectady, was the next witness. His examination of Mrs. Shaw's stomach indicated that she had ingested a sublimate of metallic-mercury. Under cross-examination Perkins said he had not actually found any of the sublimate in Julia's stomach. Perkins attributed the lack of sublimate to the reaction of the chemicals in her stomach. According to Perkins the sublimate had already been broken down. He was able to find traces of metallic-mercury, the by-product of the acids in the stomach and the sublimate.

In an effort to establish that Charles Shaw had threatened his wife for some period, several witnesses were called. Among these was Norman Fowler, cousin of the man who owned the farm on which the Shaws resided. Norman was present when, in the heat of a quarrel, Shaw yelled at his wife, "God Damn you won't be here the first of April to disturb me."

Blackman Fowler, the owner of the Shaw homestead, told the court that two weeks before the onslaught of the illness he and Charles had crossed paths in Cambridge. Shaw told him that his wife would not last more than two or three weeks. Charles had gone on to say that in case she should die he would want to continue to rent the farm.

The next witness proved to be an embarrassment to the prosecution. Ebenezer Larman was "not a man of great intellect." Under direct-examination for which he had ample time to prepare, Larman had almost attained the level of acceptable as a witness. He told of how he was at the Shaw house when the "ailment" broke out. Larman said that he heard Mrs. Shaw immediately accuse her husband of poisoning her and the children. Conveniently, Larman was also in the Shaw house when Elizabeth died and heard Shaw say he was "the cause of her illness." The problem was that it was not possible to prepare Larman for cross-examination. Hughes was able to totally confuse poor Larman regarding dates, times and exact quotes. In this dismal trial, Larman provided pathetic merriment at his expense.

A Victim Testifies

In a bold move, the prosecution then called nine-year-old Anna Shaw. Anna was the oldest of Shaw's children present at the time of the poisoning who had survived. After hearing from so many witnesses with limited capacity, Anna surprised the audience with her intelligence. Anna at first appeared to be a strong prosecution witness but faltered badly on cross-examination. Anna had trouble keeping track of the dates when things happened. She did hold to thee fact that the drinking of the liquor slings happened on a Monday not Tuesday, the date given by her mother, or Thursday, as given by her sister Hattie. Anna was certain that the day was a Monday because she had gone to Sunday school the day before. Anna's memory was reinforced by the memory that her father had returned from Hoosick the day before with two new shirts, a truly notable event in a poor family.

Anna went into details, which tended to support her mother's statement about the suspected drinks. Anna told the court how no one in the family was sick before drinking the slings. Although not common in her home, Anna said she and her family had been given slings prior to this Monday. What was different this time where the drinks were made. In the past, her father mixed the drinks in the pantry. On this occasion, Anna said he made the slings upstairs. Her father gave three swallows of the liquid to Ida, Libbie, Marietta, Henrietta and her mother, those who had died. Anna said that the potion caused her throat to burn and her stomach to be sick. Like her sister, Anna said a separate drink was made for Willie and her father. Unlike her mother, Anna said that her father did not drink from the same glass as everyone else.

Merchant

Sidney Wright, the merchant who had sold Shaw the shoes, was called to testify. As in the coroner's hearing, Wright swore that his family had eaten Skiff's sausage with no ill effects. It was the next portion of Wright's testimony that was new and damning. According to Wright, it was in his store that, on the Wednesday before the poisoning, Chris Shaw told his Aunt Julia: "I can tell you of something that you can fix Shaw upon." Wright asserted that Mrs. Shaw pursued the question and, after some reservations by Christopher, he finally said, "Shaw offered me $50 to poison you." According to Wright, Christopher had gone on to remark: "I told him if he had any poisoning to do he better do it himself."

Neighbors

Mrs. Electa Blakesly, Julia's employer joined the list of repeat witnesses. According to Mrs. Blakesly, on the week of the poisoning, Julia came to her house on Wednesday instead of Monday, her usual day. This would have been after the poison was administered. In response to Julia's complaint of feeling sick, Mrs. Blakesly had prepared her some breakfast. Julia was unable to eat any of the solid food but did drink some coffee. During that same morning, Julia had to go outside several times to vomit. Electa retold the story of Shaw coming the following Saturday after Elizabeth's death and saying, "no one is to blame but myself."

Hiram Bentley, the owner of the hotel at Wait's Corners, testified that on Thursday Shaw came in and said he wanted whiskey for his family. According to Bentley, Shaw told him the family had a bad cold and he preferred whiskey to "doctors stuff." The day Shaw administered the whiskey is very significant. If it were Thursday, then it would have been just hours before Libbie's death **and** after Julia had complained to Mrs. Blakesly about feeling sick **and** after the doctors had been to the house.

There are several observations that need to be made regarding Bentley's testimony. The use of whiskey as a medical treatment was fairly common in the area at the time. It was widely held that if it burned going down, tasted bad and made you tired, it had to be good medicine. Cheap whiskey, the type Shaw would buy, would fit this description perfectly. Further, Bentley was a prosecution witness who would have been fully briefed prior to testifying. It is perplexing why the prosecution put on the stand a witness who said the whiskey was purchased on a Thursday when both Mrs. Shaw and Anna said Shaw went for the whiskey earlier in the week. The jury must have considered the issue as Bentley and Hattie said the whiskey was purchased on Thursday. If Bentley's testimony is believed it effectively eliminates the whiskey slings as the source of the poison. It was Wednesday night that the family was so sick that Shaw went for the doctors.

Family Members Testify

Burton Mattison, Shaw's son-in-law, was the next witness. His testimony on this occasion added his hearing of a confession by Shaw. According to Burton, the previous fall he had accompanied Shaw on a wagon trip. While they were chatting, Shaw had told him of his sexual escapades with Mrs. Briggs. Prepared for this testimony Burton's language was not as crass and repulsive as his previous testimony before the coroner's jury.

The tale told by Fannie Mattison on the stand was that of a despondent daughter sharing with her community the tragic circumstances under which she had been raised. According to Fannie, she had shared a roof with her angry father, a man who had said of his wife, "I will have a bill (divorce) or her life." Fannie told the court that her mother had told her that none of them were sick until they drank the whiskey sling that had been given to them by Shaw. Throughout her three-hour cross-examination Fannie never faltered materially in what she held to be true.

Court was then adjourned because Fannie's testimony ended on Friday afternoon. It was noted that the trial was taking longer than expected. Since the prosecution leads off the case, the first week had been its turn to shine. The district attorney had put forward a logical, if primarily circumstantial, case. Without direct witnesses or even the poison, there remained two unproven questions. Who had administered the poison and how? Looking at the sequence of when those affected became ill, the sausage would seem to be the logical vehicle. The problem for the prosecution was the victim, Mrs. Shaw, had held the poison was in the whiskey. The whiskey as a source had the problem of when was it purchased. If the defense was right that the sausage was the vehicle, the prosecution had not shown how or when Shaw had access to it. It was obvious that this was not going to be a clean case.

The trial was to reconvene on Monday at noon. Over the weekend, a series of severe storms struck the area, making roads muddy and disrupting train schedules. Since the main form of transportation was either a train or buckboard, the judge waited until 2:00 o'clock to open court. Even with the delay, two of the prosecution witnesses had still not arrived.

Seventy-one-year-old Fanny Wolff, Julia's mother, was the first witness of the abbreviated day. She added few facts. Fanny was called to tell of her daughter's last comment. Fanny said that Julia had told her that she (Julia) "'xpected she was poisoned and that Charles and Mrs. Briggs did it." This is in direct conflict with the other two statements made by Julia in which she held Charles was not involved.

Julia Mattison, Burton's mother, was the last witness called before the case was turned over to the defense. Mrs. Mattison had visited the Shaw house many times during "their sickness." She had asked Mrs. Shaw if it was Shaw that gave her the poison. Julia had answered it was "him and Mrs. Briggs." Julia had told Mrs. Mattison that he had given it to her and the children in the whiskey sling. Julia Mattison was there on the Sunday that Deputy Archer had brought Shaw to visit his family. According to Mattison, Shaw had asked his wife if she thought he had poisoned her. Julia's response was, "Charles, you know." Mrs. Mattison went on to say that then Julia had turned and said, "Why couldn't they kill me and let my poor children alone?"

The prosecution still had two witnesses that they wanted to present to the jury. Neither was in the court so by mutual agreement the court turned the case over to the defense with the stipulation that the two witnesses would be called upon their arrival. This agreement did not serve the defense as the attorneys revealed their theory in their opening. The calling of witnesses after the opening allowed one of the late witnesses to contradict the defense's theory.

The Defense Opens

Daniel Westfall, in his opening, pointed out to the jury that he and Hughes had not been hired but rather appointed by the court to defend a man who, if guilty, was a criminal unparalleled in history. Westfall assured the jury that the two attorneys had accepted the responsibility "timidly and cheerfully." Despite his professing to the contrary, it is doubtful that either attorney was ever timid in a courtroom. Westfall went on to say that as attorneys their biggest concern was that they might leave something undone which would prejudice the jury against the prisoner. He pointed out that their cheerfulness was based on a sincere belief that Shaw was innocent of the "appalling crime with which he stands charged." Westfall pointed out that they all, the attorneys and jury, needed to act not from rumor but from honest hearts and clear investigation.

In his opening, Westfall clearly and concisely laid out the defense's theory as to what happened in the "Death House." The defense suggested that there might never have been any crime. Westfall made it clear that one of the issues they were going to put before the court was the possibility that the meat was tainted not poisoned. Over and over in his opening, Westfall argued that it was the tainted meat that caused the deaths. Westfall wanted to get the jury to have a reasonable doubt that the unfortunate deaths may not have been the result of any human's design.

Westfall then put forward the possibility it was the medicine not the meat that caused the death. He used as proof the fact that Emma and Willie had not taken the medicine and had recovered completely while those who took the medication either became worse or had died.

To the whole court, Westfall elaborated on the problems within the Shaw family. To the defense, the issue was Julia's jealousy not Charles's actions. Westfall noted that as neighbors the Shaws and Briggses had gotten along well until "the demon jealousy took possession of Mrs. Shaw." Westfall went on to induce the jury into believing that the demon jealousy was a "thousand times more dangerous and baleful that the demon of illicit love." According to Westfall, after the Briggses moved at Christmas, there had been a reconciliation between the Shaws. All was well until Charles accepted an invitation to visit his former neighbors in their new home. Again the "demon jealousy descended upon its victim leaving her moody, irascible and nearly insane under its subtle influence."

Drs. Gray and Ketchum, as principal witnesses for the prosecution, were the next victims of Westfall's verbal onslaught. As part of his diatribe, he accused the doctors of inadequate treatment. Westfall went so far as to suggest that the source of the illness may well have equally been the medicine the doctors prescribed.

Westfall closed by playing on the emotions of the jury saying, that a tremendous injustice had already taken place, as his client had not been granted the "privilege of closing the eyes of his loved ones" and "attending their funerals." As Westfall finished the court was adjourned for the day.

Testimony on Tuesday morning began with the prosecution calling its two remaining witnesses. The weekend weather had put the defense in a position of exposing their theory in the previous day's opening. Conveniently for the prosecution, the first witness of the day gave testimony contrary to Westfall's eloquent opening. Dr. Ketchum, who had testified earlier, assured the court that, while the rest of the family was suffering from symptoms of poisoning, Emma and Willie had only been sick with a cold. Because they knew Westfall's allegation of medical mistreatment, Dr. Ketchum guaranteed the jury that neither he nor Dr. Kennedy had any corrosive sublimate in stock.

Witnesses

Deputy Archer was the last witness for the prosecution. Deputy Archer was the man who had arrested and guarded Shaw. Deputy Archer was also the man who accompanied Shaw on the visits to his family. In court, Deputy Archer related a conversation that transpired between Charles and Julia on one of these visits. Charles had leaned over his dying wife, Julia, to give her a hug. She put her arm around him and said, "Oh, Charles you used to be a good man to your family." According to Deputy Archer, who heard her comment clearly, Shaw then turned to him and said, "She says I am not guilty of the charges of which I am accused." Under a grueling cross-examination, Deputy Archer would not yield. He was steadfast about what each had said.

The defense was now ready to begin with it's own witnesses. The attorneys chose to open with a man who had already exhibited his lack of valor or grace. LeRoy Briggs was recalled to the stand. Under oath, Briggs informed anyone listening that he was unaware of any illicit intercourse between his wife and Charles Shaw. Further, LeRoy explained that Shaw had never brought any gifts into the Briggs's house. This testimony, which was not really challenged by the prosecution, was in direct conflict with what LeRoy had been saying in the tavern a few nights previous.

The defense then had the post-mortem of Mrs. Shaw read into the record. This testimony had been taken the week before her death. In her death statement, she indicated that she did not believe her husband guilty of the crime. It appears this was read in to counter the testimony of Julia's mother, Mrs. Wolff. The testimony appears previously in text.

The next witness was Mrs. Carrie Shaw, Alvanza's wife and Charles and Julia's daughter-in-law. Carrie and her husband had attended Elizabeth's funeral. In the house after the funeral, she had asked her mother-in-law if she thought Charles had done the poisoning. Julia had responded, "No, but I knowed who done it, and so do the One above." Although she asked several times over the next few days, Julia refused to tell her daughter-in-law the name of the guilty party.

Mary Jane Shaw was married to Charles's "bad boy" nephew, Christopher. On the stand she told the jury that her husband had picked up some of the sausage from Shaw a day before the incident. Her family was poor and she was happy for the sustenance. Mary had cooked and served the sausage to her family that same day. Mary told how as a result of the sausage, her child was sick and vomited. Mary was also sick purging but did not vomit. According to Mary, after she had been sick for a week Dr. Niver was called. Mary added that her husband was taken sick after the doctor's visit. Like so many of the other unsophisticated witnesses in this trial, Mary was totally confused on cross-examination. In front of the court she lost track of dates and times. It is doubtful her testimony did much to support the defense.

Awaiting the Trial

The line of spectators waiting outside the courthouse for the doors to open had grown each day. The room was simply not built to house the volume of people interested in an unseemly case of this magnitude. Reporters noted that each day the number of women present had grown. The normal Victorian decorum that required men to give up their seats and allow the women to sit was not being followed. With Charles Shaw about to take the stand not one in attendance would yield whatever space he or she had staked out.

Charles Takes the Stand

The courtroom fell as close to silent as possible as the court clerk called Charles Shaw to the stand. The room remained virtually without noise even after he was sworn in. Everyone waited with baited breath to hear the voice of the man that had been already convicted in his or her own mind. The first thing noted was that Shaw came off as better educated than had been previously projected by the press. He also was more likable than most had expected.

Under questioning led by Hughes, Shaw went into great detail about the sicknesses of his family following the purchase of the sausage from Skiff. Shaw related to the jury how most of the children had eaten large portions of the sausage raw. By altering the phraseology, Shaw attempted to dispel the impact of his reported verbal threats against his wife. The defense brought out two interesting twists through Shaw's testimony. Charles maintained that he did not intend at any time to threaten his wife's life. His objective from the beginning was only to be separated from her on account of her "violent temper" and "jealous disposition." As he had held from the beginning, Shaw told the jury he had not had an affair with Mrs. Briggs. The relationship was just in his wife's imagination, which was consumed by jealousy. In the final blow, Charles suggested that if there were anyone to blame for the poisoning it was his wife.

Surprisingly, Shaw did not waiver or bend under cross-examination. He maintained steadfastly that he was a devoted father and misunderstood husband. With Shaw's testimony over, the trial ended for the day.

The Other Side of the Family

The next morning the defense closed after presenting two more witnesses, LeRoy Briggs and Christopher Shaw. Both men were called to present information regarding Charles Shaw's access to the bottles of sublimate supposedly left in the tollhouse pantry by Sarah.

This was the third time LeRoy Briggs had been called. On this occasion, Briggs testified that he was with Shaw for the entire time when they packed and loaded the contents of the tollhouse. The reason for the testimony was to assure the jury that if poison had been left on the shelf Shaw was not alone in the house to take it.

The final defense witness, Christopher Shaw, told the court he had never seen a corrosive sublimate at the tollhouse or at any other place.

The prosecution called several rebuttal witnesses. The first five: Charles Graham, Willard Lanton, Joseph Mitchell, Peter Valentine and Norman Fowler all were called to testify about Shaw's character. Uniformly they all told those gathered that Shaw was so bad by nature that they would not trust his testimony even under oath.

Rebuttal Witnesses

Lyman Clark was the first doctor to prescribe for the Shaw family. He told the court there was no mercury in any of his medications. He was called to dissuade the argument that the source of the poison, if there was a poison, was the medication.

Dr. Ketchum was recalled to testify that the previous January he - not Dr. Niver - was called to describe the symptoms in the family of Christopher Shaw. Dr. Ketchum reported that he treated Christopher for frostbite of the feet. He also treated his wife Mary Jane for diarrhea (purging). Dr. Ketchum assured the prosecutors that there were none of the symptoms of poisoning present in Christopher Shaw's family.

Leonard Fletcher, the justice of the peace in Cambridge, related the history of the Shaw family's trouble with the law. Justice Fletcher included the arrest of Shaw in December for the assault on his wife.

Deputy Archer returned to the stand to testify that Shaw was present when the statement was taken by the coroner and transcribed by Shaw's own attorney, Charles Stroud. During the entire examination, Shaw had stood four to five feet away from his wife, nodding his head to her responses. This testimony was necessary to dispel the idea that Shaw could not face his accusers, namely his dead wife.

For dramatic effect the final witness was Mrs. Blakesly. She was called only to repeat the remark made by Shaw that it was all his fault. District Attorney Grover used a brilliant strategy having the final words by a witness be the alleged confession of the defendant.

Judge Potter then ruled the case was closed. He instructed Charles Hughes to begin the defense's closing.

The Defense Closes

Even for a man known for his command of the English language and how to use it to the maximum on this day, Hughes was considered to be exceptionally eloquent. For five hours, he mesmerized the jury and the two thousand spectators as he demonstrated how the evidence did not support the claim of murder.

To Hughes, the culprit was the sausage. He pointed out the dates of the onslaught of the ailment. He showed that the family was so undernourished that the children ate sausage raw. Most importantly he tried to demonstrate that Shaw did not have the opportunity to poison the family. To dispel the possibility of opportunity, Hughes reminded the jury that after Shaw brought the sausage into his home he had not touched the sausage except to eat what his wife had prepared. Shaw, like most farmers of his time, had left the preparation of all meals to his wife.

Just before Hughes raised the standard argument that if there exists reasonable doubt the jury must free his client, he made a brief suggestion that was almost missed. In a bold uncharacteristic argument for the time, Hughes alluded to the possibility that Mrs. Shaw had poisoned a portion of the sausage. In 1873, people, especially attorneys in a courtroom, simply did not speak badly of the dead. Here stood Hughes suggesting that perhaps the deceased had intended to poison Charles and his bastard son, Willie. He attempted to raise reasonable doubt by proposing that the platter was turned in the serving and the parties ate from the opposite side intended. Hughes acknowledged that Mrs. Shaw would have known the allegations regarding the parentage of Willie. Hughes raised the question could Julia, in her jealous state of mind, have wanted Charles and the boy dead? In her "demon infested jealous obsession," the boy would have been a constant reminder of her husband's incestuous relationship with his own daughter.

When Hughes finished, it was already seven o'clock. Not one of the spectators had left the packed room. They all agreed that they had been treated to a truly fascinating closing by the defense. Judge Potter told Grover to be ready first thing in the morning.

The Prosecution Closes

Grover was only the acting district attorney when he took the floor at nine o'clock that Thursday morning. When he sat down at one o'clock in the afternoon, he was sure he would be appointed to the position permanently.

Grover said that based on the medical evidence the prosecution had proven that the illness was caused by poisoned meat not tainted meat. To Grover, it was conclusive that Shaw was driven to poison his wife as the next step in his sinister behavior. It had begun with threats, escalated to abuse, and ultimately ended with a death. Grover insisted Shaw was motivated to such violence by his illicit love for Sarah.

Grover was incensed by the argument that Mrs. Shaw could have administered the poison. He tried to turn Hughes argument and make it sound like Julia intended suicide, which is not what Hughes had said. Grover insisted that Julia cared for her family too much to kill herself and let her children live with the woman responsible for the demise of their happy home. She never would have wanted Shaw to be with the woman she despised. To Grover, Shaw was the only logical candidate and all the evidence proved the case.

In his closing, Grover was rated by those in attendance as able, convincing and eloquent, perhaps not so much so as Hughes, but that was a tall tree to climb.

Judge Potter ordered an hour and a half recess to give himself time to prepare the charge to the jury.

THE VERDICT

Potter's charge went on for an hour and a half and was considered by both sides to be fair. He spoke of the presumptions of innocence and reasonable doubt. He instructed the jury in ways to argue the evidence, careful not to put forth his own opinions. He narrowed the issues to two, which needed to be resolved in order. First, was the death the result of poisoning? If so, was there sufficient evidence to indicate that Charles administered the poison? The jury was retired at four in the afternoon.

And the Verdict Is?

At 7:45 that same evening, a tired, drained, and hungry Judson Maynard, the foreman of the jury, stood in the packed courtroom. It appeared to those gathered that half the hamlet of Sandy Hill had come out upon hearing the courthouse bell being rung a half hour earlier. Not used to speaking in public, Judson Maynard's voice trembled as he informed the judge and those gathered that the jury had found the prisoner guilty of the charge of murder in the first degree.

Charles grasped his head with his hands, as if not ever anticipating this outcome. He was clearly stunned, as were many in the audience. It had been expected that the best the prosecution could hope for was a hung jury. Most felt it was a case of poison but that there was not enough direct evidence to convict Shaw.

Hughes requested that the jury be polled. They all asserted the same verdict. The judge then released the jury setting the sentencing for nine o'clock the next morning.

THE SENTENCE

Charles Shaw came into the packed court on this fateful Friday a broken man. It was obvious he had not slept. That day, Shaw wore his 40 years more like they were 80. When he left the courtroom, after Judge Potter's tongue lashing, he walked more like he was 90 years old.

Judge Potter pointed out that, in his opinion, through his attorneys Shaw had virtually picked the jury himself. Despite his control over the selection, the jury had found evidence to convict him on the charge of murder in the first degree. Before the formal sentence was passed down, the judge asked if Shaw had any final comments.

Despite his exhausted appearance, Shaw's words were firm and loud enough for the entire assemblage to hear. "I am innocent of the crime of which I am convicted. Thank God I am innocent of taking the lives of little children and my wife. If I die, I die innocent."

Judge Potter pointed out that Shaw had been afforded the best counsel in the county. That the county had allowed him to call any and all witnesses he chose. The judge's remaining words are as he said them that cold morning.

"Those counsel have brought to your defense all the patient inquiry, earnest work, high legal attainment and eloquent advocacy could accomplish. Riches, respectability and friends could have done no more in your behalf then has been done by them. Notwithstanding all this, and much more the evidence has constrained the minds of the jury into a verdict of guilty. The court will refrain from further expression. Its words would not be heard by you with your present surroundings. Standing as you do, with the graves of your murdered wife and children on one side and your own preparing upon the other, my words could signify nothing. I will only say that in the time that awaits you think not of pardons, commutation of sentence or new trial, but devote that time to a review of the past and preparation for the future. The court now orders and adjudges that you be taken from hence to the jail at Salem; that you be detained therein until the 28th day of November next; that on that day, between the hours of ten in the forenoon and two in the afternoon thereof, you be hanged by the sheriff or other proper officer by the neck until you are dead."

Shaw broke down and cried like a child after hearing the judge order the sentence. It was a punishment he would never receive.

Postscript

Shaw was returned to Salem to await his fate. Before the court ordered execution could happen the defense team was able to win a stay pending a ruling on a new trial. It took over a full year for the new trial to be ordered.

Shaw's Interview

On October 25, while sitting in his cell on the second floor awaiting his execution, Sheriff Hall convinced Shaw to grant a reporter from the *Post* an interview. This interview was against the advice of his counsel. While in the Salem jail, the reporter was allowed to descend one flight of metal stairs and also interview Sarah in her cell.

Sheriff Hall stayed with the reporter in the cell. It was cool enough in the cell for Shaw to be wearing a cardigan sweater. Although he appeared generally composed, Shaw paced in his cell and smoked his pipe during the entire interview. At the beginning, there was a point where Shaw's demeanor broke down. It looked like a sudden pain had overtaken him. It passed quickly and the interview resumed.

Asked about the sentence Shaw exclaimed, "It's all wrong! It's all wrong!" Shaw went on to reiterate what he had said in court - that he was innocent. Looking upward, Shaw went on to say, "I never did it. My hand and my heart are as free from the stain of the blood of my family as is the Almighty God."

Shaw then spoke to the Sheriff, "if you was to let me out of this place - mind I don't ask you to; I know you wouldn't and couldn't - but if you should let me out I'd stay just where I used to. Do you think I'd run away?"

The sheriff responded, "I sympathize with you, and wouldn't blame you if you'd skedadled when you had the chance."

Shaw's response was interesting: "I shouldn't try to get away though, I am innocent, and have no reason to run away."

The reporter challenged Shaw's protestations asking how he could hold to his innocence when all the evidence pointed to him. Shaw responded, "Oh, there's boughten evidence. Money did it."

The reporter was obviously shocked by the claim. "Why, who had such a grudge against you to swear your life away?"

Shaw whimpered for a minute before he answered. "My daughter Fannie.

She has some of my furniture and she said she'd swear me to hell before she'd let me have it again."

Shaw stated that he had been advised not to have any interviews without his attorneys present. Even so he added that he was disappointed that his son Alvenza had not testified. He was sure the son would have contradicted Fannie.

Shaw went silent. Knowing that there was nothing new to be learned, the sheriff left the cell, leaving the reporter alone with Shaw for a few moments. Shaw was weeping in a way the reporter had never seen a grown man cry. In an act of compassion, the reporter reached out his hand placing it on Shaw's shoulder. The reporter wrote that if a man were to ever break down and confess it would have been at this moment. Instead, Shaw looked up at the reporter and said, "I was judged guiltless by my conscience and in the sight of heaven." Charles stared at the reporter saying:

> I didn't kill my children; I loved them all, and wouldn't harm them but if I could help it. When I die, if they hang me, I shall go to them and I'll be all right then. I haven't any bitter feelings against anybody who has brought this doom upon me. I forgive them all and hope God will bless 'em all. I don't hate them. When I do bid farewell to earth on the gallows these shall be my last words.

The moment was too perfect for the correspondent. He asked Shaw who he believed poisoned the family. "Oh, I know, but I don't like to say it's her. Oh, I know but I don't want to think it was her," Shaw responded.

With only two women to accuse (Sarah and Julie), it was the moment for any reporter to strike. This reporter, like any other, asked Shaw who he meant.

"My wife. She did it, but I hate to think she would do it. She was jealous and used to have wild fits."

As the reported left the cell, he thought about how Shaw was a weak-minded fellow, unable to understand the enormity of the crime of which he had been convicted. To the reporter, Shaw's assertions may be true but since he was the type who "will not scruple to tell falsehoods on less inducements that the desire to save one's own life," he did not believe it was the wife. To the reporter, Shaw acted like a man guilty of a crime, trying with whatever means at his disposal to shield himself from blame.

Sarah Briggs's Interview

Like the reporters before him, this correspondent was smitten by Sarah. She was described as "comely and as intelligent as the average of her station in the world." Sarah, and exhibitionist and an extrovert, began the conversation saying that she did not want to be mentioned in the papers. Given her choice, Sarah probably would have chosen different terms but she did enjoy having her name in the newspapers. "I won't believe he's guilty till he says so himself. I don't believe a man who was so fond of his children would kill them" Sarah said as her youngest son Georgie was running around the cell.

"She was a very jealous woman, and used to be jealous of other women" were the words Sarah used to describe Julia. Sarah went on to say that she believed that it was Julia who did the poisoning. In this article, the reporter referred to himself as a caller, admitting he could easily have spent several hours conversing with Mrs. Sarah Briggs. Whatever Sarah's magnetism, it was consistently felt among the men who spoke of her.

The Second Trial

The second trial had a very different presentation and outcome. Between the two trials Drs. Gray and Kennedy both died of heart failure. Their deaths left a huge hole in the ability of the prosecution to put forward a complete case. A second difference between the two trials was the reliance on the statement made by Mrs. Shaw. Before the second jury, Hughes was more convincing in showing that Julia never directly accused her husband of the act. Julia had said that Charles and Sarah were responsible - not that they committed the act. A third variance was in the defense's argument against the physicians. Hughes argued that Emma had not taken the medicine the first night. Like her sisters, Emma had eaten the sausage. She, unlike her sisters and mother, had not taken any medication. Emma was the only girl who showed no signs of being poisoned. Without the attending physicians alive to counter his presentation, Hughes argued effectively that the cause of the deaths might very well have been the administration of the medication.

The second jury was convinced a reasonable doubt existed and Shaw was found not guilty. In June 1875, Charles Shaw was released from jail.

What Ever Happened To?

Christopher Shaw, the near-do-well, was arrested twice in the next seven years on charges of horse theft. The first charge was in the town of Easton in 1877. The second, more serious incident, was in 1880. The second time, Christopher rented horse and wagon to get witnesses in North Hoosick. To prepare himself for the trip, he stopped in Little White Creek for a drink. One drink turned into many. When he got to North Hoosick, he raced the horse through the streets. Without picking up the witnesses, he returned to Eagle Bridge. Not feeling like stopping, he went on to Salem then Bald Mountain. He finally returned to Eagle Bridge and abandoned the horse and wagon. During the entire trip he had neither fed nor provided water for the poor horse. The horse hurt itself and destroyed the wagon as it attempted to get to water. Christopher's behavior had gotten the best of him for the last time. For this theft, he was sentenced to a year in Dannamora Prison.

Sarah Briggs seems to have dropped off the face of the planet. She does not appear under this name in any census that followed.

Charles Shaw remarried a woman whose first name was Angeline. The two of them were able to get Anna, Ida and Emma from the county poor house. True to his word, Charles Shaw remained in the Cambridge area through the 1891 directory.

Reflections

This case shows the difficulty our criminal court system has in providing true justice to the poor and under-educated populace. Obviously, Charles Shaw and Sarah Briggs lied at times, perhaps even most of the time. Whether this was an intentional act or a learned survival skill will never be known. Watching trials today we can see the same behavior evident in those charged.

There are elements of this unsolved murder that warrant additional consideration. First and foremost, Shaw and his wife watched as their children died. To parents, the death of their child is the most dreaded event imaginable. The fear of a child's death exceeds the parents' anxiety over their own death. How could any parent handle watching the slow painful death of a child, especially if he or she were the cause. Could this have been the reason Mrs. Shaw kept asking for others to pray for her? Shaw was never described in anything that would be considered a glamorous way. Yet he never acted like he had regrets. How could any person, male or female, act sane after administering a slow acting poison to his or her own children?

Shaw's behavior leads to an important after-effect. Shaw resided in the Cambridge area after his release. The late 1800s was a time when many men moved West to redefine themselves. Would a guilty man return to the community that had unofficially found him guilty unless he really was innocent?

Did Julia so fear the possibility of her children having Sarah as a stepmother that she deliberately poisoned them and herself?

Did the doctors commit a medical treatment error when they refused to come to the house the first time they were asked? Would the doctors then cover up the mistake to protect themselves and their own reputations?

This is one case where justice will be found in eternity.

Visiting the Sites Today

Cambridge, New York, is one of those beautiful little communities fortunate enough to have escaped the ravishes of modernization. By using one's imagination to change the cars, one can look down the streets today and picture exactly how it must have looked in the 1950s or even the 1920s. A visit today places the traveler in the footprints of all the characters in this story. The best way to reach Cambridge is either route 22 or 378. For those interested in experiencing village life, a visit to Cambridge should be mandatory for those traveling to Manchester, Vermont.

To get to the Turnpike Road turn south off Main Street on either street between the library and the hospital. The roads converge and form the Turnpike. The house was on the right side of the road as one goes south near the base of Owl Hill.

The Center White Creek Baptist Church, where the services were held, is just off route 22 about four miles south Cambridge. The family's graves have not been found in the cemetery across the street.

The two places where Charles Shaw was incarcerated, the jail in Salem and the Union House in Cambridge are still standing.

One historical note, at the time of the trials, the Village of Hudson Falls was called Sandy Hill. This name change often causes confusion for people not from the area or new to local history.

Nathaniel Moak

Judge Potter

The former Washington County Courthouse was only recently completed when Charles Shaw was on trial in 1873.

Lowenstein:

Murder is a Capital Offense

(Or Men are Fools)

The Discovery

When George Warner left for work on the morning of Thursday, August 7, 1873, he may have expected to see a cluster of flies but he was totally unprepared for the source of their attraction. Warner, originally from Ballston Spa, had, for the last four years, been a boarder at a farm outside of Albany near the Schenectady Turnpike (Central Avenue). The farm belonged to Isaac Jones, a reasonably successful farmer who, for extra income, had several male boarders lodging at his home. That morning Warner did not leave for work until between 9 and 10 o'clock. As was his practice, Warner took a shortcut along a fence that led southeast from the barn to the main highway. Even this early in the day, the August heat was building, so in a cool ravine he took a moment to sit on the fence. Hearing birds, he looked to the side and noticed something white about a 100 feet from the fence. In the heavily wooded ravine lay a one-armed man. The man was lying on his side with his back to the fence. The man's legs were curled up as if he were in a deep sleep. Since it was already mid-morning, Warner did not think the man would still be sleeping, so he assumed he must be injured. Not knowing the extent of the person's injuries, Warner walked part way down hill before he was able to distinguish an extensive amount of blood in the area. Immediately, Warner realized that the man was probably beyond help. Even from a distance of eight to 10 feet Warner could see the person's throat had been cut. Warner hurried back to the Jones's farm, hitched a horse to a wagon, and started for the city of Albany to look for the coroner.

It was about noon when Warner got to Coroner John Harrigan's home. The house appeared empty. Warner left a message in the mailbox then went back to the Jones farm to wait for the coroner. Warner's return to the farm was based on his sense of duty to the body on the farm. He felt that he should insure no one bothered the body before the coroner arrived.

The Coroner

Coroner Harrigan was inside reading the newspaper and did not want to be bothered by this laborer. The coroner watched as Warner put something in his mailbox. After he finished his newspaper and tea, Harrigan went out to retrieve the note. Wanting support Harrigan picked up his brother before he went out to the scene.

It was about an hour before John Harrigan and his brother, Daniel, got to the Jones farm. Warner had spent the intervening time discussing his find with some of his fellow boarders. When the Harrigan brothers arrived at the farm, Warner assumed his responsibilities were over. Instead, Coroner Harrigan insisted that Warner accompany him to the site.

Assistance

Several of the other men, who boarded at the Jones farm, realized that the discovery of a body was one of the most interesting things that was going to happen in their lives. These men joined the coroner and their friend, Warner, on the trek to the ravine. For today's detectives, the crime scene would be considered seriously damaged by the number of men roving around the site that day. This was 1873 and forensic evidence was in its infancy.

THE INVESTIGATION

When the men got back to the scene they all theorized that the person had started to commit suicide at the top of the embankment and, once injured, had fallen or stumbled to the bottom. These deductions were based on the placement of a neatly folded pile of clothes at the top of the ravine and the trail of blood down to the place where the body was found. The men all agreed that the embankment was very steep, so inertia would have carried a body down fairly easily once it started its descent. The distance from the pile of clothes at the top of the ravine to where the body was found was a distance estimated at 65 feet. At first examination, suicide was considered the cause, as the person's neck had been cut almost completely across. The wound, although long, was not deep enough to reach the jugular vein. This slower loss of blood had made it possible for the mystery person to somehow get down the embankment before he died.

In the pile of clothes was found a black alpaca coat, vest, straw hat and a New York City *Sun* newspaper dated August 5th. The body was dressed in a blue coat, not quite white shirt, pants, suspenders and boots. Over the off-white shirt was a false bosom or dickey that tied in the back. There were a pair of glasses attached to the suspenders. In effect there was little doubt that the clothes all belonged to the dead man.

A boarder named Cookham noticed that the victim had only one arm and mentioned it to everyone.

George Warner was called upon one more time. He had to help Coroner John Harrigan and his brother, Daniel, place the body in a makeshift box that the coroner had brought in his buckboard. In front of everyone, the coroner searched the body finding a two-dollar bill and 10 cents in coins. Inside the vest pocket was a business card. The card read:

Theo. Grunewald
Shaving and Hairdressing
No. 35 Atlantic Avenue
Brooklyn

The body was so covered in dried blood that it was impossible to determine the person's race. At the coroner's request, Warner got a hat full of water from the stream that ran through the bottom of the ravine. Warner brought the water to the wagon so Harrigan could wash the victim's face.

While Warner and Harrigan were at the top of the ravine washing the face, the other boarders and some other men, who had happened to see the crowd and decided to join in, were searching for evidence as to what occurred. Jim Cavanaugh, a railroad man and fellow boarder at the Jones homestead, found an open straight razor about four feet from the where the body had lain. Cavanaugh placed the razor on the lower rail of the fence where Daniel Harrigan later picked it up. When Harrigan picked up the razor it looked like it had blood on it so he cleared the blade to see if there were any identifying marks. The coroner's brother noticed the mark L VII on the blade. Harrigan then placed the razor in an envelope he had brought to the scene.

As Coroner Harrigan ran water over the person's face he noticed that there appeared to be a hole in the middle of the forehead. As more of the face was washed clear of the caked-on blood, the coroner thought he perceived powder burns. Powder burns would be the result of gunplay at close quarters. As still more blood washed away, Harrigan thought he noticed a second hole in the area of the temple. Harrigan found a small piece of glass lying on the ground and used it to probe the holes. He was not able to find anything inside the wounds with the makeshift probe. Harrigan noted that the victim was clean-shaven and that he could smell perfume in the person's hair (a sign that the person took reasonable care of himself).

At about 5 o'clock in the afternoon they felt they were finished at the scene so Coroner Harrigan and his brother took the body to the dead house building at the county's Almshouse (the 1870s name for the poor house). The coroner took with him all the clothes that had been in the pile. On his way back home, Harrigan left a message for Dr. Haskins to conduct a postmortem with another doctor present.

The Press Draws Conclusions

The reports the first day were that it appeared a drifter had committed suicide. This was not an illogical conclusion. The body was found in a secluded spot near the rail yards. This would have been a natural selection for a homeless person riding the rails to try to get a quite night's sleep. The man had some money on him, implying he was not robbed. The person did not have much money - meaning that he may very well have fallen on hard times causing depression and therefore slit his own throat.

On Sunday afternoon, the coroner returned to the Almshouse to collect the clothes the man was wearing at the time the body was found. While he was at the Almshouse, John Harrigan visited with Dr. Haskins, where it was confirmed the man had been shot numerous times. Harrigan was not surprised that Dr. Haskins had determined, for himself, (an inquest had not yet been held) that the cause of death was murder. Since no gun had been found, the two men went to the Jones farm and examined the site together to try determine what had happened and to see if they could find the gun. The hour-long search yielded nothing.

Discoveries at the Autopsy

Dr. Henry Haskins had been a surgeon and physician in Albany for 13 years. During that time, he estimated that he had done over 300 postmortem examinations. When he heard that Coroner Harrigan had asked him to do an examination and with a second doctor present, he called on an old associate, Dr. Lansing. The two arrived at the Almshouse on Friday morning. A simple visual examination of the body caused the doctors to suspect that the one-armed man had been murdered.

The doctors noted in their report how the man found in the gully was dressed. The man was only five feet one inches tall and estimated to be about 35 years of age. He had weighed 120 pounds. The man had dark hair and eyes and a sandy mustache. His arm had been surgically removed at the shoulder. One very noticeable quality was that the man's teeth were irregular, described by one of the doctors as "defective."

The doctors measured the slit in the throat. The cut went from the upper part of the back of the neck all the way across in a downward slit to the front of the throat. Amazingly, the incision was shallow, missing any major arteries. The doctors also noticed two other head wounds. On the opposite side of the neck, the doctors found a second incision three inches long. The second neck wound opening appeared to be caused by missiles (bullets). Another opening, which the doctors attributed to a missile, was in the center of the forehead. The doctors found two flattened bullets in the cavity of the brain. This was still in the time of lead bullets, which rarely, if ever, held their shape upon impact. The doctors noted that either of these head wounds would have caused death. Further, if the death was not instantaneous then the nature of the wound would have rendered the person insensible and therefore he could not have fired the second round. To the doctors, the question of suicide was now answered. This had to be a murder.

The doctors were not finished with the examination, as several other wounds were present. The two doctors noted a third wound on the side of the head. They followed the path of the missile, finding the bullet near the back of the skull beneath the skin, but outside the bone. A fourth bullet was found at the back of the left eye socket.

Another wound was found below the left ear. When it was traced it did not lead to the finding of a bullet. The same was true for a wound behind the right ear.

As if the doctors had not discovered enough, they also checked the lower body where they found two chest wounds. One was just below the left nipple and proceeded in a downward track to the back. The second was between the ribs and this ball penetrated the heart. In all there were eight wounds found in the areas that would be considered vital. The doctors determined that the two wounds to the chest were almost certainly fired after the person was dead, as there was little blood inside the chest cavity.

A ninth wound was in the back of the right (and only) hand. This ball was found at the base of the thumb.

The jaw had been broken but the doctors were not sure if this was from another wound or from a punch that may have proceeded the slicing of the neck.

Besides the missing arm, the poor victim had two distinctive physical traits that could help in his identification. First, the teeth were very widely spaced, making them appear jagged. In addition, the second finger on the only hand also could bend backward at the middle joint. This appeared to be a natural phenomenon not attributed to any wound.

Based on the limited amount of powder burns and the condition of the bullets, the doctors assumed most of the gun shots had been at a distance. Some of the shots, probably the two that entered through virtually the same hole in the forehead, were fired later and closer.

A more Thorough Search

On Tuesday morning, Coroner Harrigan went back to the scene for a third time. He arrived about 9 o'clock in the morning and asked George Warner and another of the boarders to cut down the grass and weeds in the ravine. Harrigan was again looking for a revolver. With scythes the men cut down an area about 80 feet in diameter. The three searchers scoured the scene of the murder, but were not able to locate the missing gun.

The Press

This story grew in news coverage as it grew in intensity. By the second day this case even had acquired its own epithet "The Schenectady Turnpike Mystery." In the afternoon papers of the second day, the reports of suicide were replaced by stories of a possible murder. The Albany *Argus* led the charge to outrage the public by describing the qualities of the murder. Referring to the autopsy report the paper said, "These developments show about conclusively that a cruel and cowardly murder has been committed, but by whom, and upon whom remains shrouded in mystery."

The newspapers and police were having a major problem identifying the victim. The fact the person only had one arm would have seemed a major factor except for the time period. It was only eight years after the Civil War and many men had lost limbs in the fighting.

The Albany police detectives, following normal procedures when the body was that of a possible vagrant, interviewed employees of the Almshouse. The policemen believed they had their first lead as several of the workers said that a one-armed man had tried to visit a resident of the insane asylum building at the Almshouse the night of the murder. The one-armed man had been denied admission because of the late hour.

Each week we have newspapers that are at least an inch thick because of the inserts. As difficult as it is to believe, there were no Sunday papers in the 1870s. After a day of major headlines, the story rested until Monday, August 10th.

On Monday, the mystery of the one-armed man who had turned up at the Almshouse the night of the murder was resolved. If people call Albany "Smalbany" now, just think what it was like a hundred and twenty five years ago. Albany, like all small to medium-size communities, had its local characters. "Nickey," a local eccentric, was the man identified as being at the Almshouse. Nickey was seen on Saturday stumbling his way across the bridge to Troy so it was established that he was not the man murdered.

Another Possible Clue

The railroad was installing a second set of tracks to meet the need of the expanding commercial and personal traffic that flowed to the west. A local Cohoes contractor named Trull had been given the contract to build the new double track. The loose gravel used in the construction had showed a set of footprints coming from the area of the murder. Many felt the footprints would help in the detection of the murderer.

On Monday there was yet another connection to the construction gang explored. Four of the rougher characters in Trull's employ had been "drinking and carousing" around West Albany. On Saturday the four seemed in a big hurry to get out of town. Hearing of this, two Albany detectives showed up at the railroad station. The police impounded the men's luggage that had been placed in the express area. With the construction workers' permission an examination was undertaken. The luggage revealed no evidence that the men were involved in the murder, so they were allowed to "depart."

Searching for the Identity of the Victim

Based on the business card found in the victim's vest pocket, John Malloy, the chief of the Albany police sent a telegram to the Brooklyn police asking that they follow up on the only lead. On August 9, 1873, Malloy received his answer. Telegrams were paid for by the number of words so government messages were kept short.

"Grunewald knows nothing of any such man. One of his men says he thinks that some four weeks ago a stranger with one arm got shaved there.

John Folk, Acting Chief."

As would be expected in a case with as much newspaper coverage as this one had garnered, there were those who feared that the unidentified murdered man might be a relative or friend. A man named John Brown, of Troy, was one such person. He came to Albany's Almshouse fearing for his brother, Abraham, who had been missing from about the time of the murder. The Almshouse employees would not talk to Brown without a detective present. When detectives arrived they showed Brown the clothes the missing man had been wearing. It was immediately obvious that the murdered man was not the missing Abraham Brown. Brown's brother was at least nine inches taller than the man whose body had been found. Brown left assured the murdered man was not his brother, but still concerned as to his missing relative's whereabouts. Two days later, Abraham Brown was positively identified in Gloversville.

In what was always going to trouble the criminal case, the body of the one-armed man was ordered buried by Patrick Murphy, an employee of the Almshouse. On Saturday, August 9th, the body was buried without any family member having made a positive identification. To show how badly the error was, at the trial Murphy had to admit that in addition to ordering the premature burial, he had no idea as to the burial site.

The *Argus* closed Monday's article with the following quote: "This horrible affair consequently remains shrouded in the same impenetrable veil of mystery that has enveloped it since its first sickening details came to light."

May have Lead on Victim

The next day another possible identity was raised for the murdered man. A farmer who lived in the general area of the murder came to police headquarters and related a story about having picked up a one-armed man the previous Wednesday (the day before the body was found). According to the farmer, the man had asked that he stop the wagon near the railroad bridge. The farmer said that the man seemed to be under the influence of alcohol as they conversed. The one-armed passenger said that he came from Fonda and knew Mr. Hevenor, a lawyer in the city of Albany who had represented him in a suit some years before. When the police checked with Hevenor he had no recollection of a client that fit the description.

Moak Seeks Reward

With no one coming forward able to identify the body, District Attorney Nathan Moak went to Governor Dix asking that the state offer a reward. Moak's argument for the state to issue the reward, rather than the county, was based on the sincere belief that the murdered man was not from the area, and, since he was not a native, any cost should be borne by the state, not the local community.

Coroner's Inquest

A week after the body was discovered the identity of the murdered man had still not been determined. Coroner Harrigan felt he could wait no longer so he conducted an inquest with respect to the case. The finding of the coroner's jury did not surprise anyone. They held: "That the unknown man found on the morning of August 7, in a ravine on Isaac Jones's farm, came to his death by a pistol shot wounds at the hands of some persons unknown to the jury."

Reward --- False Lead

The day it was learned that Governor Dix had approved a reward for $500, District Attorney Moak received a telegram suggesting that the murdered man may be Henry Hevenor of Fonda. Detective Malloy was sent to Fonda only to find Hevenor still residing in that canal village and in good health. The newspapers never noticed that Hevenor is the same last name the farmer had reported as the name of an attorney known by a one-armed hitchhiker the week before.

Rewards

The implications and impact of the reward needs to be fully understood. In 1873, unlike today, detectives were allowed to receive a portion of any rewards offered. This practice caused two problems. First, detectives were hesitant to do investigations where there was no reward. After all why waste the time? Second, rewards were only awarded if the person was convicted. Therefore, there was always a question of honesty in the testimony of those eligible for a portion of the reward. In this case that included the detectives from Brooklyn and Albany and Albany's police Chief Malloy. It needs to be noted that the reward offered by Governor Dix did not name a suspect, but instead was predicated on a conviction for murder.

Mystery of Mysteries

By August 15th, and probably because there was now a reward posted, the case was beginning to gather some clarity. The *Argus* carried a story that called the case "the mystery of mysteries." Yet in the next paragraph it named the murdered man and the suspected killer. The concept behind the "mystery of mysteries" headline was attributed to what caused the murdered man to go to such a secluded site.

The newspapers were all noting that only one set of footprints went through the oat field leading to the ravine. The automatic question became, what would be the reason the murdered man went to the ravine alone? The second question was, how did the killer get to the scene and then get away again after without leaving tracks?

Weston Murdered - Lowenstein Sought

The Albany police got their first concrete lead the same day the reward was offered. The Brooklyn police sent a wire that they had reason to believe the one-armed man was John Weston of Palmetto Street in Brooklyn. The alleged murderer was Emil Lowenstein, a German barber, who had on occasion gone by the name Livingston. As is regularly noted in this book, the 1870s were not politically correct. It is important to note that the religion of Lowenstein (Jewish) was also listed in almost every article. Although his religion would have nothing to do with his arrest, it may have impacted the outcome of the trial. The Brooklyn police's telegram said that Lowenstein was missing. They described him as five feet six inches and weighing 140 pounds with dark hair and a mustache. The last time Lowenstein was seen he was wearing a Panama hat, light suit, and gaiters. The real reason for the murder was suspected to be in the last words of the telegram. "May be in the company of a woman and three children."

A Second Telegram

Later the same day, the Albany chief got a second telegram. With a reward for capture and conviction, the Brooklyn police were taking the matter more seriously and following up on all leads. They told the Albany police that according to their sources the parties had left New York City for points west. The Brooklyn police believed they had purchased tickets for St. Louis. The woman believed to be accompanying Lowenstein was 27 year-old Mrs. Mary Weston, wife of the murdered man. Sandy-haired, Mrs. Weston was the mother of three children, the youngest being 17 months old. The reason the one child's age was given was because the police believed that the mother might let older children travel on their own but the youngest would be with her. When last seen, Mrs. Weston was wearing a lavender linen suit with a polonaise blue hat. Her weight was listed as one 110 pounds.

Knowing nothing more than this, the Troy *Times* carried the following paragraphs concerning the murder of Weston. It must be noted that the reporter had not interviewed anyone except some of the police officers connected to the crime. This type of highly speculative story was common in the area. Such stories, which had no factual basis, were printed and widely read. Potential jurors reading such tales would naturally assume it was true. This editorial license had prevented true justice in many cases.

HOW THE MURDER WAS COMMITTED

It has been said, although the statement receives little attention, that Weston was murdered in Brooklyn and the body brought to the spot where it was found, but the pools of blood found there and other circumstances entirely contradict such a theory. The more likely story is that Weston was inveigled to the ravine on Jones's farm, and there met his death. It is understood that Weston and Lowenstein were apparently friends; that the latter frequently visited the house of the former, and there met the wife of Weston, who became enamoured with the barber, and there is every reason to suppose a criminal intimacy existed between them. Weston had some money, and it may be supposed the pair plotted the poor, unsuspecting crippled husband's death. How to do it must have been their thought and study. Finally, it is supposed, that the one-armed man, little dreaming the fiendish treachery of his professed friend, was prevailed upon to go with Lowenstein on a speculating expedition; perhaps to buy cattle at West Albany, and never having been in that vicinity it would be easy enough for his companion to lead him without

THE SHADOW OF SUSPICION

Across the fields into the dreary clump of pine trees; and then the murderer, steeling his heart against all pity, took hold of his victim, and before he could offer a prayer to his Maker, shot him, once, twice, thrice; a dozen shots rang out clear and sharp on the midnight air, woke up the nodding watchman on the track half a mile distance, and made the farm laborer, who sat in his room late, wonder what so unusual sound could be at that "witching hour." Weston was dead, shot through the heart and brain, and he lay at the feet of his murderer a mass of inanimate clay. But the fiend was not satisfied, so he took from his pocket a razor, and cut the throat of his victim; then, not daring to leave the body on the brow of the hill, he dragged or carried the ghastly burden over the growing shrubbery, staining the green leaves with the life

Blood of the Murdered Man

And then he tossed it near the ravine, and after taking all that was valuable, but leaving behind that which would hang him, the murderer fled, leaving his work well done, and the great pine trees, in whose shadow his victim lay, to moan a requiem over one so cruelly sent to his long home.

Returning to the *Argus* article we learn that no sooner had the Albany police sent dispatches to Cincinnati, Indianapolis, Springfield, Illinois and St. Louis, then the case took yet a different turn. The reporter for the *Argus* provided such a beautiful story it deserves to be told in his words. Keep in mind his only source was the telegraph quoted previously

No one would have been surprised if some startling developments had come to light after this. It really seemed as if the murderer must surely be captured. But the bright cloud through which the sun had been shining so brightly was quickly followed by a dark cloud, whose thickness at first seemed to scarcely impenetrable. Click, click, over the wires came the following:

John Malloy Chief of Police:
Mrs. Weston has been arrested.
P. Malone Detective.

This was all the dispatch contained. It did not say she was arrested in Brooklyn, but such is probably the case.

But the enigma now appears greater than ever to solve. Mrs. Weston and Lowenstein without a doubt were together. How, when and where did they become separated? What has become of the children? Not a word of their whereabouts. Was there ever such a mystery? This is the strangest part of the case. It is perfectly evident that the murder was committed so the murder and his victim's wife might elope. It is clear they were together and now one is arrested and the other is not to be found. Had they remained together and had the children with them they could have easily been detected, but now that they are separated, the detectives are again thrown in the dark, and are at even a greater loss than ever to conjecture where 'Emil is.'

The *Argus* went on to express its congratulations to the police in both Brooklyn and Albany.

Mary Weston's Arrest

The next day the story surrounding Mary Weston started to develop. It appeared she was arrested in Brooklyn and taken to the precinct house on Washington Street. The police ransacked her trunks and a large bundle of articles were found inside. When contacted by the Albany area newspapers, the Brooklyn police would provide no further details but rather wished that information about her arrest had not been released.

Mrs. Weston and Others

It turns out that when the Brooklyn police arrested Mary she was not alone. The police did not have to look far to find her, as she was taken into custody at her apartment in Brooklyn. The apartment was half of a duplex and Emil Lowenstein and his wife lived in the other half of the house. The early messages out of New York held that Mrs. Hannah Lowenstein was also detained as well as a Miss Mary Cochrane, who was reported to be visiting Mrs. Weston at the time. Following the arrest of Mrs. Weston the associated press [it did not yet have capital letters] released a dispatch with what it believed was the situation relating to the women. More important than the women at the time was the discovery by the police of two revolvers in the women's possession. Mrs. Weston had in her possession a seven shot revolver with all the chambers discharged. In Hannah's half of the house was found a second revolver, from which five shots had been fired. It was unclear the source of the associated press story but it went on to say that upon their arrest it was believed that Mrs. Weston had in some way assisted in the murder and the other two women were "cognizant of the affair." All three women had been sent to Albany by boat.

It was also learned that Mr. Weston was a one-armed veteran having lost his arm in the Civil War. Reporters had also learned that on the day before he disappeared, Weston had withdrawn large sums of money from his accounts.

Identification of Lowenstein

The police were able to learn of two other ways their counterparts in the west might be able to identify Lowenstein. Before the exclusive use of buttons, men used studs that went through a pair of holes to hold the front of their shirts together. Most studs were white or black. It appears his ego was strong as they sent telegrams telling that he was wearing red shirt studs that would be equivalent to driving a red convertible today. The other identifying mark was much more specific. The police were now saying the index finger on Lowenstein's right hand was black, like it had been bitten. It was felt the black finger would lead to his arrest.

Condemning Each Other

The Troy *Times* called an editorial in the *New York Times* unwarranted and unjust. The *New York Times* had been critical of the way the Albany police had handled the investigation. The *New York Times* editorial said that the body should not have been buried without being properly identified. The editorial pointed out that without a positive identification the murder of an individual would be difficult to prove at the legal level of beyond a reasonable doubt. The editorial went on to say every effort should be made by the police to bring the person to justice. The implication was that every effort was not being made to bring the murderer to justice.

Moak Interviews Mrs. Weston

When interviewed by District Attorney Moak, the story of Mrs. Weston's potential involvement in the murder changed radically. It needs to be understood that up to this point there was merely a logical assumption that the one-armed man was Weston. Moak showed Mrs. Weston the murdered man's clothes, which she said were the ones her husband was wearing the last time she saw him. Mrs. Weston was also able to assure Moak that she was in Philadelphia at the time of the murder. The motive for the murder shifted from illicit love and was now believed to be exclusively money.

It was unclear how, but the three women were also able to provide a lead that Lowenstein might be found in Canada.

A Little About Weston

In 1840, John Weston was born in small community in Chester County, Pennsylvania. The hamlet was about 30 miles from Philadelphia. From birth he had two distinguishing features. His fingers had oversized joints and the second joint on his second finger could bend backward. The finger abnormality was a congenital condition, shared by his brother, Joseph. John also was born with "two scars above his lip" (hair lip) which he kept covered with a mustache.

Prior to the Civil War, the Weston family moved to New York City where John earned a respectable, if somewhat humble, income working as a painter. With the outbreak of the war, John and his older

brother enlisted in the 14th New York Volunteers. John's enlistment was very early in the war, June 30, 1861. He began his service in Arlington Heights, Virginia, serving under a Captain Walter Gill. Gill would play into Weston's life from this time forward.

Weston served in Company I until the battle of Gettysburg in early July 1863. In this battle, Weston's left arm was struck by an enemy rifle ball, the wound required the surgeons to amputate the appendage just below the shoulder. A few days after the battle, Mary Coon, John Weston's mother, hearing of her son's injury, had gone to Gettysburg and brought him home.

In October 1863, Weston became a throwaway soldier, having been wounded in the service of his country, he was discharged from the army with a minimum pension. The loss of his arm must have been even more of an issue for Weston who, despite his short stature, was considered to be one of the strongest men in the regiment.

Weston used the pension to buy a small paper route, making a reasonable income. After a year Weston found the paper route unfulfilling, so he approached his old captain asking if he could aid Weston in getting work at the Old Navy Yard in Brooklyn. Gill was able to help and Weston worked at the Navy Yard for two years saving enough money to buy a two-family cottage on Palmetto Street, where he resided until his death.

After two years Weston again returned to the profession of peddler. This time he sold newspapers, books, and other light items on the horse-cars. His economic condition varied radically. He would often borrow money, especially from Gill, but he always repaid any debt. Part of his problem, as a vender, may have been his incommunicable nature and mannerisms. In the army he had been called Corporal Crab. The tag came from his peculiar way of walking and the shape of his hands. Corporal Crab was the butt of ridicule and was generally out of favor in the regiment. Whether because he was called names or some other personality issues, he chose to take his meals alone. He also had a bad temper resulting in several fights with members of his regiment. As a joke or in meanness, the men of his regiment even pulled his tent down on him on one occasion. Weston countered by grabbing his musket and pointing it at the group gathered to laugh at his misfortune. There was little doubt in anyone's mind that he would have fired the musket had it not been pulled from his hands.

On January 26, 1865, 25 year-old John Weston married his 19 year-old fiancée, Mary Ann. Over the next eight years the couple had three children.

There is not a question about whether Weston was a peculiar man, the only question was the nature of his idiosyncrasies. Weston was consumed by his fear of death. He had sunstroke a few months before his death and that incident seemed to change him for the worse. Fearing death, he would not ride on ferryboat or rail trains. He would only travel on horse-cars, never motorized trains. He would complain to his wife that his hair was turning gray and he would not live much longer.

His tenant, Lowenstein, had refined a method of playing on Weston's paranoia. Lowenstein was always scheming and dreaming of ways to make a quick fortune. He would separate Weston from his wife and then tell him of ways to double his money in days or weeks. The most prevalent theme was to go to California and make his fortune. When Weston would tell his wife of his plans she would protest and tell him to stay away from Lowenstein. This sound advice was from a woman who, a month later, would be accused by the newspapers of being an adulteress and accomplice to murder.

Six weeks before his death, Weston called upon his former captain. He was again seeking work. Weston claimed to Gill that his house was heavily mortgaged and he needed a loan. Weston also claimed to have been promised a job but it had fallen through.

Money

The police believed that the little corporal had withdrawn his life's savings the day before he disappeared. In fact, they listed one bank where he withdrew $458 and a second where he had withdrawn $102. It is believed Weston left Brooklyn on August 5th with the money. On August 7th, just over $2 had been found on the body in the ravine.

A Little About Lowenstein

The suspected murderer was a 24 year-old German man who spoke very broken English. He had dark hair and a mustache. When he was 18 years old, Lowenstein had immigrated to this country with his mother, brother and three sisters. His family followed a typical immigration pattern. His father had been in the country three years, saving money to bring the rest of the family over from Europe. The family was reunited in New York City, moving immediately to Germantown near Philadelphia. Lowenstein's mother died in September 1873, while her son was in the Albany County Jail. At the time of his arrest, Lowenstein had one brother and two sisters living in Philadelphia. The other sister was living in New York City.

A Man on the Move

After the first year of residency in this country, Lowenstein had moved around quite a bit. He had worked as a waiter in a hotel in Sacramento for a year where he earned $50 a month plus room, board and laundry. On his way back East Lowenstein stopped in Salt Lake City for eight months where again he worked as a barber. While he was in the Wild West, Lowenstein purchased an old pistol. The pistol was cantankerous and would not always fire. Even when he moved back East, Lowenstein was in the habit of carrying it in his pant's pocket.

When Lowenstein returned from the West, he lived near his family in Philadelphia. He took some of the money he had saved and bought a barbershop, which he owned for 15 months. Eventually, he sold the shop for $185 so he could go to Sault St. Marie, on the Upper Peninsula of Michigan. There he worked on a farm for two months and in a mine for another two months. As he returned from his excursion to the North Country, he came across Canada and took a train south through Albany. This, he would later claim, was his only connection to Albany. Despite rumors to the contrary, Lowenstein maintained he never worked as a barber in West Albany.

When Lowenstein returned to Philadelphia from Michigan he had trouble with the law. He was convicted of petit larceny for steeling a watch and chain and sentenced to five months in Moyamensing

Prison. He was released in January 1873. Lowenstein would maintain that the man who filed the charges was later sent to prison for making a false statement against him. The man was also ordered to pay Lowenstein $50 in damages. Because of his problems with the law, Lowenstein had become estranged from his family and went by the name Livingston. To avoid confusion, only Lowenstein is used in this text.

Lowenstein was known to have a strong desire for money. The real questions were Lowenstein's reasons for seeking money; they were, at best, limited. It seems Emil Lowenstein had a compulsion to own his own barbershop.

In the spring of 1873, after working for a few months as a barber, Emil Lowenstein returned to Germany to visit relatives. In Germany he visited two of his uncles in Felfe-on-Mill. He was in Europe almost three months, returning on June 13th. Knowing he was not welcome in Philadelphia, Lowenstein stayed in New York where he went by the name Livingston. On June 22nd, six weeks before the body was found, and nine days after his return from Germany, Emil Lowenstein married 19 year-old Hannah Davidson.

The Young Couple

For the previous eight years Hannah had lived most of the time in the home of Joseph Weston, John's brother. Her occupation was a domestic, not for the Westons but for other families in Brooklyn. The Weston family was so close to Hannah that her wedding to Lowenstein took place in Joseph's house. The couple had only known each other for a brief period prior to their marriage.

The young couple moved into their new home on the second floor of 116 Palmetto Street in the apartment above John Weston. The apartment had so little furniture that for the first two weeks Hannah had to cook on Mary Weston's stove.

A Razor

On the 29th of July, Joseph Weston was at his brother John's when he noticed Lowenstein sharpening a number of razors. As the men talked, Lowenstein offered one of the razors to Joseph who accepted it. When he got home, Joseph's wife, Cornelia, placed the razor upon the mantle, where it remained until it was given to a detective to help in the identification of his brother's body. Engraved on the razor's steel blade was L VIII

Lowenstein in Flight

Now that Lowenstein was believed to be in flight, it was believed that, to avoid detection, he would change his appearance. The memos to the police in the various mid-west cities said it was speculated that he would shave the mustache and get his hair cut very short. The telegram also included the fact that Lowenstein had been in a fight, the right forefinger had been bitten and the nail was seriously discolored and about to fall off. It was also believed he was short of money and would be seeking work as a barber. Lowenstein had had his photograph taken the night before he disappeared and the photo was included in many of the dispatches.

Even though Emil Lowenstein was still on the loose, the Troy *Times* wrote an article with compliments for the Albany police. "Rarely if ever before has the crime of murder been so well executed; rarely, indeed, in the history of our State, has it been so well tracked out and its authors brought to the light of day. The detectives well deserve the public gratitude."

The newspapers reported sightings of Lowenstein in communities from Oswego to Milwaukee.

Lowenstein Arrested

Eleven days after the body of the murdered man was discovered, the case appeared to be about to close. Chief Malloy had received a telegram notifying him that Brooklyn detectives had arrested Lowenstein in St. Catharines, Ontario. There was tremendous speculation as to why the Brooklyn detectives made the arrest and even more questions as to why they were in Canada.

Arrest too Easy

Lowenstein's arrest surprised most people. It was believed that he was a shrewd man who had enticed his victim to go to a community where neither of them was known. Somehow he was able to lure him to an out of the way place. A place so isolated and away from the beaten path that, if it had not been for a shortcut taken by a worker, his body may not have been found for years. The readers following the case had to wonder how a man this clever could be captured so easily by the police.

The arrest was a surprise to Lowenstein who was living in St. Catharines under the name of Louis Davison (his wife's maiden name was Davidson and Emil had broken English, which probably explains the leaving out of the d). On August 19th, Brooklyn detectives, Corwin and Folk, arrived in St. Catharines on the 2:00 train. Following protocol they went to the chief of police in the city and told him they had reason to believe Emil Lowenstein was working in the city probably as a barber.

Aid From St. Catharine Police

Chief Cumming of the St. Catharines police immediately started inquiring as to the whereabouts of a man fitting Lowenstein's description. The chief soon learned that such a man had just started work at Kittow's Barbershop.

Detective Corwin immediately went to the St. Catharines House, a hotel in the area and the logical residence for Lowenstein, to make inquiries. After asking the clerk several questions, Corwin noticed a man silently leaving the hotel. On a hunch, Corwin followed the person who, luck would have it, went directly to Kittow's Barbershop. Seconds later a man matching Lowenstein's description emerged from the building and walked rapidly down the street. Immediately, Corwin began following the suspect, taking out his pistol at the same time. As Corwin caught up to the man he placed the barrel of the pistol at the man's head saying "Emil come with me." The search was over.

St. Catharines

The reason for the search moving to St. Catharines was Lowenstein's love for his wife. She had received a letter addressed to her maiden name and mailed to her former employer in Brooklyn. The police had tried to get the letter at the post office but the postal worker refused, saying he could only give a letter to the addressee. The detectives claimed they had been able to get the postal worker to give them the return address on the envelope. The lead to look for a letter came from Mary Cochrane, Hannah's houseguest at the time the police went to the residence in Brooklyn. Cochrane had told police that Lowenstein had promised to write to his wife using her maiden name.

The Letter

There was a great debate about whether the police had gotten to read the letter. Some newspaper articles actually carried what they claimed was the text of the letter. The police involved in the arrest said they only had access to the return address. This question was answered several months later when it was learned that the police did read the letter by forging a search warrant and giving it to the postal employee who provided them the letter.

The text published in August was the same text entered into evidence in January. In all probability, the postal worker realized what had happened and either for fear of his own position or just to help he covered for the police. The text has the grammar and spelling as published in the original.

SaintCatherines,
August 14

Dear Hannah,

You must excuse me for not writing sooner to you my child, but I always thought I would get well again and come to you, but now I see I can't. So I thought I would write to you and see if you could come to me and attend to your aged father. You know I loved you most of all my children and do still, but now my child come right of before I die. I got a comfortable home for you and me; right and tell me what train you take and if you have not got money enough let me know I will send you some at once. I will send 10 dollars. Take the 9 o'clock train in the morning and you will be here by midnight. Now my child a father is begging of you to come to him; write me as soon as you get this letter.

Lewis Davison

P. S. In case you cum instead of writing, which I shall like best for you to come yourself go to the St. Catherines House and enquire for me.

Who Wrote the Letter

There was always an issue of Lowenstein's handwriting and whether he had personally written the letter to his wife. Lowenstein could write but maintained that the letter addressed to his wife was written by Mrs. Kittow, the wife of his employer in Canada. Lowenstein never said why he did not write the letter himself.

While in St. Catharines, Detective Folk gave an interview to the newspapers in which he said that the evidence gathered against Lowenstein was overwhelming. He said that in searching the room Lowenstein rented, he had found cuff links that were worn by Weston. Folk told the reporters Lowenstein had given conflicting accounts for the incidents of the night of August 5th and August 6th. It was understood he was back in the New York City area on the sixth but where was he on August 5th?

An Arrest on Canadian Charges

Albany County District Attorney Moak had to deal with the extradition of Lowenstein. The law regarding the exchange of prisoners between Canada and the United States had recently changed. Under the old law, the chief of police in any jurisdiction in Canada could have made the necessary arrangements. The new law required a county judge to sign the warrant. The judge was on vacation. With the judge out of the area there was a real concern that Lowenstein would claim habeas corpus and be released. He had, after all, not committed any Canadian crimes. Detective Folk dealt with this contingency by filing a charge of petit larceny against Lowenstein. Folk claimed the cuff links were Weston's, so they must have been stolen. Therefore Lowenstein was in possession of stolen goods, a crime in Canada. Since Lowenstein had only six dollars at the time of his arrest, he would not be able to make bail.

The man arrested in St. Catharines fit the descriptions of Lowenstein that had been circulated almost perfectly. This is a compliment to the descriptions not to Lowenstein. The primary difference was that Lowenstein had grown a short goatee. The index fingernail was damaged and discolored. Lowenstein even had with him the red shirt buttons that were mentioned in the wire sent by Albany Chief Malloy.

False Charges

Lowenstein's young defense attorney, Herrick, would say that the charges filed against his client, which resulted in the trial, were built on a false statement and continued on the same. He was referring to the issue of the arrest of Lowenstein in Canada. Detective Folk filed charges for possession of stolen property based on what he had claimed were Weston's watch and cuff links. It would later be shown that neither belonged to Weston. In short, Lowenstein should never have been held in Canada. The second serious example of police abuse of power was the letter from Lowenstein to his wife. When the police wanted the letter from the post office they were told they needed a warrant. The warrant produced to obtain the letter was forged, but neither officer would admit to having committed the forgery.

The Events of August 4th through August 18th

The accounts of Monday, August 4th through August 18th are from the testimony of Mary Weston; her sister-in-law, Cornelia Weston; Mary Cochrane; Emil Lowenstein; Clarence Percival and others who worked with Lowenstein.

Monday August 4, 1873

Emil Lowenstein had the day off from work so he and John Weston spent most of the day together in the front room of the Weston's flat. As evening approached, the men came up with a grand plan to take their wives out for the evening. Weston went into the kitchen to tell his wife, Mary Ann, that he wanted her to join the Lowensteins and him for a night at the theater. The mere idea of an evening at the theater was an incredible treat to Mary Ann Weston, who had never before been to a show.

An Evening Out

With the evening's plans confirmed in the Weston home, the men went for a walk. When they got back to the house both Lowenstein and Weston had a treat of a half-pound of tea and a half-pound of coffee for their wives. After giving his wife the present, Emil asked Hannah to go to the theater. Hannah protested, saying they couldn't go as they only had $2.20 left to get through the week. Her feeble objections fell on deaf ears and the two couples went to see Hooley's Ministrels. By a previous agreement, the theater tickets were paid for by Weston. On the way home, Emil Lowenstein treated each person to a soda water.

The party arrived home around midnight. When they returned to the house, Weston gave Lowenstein a pinch on the arm and said "remember tomorrow morning."

The Babysitter

John and Mary Weston had three children so to go out they needed a babysitter. Their sister-in-law, Joseph Weston's wife, Cornelia, had performed this duty. Because the hour they returned was so late, Cornelia stayed over rather than walk home. The two Weston wives slept in the bedroom with the three children while John Weston spent a restless night on the couch.

The next morning, at around 6 o'clock, John went into the room where his wife, children and sister-in-law all slept. He told his wife he was going away with Lowenstein and asked his wife the whereabouts of some of his shirts. She never spoke but instead just looked up for a moment. She said that she heard Lowenstein coming down the back stairs at this same time. After retrieving the shirts without her aid John quietly went out the back door and disappeared into oblivion. The date was August 5, 1873.

The fundamental question of this case is what happened on August 5th. This needs to be looked at from the perspective of the prosecution whose presentation appears in the trial portion of this section. At this time we will look at Lowenstein's explanation of what he did on the fifth of August.

Before August 5th

In July 1873, Emil Lowenstein took a position in the barbershop owned by Theodore Grunewald. Grunewald was a local entrepreneur in Brooklyn owning both the barbershop and a cigar store. Grunewald paid journeyman Lowenstein $14 a week for his services as a barber. Lowenstein's work habits in the early days of his marriage were, at best, questionable. For the period between when he took the job and August 3rd, his last day at work, Lowenstein only earned $34. In the month of July, Lowenstein "went off" nine days saying his wife was sick and needed him. In fairness, his record was improving as the last 10 days he was supposed to be at work he was present. Lowenstein was not scheduled to work on Monday, August 4th, so Sunday, August 3rd was his last day of employment for Grunewald.

The men at the barbershop had an interesting way of passing the time. When business was slow they would take a pistol owned by Lowenstein and shoot at the rats in the shop. Grunewald, the owner, had taken part in this amusing pastime on three different occasions.

Going for Money

On August 5th, Emil had woken up with plans to go to Philadelphia and get money that he had hidden in the stone wall that surrounded Moyamensing Prison. Lowenstein had been traveling the United States extensively since his immigration. In his travels throughout the western United States Lowenstein would hold he had accumulated an enormous amount of cash ($650). Unfortunately for Lowenstein, he did not have much faith in banks, so when he returned to Philadelphia about 1871, he looked for a safe place to hide the money. Walking along the outside of the prison he noticed what he believed to be a loose stone. Lowenstein looked on the ground for something with which he could pry the stone free. Eventually he found a small piece of iron. He picked at the mortar around the stone until it came loose. As Lowenstein had suspected, behind the rock was a small area where his money could be carefully hidden. He wrapped the money in oilcloth and replaced the stone. During the intervening years he had visited the site several times taking money out when needed and replenishing it when he had extra.

Before he went to Europe in the spring of 1873, Lowenstein had revisited the hole in the wall. He found his money safely encased behind the rock. Lowenstein took out $200, the amount he expected to need for his trip, and left the rest. Now a newlywed with real responsibility he wanted the remaining $450. Lowenstein had every intention of using the money to open his own barbershop.

Taking the Tools of His Trade

He started the day, August 5th, by going to his current employer's shop (Grunewald) to gather the tools of his trade. Lowenstein maintained he left his home at 5:00 o'clock in the morning to walk the little over four miles from his home on Palmetto to the barbershop on Atlantic Avenue (it would have taken that amount of time). There is no disagreement between the time Lowenstein says he arrived at the shop and the time given by Grunewald. Up to the time of Lowenstein's leaving the barbershop there is no disagreement as to what occurred except Mrs. Weston's claim that he left a little after six in the morning. If he did leave at 6 o'clock he could not have reached the barbershop in time, unless he took the horse-cars.

Grunewald claimed that at 6:30 on the morning of August 5th, Lowenstein came in the cigar store and picked up the key to the barbershop. A little before 7 0'clock that morning the other journeyman who worked in the barbershop passed Lowenstein on Atlantic Street. At the time, Lowenstein was walking in the direction away from the shop. When the journeyman arrived at the shop he found both doors unlocked. Realizing something was amiss, the journeyman planned to leave and tell

Grunewald. When the journeyman got to the door to the barbershop there was a short man asking for Lowenstein. The journeyman told the stranger where he had seen Lowenstein. The stranger walked off in the direction Lowenstein had last been seen. The journeyman went to Grunewald telling him what had occurred. Returning to the barbershop the journeyman noticed that all of Lowenstein's razors were missing. Taking a quick inventory, he noted that one of Grunewald's razors was also missing. The journeyman noted that the missing razor was one that Lowenstein had been trying to buy from Grunewald. (Hannah Lowenstein would return Grunewald's razor, to the shop the week of August 10th.)

Getting to Philadelphia

It took the entire day for Lowenstein to make the trip to Philadelphia. The journey began when Lowenstein took a ferry from Brooklyn to Manhattan. He spent a couple of hours in the morning walking the streets and taking horse-cars to get to the ferry that would take him to New Jersey. From Jersey City's train station he took the noon train to Philadelphia, arriving between 4 and 5 o'clock in the afternoon. He walked his old neighborhoods for a while then for thirty cents had a beefsteak dinner in a restaurant he had frequented several times on Gallow Hill. Lowenstein could not remember the restaurant's name but said it had a bar area in the front and was run by a man named Fritz (such a restaurant was found to exist). On the way out Lowenstein stopped at the register and purchased a cigar for a nickel. Lowenstein then walked over to the prison wall, but decided against going to the stone in so much daylight. Across the street from the prison was a cigar store that he had shopped in previously. Knowing he would soon have lots of money, Lowenstein went in and purchased six more cigars for twenty-five cents. He talked to the lady working the cash register for a few moments. After he left the cigar store, Lowenstein went back to the prison wall for a second time and removed the stone. To his relief the money was where he had left it in the spring.

Lowenstein then walked back to the Philadelphia train station. About 1 o'clock in the morning he caught a train for New York City. There was a young German man on the train who Lowenstein engaged in a conversation. The man offered to sell Lowenstein his watch and chain for eight dollars. Feeling wealthy, Lowenstein indulged himself, accepting the man's offer. At 5:30 in the morning the train arrived back in Jersey City. Lowenstein walked down to the ferry, which he took Manhattan. After he walked across Manhattan Island, Lowenstein caught a second ferry to the Williamsburgh section of Brooklyn.

By the time Lowenstein reached the block on which he lived, he was getting tired. The man who had the grocery three buildings down from the duplex Weston and Lowenstein shared had to call out to him twice before Emil heard him. The grocer told him no one was at the house. According to the grocer, the women had all left the afternoon before. When Lowenstein asked about the whereabouts of his wife, he was told she had returned to the residence of her former employer about a mile east of the grocer's store. Rather than walk to get his wife and then walk her back carrying her luggage, Lowenstein paid the grocer a dollar to take his wagon and go get Hannah. As the grocer was hitching up his wagon he told Lowenstein that Weston had abandoned his wife. According to the grocer, Mary Weston had told him that she was sure that he and Weston had gone off together, Lowenstein claimed no knowledge of the event.

After the grocer left in his wagon Lowenstein talked with the grocer's wife for a while on a variety of topics. With some degree of regularity the conversation would return to Weston's whereabouts. It was obvious she was the local gossip and was trying to determine what had happened to John Weston. Eventually, Lowenstein gave up on the conversation and left for home.

Lowenstein had only gotten about 50 feet from the store when the grocer's wagon pulled up and let Hannah out. Reunited, the Lowensteins walked back to their home together. Emil stayed in the apartment until early afternoon, then went to Grand Street and bought himself a new light colored suit and two rings one for himself and one for Hannah. The total for all three items was $21.

The First Confrontation

When he got home at 3:30 that afternoon both Cornelia and Mary Weston were in his apartment waiting to talk to him. They asked in unison if he had seen John Weston. Lowenstein responded in the affirmative. It seems that each day as Lowenstein was leaving for the barbershop he would turn and give his wife a final wave goodbye from the corner. Like so many newlyweds, she stood in the window waiting for this symbolic gesture. He told the ladies that the day before as he waved to his wife he had seen Weston in the downstairs doorway. Lowenstein explained that was the last time he had seen Weston.

What the Others Said

August 5, 1873

Mary Weston arose about a half-hour after her husband left the house that morning. She went into the closet and noticed his gray satchel was gone. On the kitchen table was $20 John had left for her. She dressed and went to the local police station house to ask to have her husband detained. When the bank opened she went down and discovered that her husband had withdrawn their money the day before. Mary would later tell the court that she had brought into the marriage the money that was in savings. She never said how she had come by that amount of money. It would also be learned that the house and lot had been transferred into her name. Having real estate in a wife's name was very rare in the 1870s.

Feeling somewhat desperate Mary went to Manhattan to see her childhood friend, Mrs. Flannery. Her friend was not home but Mary did visit with her friend's husband for 20 minutes. Mary then went to Mrs. Flannery's mother, Lizzie Burke. This is where she spent the night of August 5-6th.

Wednesday August 6, 1873

Thomas Wilkin was the owner of the grocery store that was about 350 feet from the house occupied by the Lowensteins and Westons. Both of the families traded at his store. The Lowensteins had only lived in the apartment over the Westons since shortly after their marriage. The couple actually moved in on July 8th. During that time the grocer had seen Emil Lowenstein about eight times. The last time Wilkin spoke to Lowenstein was at about "half past eight," on the morning of Wednesday, August 6th. Emil walked past Wilkin's store on his way to the house. Wilkin had called out but Lowenstein either didn't hear him or ignored his call. A few minutes later Lowenstein walked back past in the opposite direction. Wilkin called out to him a second time. This time Lowenstein heard him and crossed the street and entered the store asking in broken English, "Where my wife?" Wilkin told Lowenstein that his wife had gone back to the Philip's house in Ridgewood. This is where Hannah had worked prior to her marriage. At the time Wilkin was struck by how pale and fatigued Lowenstein seemed. Lowenstein asked Wilkin to take his wagon and go for Hannah. The excuse Lowenstein gave Wilkin for not going himself was he did not feel he looked presentable. Lowenstein was dressed in the same dark suit Wilkin had always seen him wear.

Lowenstein told Wilkin he would pay him a dollar for fetching his wife. Not knowing his wife's mood or the real reason for returning to her old position, Emil said, "If wife doesn't return wid you tell her she never see me 'gain."

As Wilkin was hitching his horse to go for Hannah, he had gone on to say to Lowenstein that Mary Weston had assumed her husband had abandoned her. Out of desperation, Mrs. Weston had spent the night her husband first went missing with Lizzie Burke, the mother of her childhood friend. It is not surprising the grocer knew all this since in 1873, the local store was the hub of neighborhood information (now we have to go to work to get the good gossip).

After returning with Hannah, Wilkin noticed the thickness of Lowenstein's wallet as he extracted the dollar to pay for the service. Wilkin remembered later thinking to himself the wallet was "well filled." While putting the money in the cash drawer Wilkin again told the Lowensteins that John Weston had abandoned his wife. He went on to say that Mary Weston had been in the store telling the grocer that she had been to the police to see if they could help find her missing husband. Mary Weston had told the grocer she knew that her husband had withdrawn their money from the bank and she feared he had run off. Lowenstein remarked back that he was unaware of the situation.

That evening, August 6th, Lowenstein was in his apartment with Hannah, Mary Weston, and Cornelia Weston. Cornelia asked Lowenstein where he had left John. Lowenstein said that John had given him $50 to take him to the Gates Avenue horse-cars to get away. Weston's sister-in-law then attacked Lowenstein telling him he was the last man to see John. She went on to say he (Lowenstein) was a mean man to take the money and a man away from his family. As Cornelia continued her assault, the seated Lowenstein looked down and his nerves twitched. Eventually he got up and walked to the mantel, moving objects around, but he did not respond further to the onslaught.

One of the more interesting characters in this case was 19 year-old Mary Cochrane. Mary mysteriously joined the story on Wednesday afternoon, August 6th. At that time she suddenly appeared at the Weston's apartment inquiring about her old friend Hannah Lowenstein. This would have had to have been at the time Lowenstein and Hannah were out buying clothes and the rings. Cochrane claimed to have known Hannah for three or four years but had not seen her in a year. When Mary Cochrane learned Hannah was not home she left the neighborhood on the sixth to return on the seventh.

There was considerable debate as to Cochrane's source of income. She maintained that she had worked from the time she was 14 as a domestic servant except for interludes when she was a sales associate in a lace store. At the trial the defense would push that Mary's real profession was that of a prostitute. Under oath Mary would claim that she never lived in a house of "ill-fame."

In order to appreciate Mary's character, we will jump ahead to February 3, 1874, when Mary testified at Lowenstein's trial. Mary was no longer Miss Mary Cochrane but was now Mrs. Mary Walker. The marriage happened on the sixth of September. On that day Mary Cochrane had married Officer Walker of the Albany police. Officer Walker was one of the men assigned to go to New York City to bring Mary back to Albany with Mary Weston and Hannah Lowenstein. The two of them had met on the trip, which was on the 15th of August. They had known each other only three weeks.

August 7, 1873.

Thursday morning started with Mary Weston going up the back stairs to confront Lowenstein for a second time about her husband's whereabouts. Mary said that this time Lowenstein said he had last seen her husband in Troy.

Later in the same day, Mary Cochrane came to the Lowenstein's apartment. When she arrived Emil was not home. She spent hours visiting with Hannah. Lowenstein came in while they were visiting and the three had tea together. In the evening, they all walked down to Broadway where Cochrane had heard there might be a "situation" for her. Since she did not get the new job the Lowensteins, walked Cochrane to a house on Bushwick Avenue where she spent the night.

Lowenstein Starts Spending

On Friday, August 8th, Emil Lowenstein started a spending spree that would be very difficult to explain. One either believed his position that he had money hidden in the prison wall or he must have taken Weston's.

At 9:00 a.m. on the eighth of August, Emil Lowenstein entered the office of John Koerber, a real estate broker in Manhattan, and asked if he had any barbershops for sale. Based on his new client's appearance, Koerber was not impressed with the prospect of a sale. Lowenstein was dressed in old worn clothes including a dark coat. Koerber informed Lowenstein that he had a listing for a barbershop on 18th Street. Without waiting, the two men went to look at the shop. Emil was pleased with the prospects of the business, which had three chairs. The two men and the barbershop's owner, Louis Daig, went back to Koerber's office to complete the paperwork. The agreed upon price for the shop was $600. Lowenstein put $350 down and signed a chattel mortgage for the remaining $250. Even in 1873 the price of real estate in Manhattan far exceeded anywhere else.

During the negotiations, the agent and Daig had wanted as much up front as possible. Lowenstein had told the men he could not put more cash down, as his wife was "in a family way" and he would soon be in need of the money. Lowenstein paid the down payment for the shop with two one-hundred-dollar bills and thirty, five-dollar bills. Koerber received an additional $7.50 from Lowenstein for drawing up the mortgage. Just five days later, Lowenstein would try to sell the shop back to Daig.

On Friday, Mary Weston saw Lowenstein coming home in his new suit. She was outside and complimented him. She asked him the time and he pulled out his packet watch and responded 2:30. This is the first time she saw Lowenstein's new watch and chain. She was sure it was the one her husband had carried and she went back to her apartment and cried.

That same afternoon Hannah would show Mary Cochrane a pair of pistols that she found in her husband's trunk. They would agree that they did not want them in the apartment. Mary took the pistols down to Mary Weston for her to hold. Mary would put them in the stairway leading to the basement. There is a conflict on this critical point, as Mary Cochrane would later say she never saw the guns until Mary Weston brought them out of the cellar stairway on Sunday.

During the time between the sale of the shop to Lowenstein on Friday and the potential resale on Tuesday, Lowenstein's behavior troubled the two journeymen barbers who worked in the shop. George Bennett and Jacob Smith were amazed at the conduct of their new employer. Lowenstein had come into the shop on Friday afternoon and announced himself as their new employer. He asked each of the journeymen if they wanted to stay for $14 a week.

Thinking for only a moment, they both agreed to stay on for that rate. Business in Manhattan was slow on this summer weekend. The journeymen could not get over how Lowenstein paced around the store, as if strolling would attract customers. At the end of the day on Sunday, Lowenstein had to pay the men. There was not enough revenue during the three days to meet even this meager payroll, so Lowenstein had to pay the men out of his own pocket.

The two journeymen in Lowenstein's shop would say that, at the time he came into the barbershop in the afternoon on Friday, Lowenstein was wearing the same old dark suit that he was wearing earlier in the day. The dark suit testified to by the journeymen, was in direct conflict with the light-colored suit Mary Weston said he was wearing on Friday.

Saturday, August 9, 1873

One of the key pieces of circumstantial evidence in the case was the razor that was found near Weston's body. When people go into a beauty shop today they must first walk past a display of hair care products. In the 1870s, barbershops kept the cash container at the entrance, usually on the bottom shelf of a display case full of razors. Barbers sold razors as a sideline just like beauty parlors sell hair products today.

The blade of the razor found at the crime scene was engraved L VII. It would be learned that at the time of his arrest Lowenstein had a large collection of razors with him, including a set engraved L I through L VI. Everyone agreed that L VIII had been sold to the victim's brother, Joseph Weston. On Saturday, August 9th, Lowenstein's journeymen watched as he purchased two new razors from a peddler. Lowenstein would claim later that he bought and sold the razor for extra income. According to Lowenstein, razor L VII was sold to John Weston quite some time before the murder.

On Saturday, Lowenstein was still dressed in the drab "rusty suit of black" when he left for work. According to one of his journeymen, when he came to the shop he brought a gray canvas satchel in which were several razors, a pair of slippers and a pipe. Lowenstein would say that he brought the items just not in a satchel.

Sunday, August 10, 1873

This was the most unexplained day in the entire case.

Jacob Smith had Saturday off but was impressed on Sunday when he saw his new boss in a light-colored suit with a Panama hat. He continued to wear the same new suit until Tuesday night, August 12th, the last time either of the men saw Lowenstein until the trial.

When Emil came home from work on Sunday the three ladies, Mary Weston, Mary Cochrane and his wife, Hannah, had just returned from a walk. They were accompanied by a complete stranger named Clarence Percival from St. Albans, Vermont. Where he came from was never explained. He just suddenly accompanied these ladies to their house. That evening, when Lowenstein came home from the barbershop, he was less than thrilled to see his wife with another man and some warm words were exchanged.

Dancing

Lowenstein quickly overcame his issue and agreed to play the harmonica so the others could dance. He played a series of waltzes while Percival and the three ladies danced together. After they danced for a while, Mrs. Weston decided it was time to get rid of the pistols and, without Lowenstein knowing, gave one to Mary Cochrane and the other to Percival. At the trial, the defense was extremely troubled by why a woman strapped for money suddenly gave away two pistols, each of which was worth about $15. To make matters worse, she gave them to complete strangers.

Monday, August 11, 1873

On Monday, the situation seemed to deteriorate rapidly for Lowenstein. Smith had the day off so only Bennett and Lowenstein worked in the shop. About 3 o'clock in the afternoon, a proud Hannah brought her friend Mary Cochrane to the shop. Since business was off, the two women stayed in the shop until 5 o'clock visiting with Lowenstein. Lowenstein took a few minutes off to join them as they went looking for furniture. He returned to the shop after about an hour, disappointed that the furniture store they visited would not sell on credit.

After the two women left Lowenstein near the barbershop, they stopped to buy a loaf of bread. The ladies took the ferry back across the river. On the trip back, Mary Cochrane dropped the pistol in the river near the Brooklyn side. When they were back on shore, Mary looked at the copy of that morning's *Sun* that was wrapped around the loaf of bread to keep it fresh. Mary noticed a story about the body of a one-armed man having been found in Albany. The description so closely matched that of John Weston the two women decided to go back to the shop and confront Lowenstein.

The two ladies returned for a meeting with Lowenstein, which lasted only a few minutes. Mary and Hannah left the shop for a second time at approximately 7:30 that evening. About 15 minutes after they left, Mary came back to the shop alone and told Lowenstein he should put on his hat and come with her. When they met on the street Hannah, perhaps bolstered by Mary, told Lowenstein that, "John Weston was murdered and you have done it."

Lowenstein responded, "Do you believe I have done such a deed?" Lowenstein continued to protest his innocence dropping to his knees and threatening to shoot himself if she really believed he had committed such an act.

Hannah was feeling very faint so Lowenstein returned to the shop to get her a glass of water. About 8:00 o'clock that evening, Lowenstein returned to the shop alone. He told Bennett that his wife had fallen on 17th Street. Bennett was struck by how agitated Lowenstein appeared when he returned. Lowenstein told his journeymen to close up early and left to rejoin the women.

When Lowenstein joined the two women on the street he began talking with his wife in German. According to Mary, Hannah insisted he switch back to English. According to Mary, who now understood the conversation, Lowenstein offered to take Hannah wherever she wanted to go. The three walked back to the ferry. Mary testified at the trial that Lowenstein fell asleep on the ride across and she noticed a pistol in his jacket pocket. Mary said that the three of them got back to the apartment at 11:00 o'clock. She never said why it took three hours to make the trip.

It would later trouble the defense that under the stress that was described why or how had Lowenstein fallen asleep? Cochrane's observation also implied there was a third pistol.

By now the living arrangements had changed and Mary Cochrane spent the night on the couch in Mary Weston's apartment. This is interesting, as Mary Cochrane had only know Mary Weston four days.

Tuesday, August 12, 1873

On Tuesday morning, when Lowenstein arrived at the barbershop, he announced to his journeymen that the reason his wife had fainted the previous afternoon was that she had gotten a letter from her father in St. Louis. The letter had informed her that he was very sick and needed her to come to him immediately. He seemed dejected as he told the two journeymen that he had to sell the shop or his wife would die of the "brain fever."

Lowenstein spent the rest of Tuesday pursuing every avenue he could think of to sell the barbershop. Journeyman Smith was there when the shop opened at 8:00 in the morning. Lowenstein offered to sell him the shop for $200 and the assumption of the mortgage. Smith was firm in telling Lowenstein he did not have the money nor any interest in buying the shop. When George Bennett, the other journeyman, came in just before lunch, Lowenstein dropped the price to $150 plus the assumption of the mortgage. Bennett informed Lowenstein he was not interested in owning the shop. From conversations that they had had since Friday, Lowenstein knew that Bennett had access to the money needed to purchase the shop. Realizing Bennett was a solid lead, when Bennett returned from his dinner break, Lowenstein unilaterally dropped the price to $100 plus the assumption of the mortgage. Bennett reassured Lowenstein that he did not want to buy the shop.

The hour was getting late so Lowenstein changed his strategies. He paid Bennett twenty-five cents to go to Daig's house and ask him to come to the shop. While Bennett was gone, Hannah and Mary Cochrane came to the shop. Smith watched as Lowenstein paced nervously back and forth in front of the ladies who were sitting in the chairs in front of the windows. The reason Lowenstein gave for pacing was his anxiety over Daig's delayed arrival. Occasionally, Lowenstein would wander to the door looking for Daig and Bennett. Whenever he was away from the ladies too long, his wife would say, "Emil come here, I want to talk to you."

Getting Daig

It was 6:30 in the evening on Tuesday, August 12th, when Bennett arrived at the home of Louis Daig to tell him that Lowenstein wanted to see him. Daig felt it was improper for Lowenstein to send for him at such a late hour, but he went to the shop anyway. When Daig arrived, Lowenstein was giving a man a shave. There was no sign of Hannah or Mary Cochrane. Lowenstein told Daig that he wanted to sell the shop back to him. He went on to explain that his wife had received a letter from St. Louis stating that her father was sick and needed their presence. Lowenstein, never one to let a point drop, went on to say his wife had fallen the day before on 17th Street and that she was brought to the shop by a police officer. Daig informed Lowenstein that he had no money on him or at home. Daig went on to say that even if they could agree on a price and payments he would have to talk to his wife before he could take the shop back. Lowenstein negotiated against himself, saying he only wanted a little money for now.

Ever hopeful the shop would sell; Emil walked Daig back to his home. Lowenstein was trusting fate that Daig would get permission from his wife to talk about the purchase of the shop. Lowenstein waited in the family's saloon while Daig went to a back room to discuss the idea with his wife. Eventually, Daig returned and told Lowenstein his wife was not interested in taking back the shop. Under pressure, Lowenstein asked him to run the shop for $15 a week and to list the shop for $400. Under the agreement, when the shop sold, Daig was to deduct the mortgage ($250) and send the rest ($150) to Lowenstein. The two men shook hands and bade each other goodbye. Under the terms of the agreement, Lowenstein started with $350 cash and would end up with $150, if the sale were for the full $400.

Mary Cochrane's Tale

Mary Cochrane told a slightly different story about Tuesday's events.

According to Mary, on the Tuesday visit Hannah told Emil that Mary Weston had suspicions that he had killed her husband and that she was going to file charges. Cochrane testified that Lowenstein disagreed, saying "there is too much muss about it. I shall move out of the house." Hannah told her husband he couldn't move or it would look suspicious. Lowenstein told Hannah he was going to sell the shop so they could go away. Hannah said he would have to stay to prove his innocence. Lowenstein said no if he stayed even though he was innocent he would be "put in prison for three months." Lowenstein offered his wife the watch and rings to sell so she would have money to last until he would send for her. He had originally told Hannah the ring cost fifty cents, he now told her it was worth seven dollars. As they said good-bye on the street Hannah said, "Emil I will never see you again." He said he would write her at the address of her former employer. The letter would be addressed with her maiden name. He told her he would send money for her to come to be with him.

There was a part of the conversation that Mary testified to that made no sense. She said that Hannah asked Lowenstein about the guns he had placed in the stairway leading to the basement. According to Mary, he said he didn't want them in the apartment, so he moved them to the stairway. But, Mary Weston testified that Mary Cochrane moved them to the stairway either Friday or Saturday evening.

Mary Weston had gone to Philadelphia that day so Mary Cochrane helped herself to the couch in her living room as a place to sleep. After that night, Cochrane moved in with Hannah where she stayed until the trial in February.

The Trial

It was the season of cold, miserable weather that Upstate New York is famous for in January when the Lowenstein trial began. Surprisingly it took only one day to select a jury. When the list was finally accepted it was comprised of nine farmers, one carpenter, one mechanic and a twelfth member whose profession was not mentioned.

The trial opened with a major argument. The defense wanted the witnesses excluded from the courtroom when the prosecutor, Nathan Moak, made his opening remarks. It was a well-known fact that Moak was gifted at weaving a thread through a complex set of facts to develop a blanket that covered the case. The skill was not the issue, that was just something to be dealt with. The issue raised by the defense was that when witnesses saw where their testimony fit the overall explanation they might change some portion to assure Moak's theory was established. Moak argued that the witnesses were honest people whose testimony to the facts would not be jeopardized by his "simple" words. The court ruled for Moak and the witnesses were permitted to hear his opening.

The opening was classic Nathan Moak - a hypothesis based on sound undisputed facts - just not all the facts. If the jurors had been polled following Moak's opening they would have been foolish not to hold the defendant guilty. Like Moak would do in other cases, he was gifted at ignoring anything that did not fit neatly into his theory.

Moak wove into the remarks a statement that tells us much about how he saw several of the witnesses. He said they represented "every class of society." Since everyone who testified, except Clarence Percival and the women introduced previously, had respectable jobs listed, this comment must be interpreted as how he saw those gathered that Sunday night, August 10th, to dance while Lowenstein played the harmonica.

The prosecution's case rested exclusively on circumstantial evidence. Moak's first job was to determine the identity of the victim. This was only an issue because of the early burial, since no one who knew John Weston had positively identified the body. The second obstacle for the prosecution was to place Lowenstein and Weston at the scene of the murder. This meant the prosecution had to account for how the two strangers got to Albany. Moak would also have to show a motive and access to the weapon. To complicate the matter, Moak would have to accomplish each of these beyond a reasonable doubt.

Getting to Albany

To place Lowenstein and Weston at the scene, the prosecution had to show that the two Brooklyn men had come to West Albany. After his opening statement, Moak started the testimony by calling the Harlem Railroad conductor followed by the Hudson River Railroad conductor. It was the responsibility of these two men to identify both Weston and Lowenstein as passengers on the trains coming to Albany on August 5, 1873.

On that day, there was a train on the Harlem Railroad that left New York City at 8:25 in the morning and arrived in Chatham Station at 2:40 that afternoon. When the conductor was approached by detectives 10 days later he was pretty sure that one of the men on the train on August 5th was Emil Lowenstein; however, the conductor could not remember any person traveling with Lowenstein. Moak considered that recognition close enough and placed the man on the stand to provide a "pretty sure" identification. The conductor had records that showed that only five tickets were sold on that trip where the passengers went all the way from New York City to Chatham. The conductor told the court that he could not remember any other passenger who went all the way to Chatham or what Lowenstein was wearing. The conductor said he remembered Lowenstein because he wouldn't look up.

The Hudson River Line conductor was more convincing as he shared his memory of Weston riding his train on August 5th. The conductor could not remember Lowenstein but did remember a one-armed man who boarded in Chatham. The man caught his attention by the way he reached for his money in his vest pocket. The man was small and matched the various descriptions of Weston including the clothing. This train arrived in Albany at 5:14 that evening.

An Albany grocer remembered being out riding in his buckboard on August 5th. While he was at the corner of Quail and Second Streets he saw two men climb a fence. He had a clear memory that one was a one-armed man because he had run a couple of steps to build enough speed to get over the fence. The grocer remembered that the man with two arms was pointing northwest in the general direction of the Jones's Farm. The grocer was not sure the two-armed man was Lowenstein.

The final witness the first day was the switchman stationed at the shack west of Albany. The switchman's name was Charles Miller. He was on duty for the night shift the week of the murder. He said that some time after midnight he heard two sets of gun shots. The first set consisted of about seven or eight shots. He went outside and heard another four shots fired in rapid succession. According to the switchman, the sound of shots even at night was not that unusual. What made this night memorable was the number of shots and the rapidity of the firing. Miller weakened as a witness under cross-examination. He admitted his testimony was somewhat tainted by Moak's opening statement. Miller really wasn't sure of the night that he heard the shots, although he did believe it was two days before the body was found. Miller admitted to the jury that his belief as to the date was based on Moak's opening statement. This is precisely what the defense had tried to prevent.

Moak left for the day feeling comfortable. In his mind he had shown how Lowenstein and Weston had gotten to Albany and then on to the actual site of the murder. He had also established a time (after midnight) for the murder.

A Motive

The testimony the second day started primarily on technical notes. In Moak's mind the motive was money. He planned to show that Weston had a tremendous amount of money on him when he left and virtually none when his body was found. The coroner testified as to the discovery of the body, the razor, and transporting the body to the Almshouse. He would be the first of numerous witnesses who said the body had only the two dollars in the vest pocket when it was found.

Two tellers from New York City testified to Weston's withdrawal of all his funds on August 4th.

Dr. Haskins, the man who did the autopsy, was then sworn in. Moak needed him to prove that the victim death was the result of homicide. For dramatic effect, Moak wanted the doctor to show by the number of bullets used that the murder was extremely violent. The doctor took a long time describing the numerous wounds and the ones that actually caused the death. The prosecution was successful in using the doctor's testimony to show the shear brutality of the murder and make it clear that it was, in fact, a murder and not a suicide.

Mary Weston would be called to the stand several times during the trail. On her first trip, she was called upon to identify the clothes found in the pile at the top of the hill as the ones worn by the victim. She claimed all belonged to her husband. Mary developed a great deal of pleasure putting the defense attorneys in their place. She used quick wit to answer many questions. Her behavior often made those in attendance in the courtroom break out in laughter. The problem with Mary's behavior was that she was a recent widow – six months – at the trial of her husband's alleged killer. Laughter, although perhaps healthy, was inappropriate for a recent widow under Victorian practices. Her choice of conduct was exacerbated by the grave illness of her youngest child. Mary brought him into the court every day – the child had a serious case of whooping cough and his cough was a subtle reminder to the court that there were children who now lacked of a male parent.

The testimony to this point assured Moak that he had established that Weston had come to Albany with a large amount of cash. Although it would have been better to have a positive identification of the body, Moak felt that through Mary Weston he had matched the clothes worn by the victim to those owned by Weston. Additionally, several witnesses had sworn the body had only one arm and the size of the victim was the same as Weston. Moak was comfortable that he had established that the man was Weston and that he had been murdered probably for his money. Now it was time to establish that Lowenstein had used the money.

The prosecution called witnesses to describe Lowenstein's behavior after the murder. Moak started by calling John Koerber, the real estate broker in New York, to the stand. Koerber retold the story of the sale of the barbershop, including the mortgage. Daig, the shop's original owner, was the next man called. Daig recounted the initial sale on Friday and Lowenstein's desire to sell the shop back to him the following Tuesday.

There was quite a stir in the court as the widow, Mrs. Mary Weston, fainted during the testimony of Bennett and Smith, the two men who worked in the shop. Bennett and Smith both told the story of their new boss pacing and looking nervous.

In court, Grunewald, the owner of the shop, Lowenstein worked in prior to the day he went missing, joined by the journeyman in the same shop identified the pistol the police had taken from Percival as looking like the one he and Lowenstein had used to shoot at rats.

During the trial there was, for one night, a stir about a bloody handkerchief found in the ladies' luggage when they came to Albany. One of the detectives testified to finding a bloodstained handkerchief in one of the trunks. The implication was that it had been used by Lowenstein to wipe the blood from the razor. The next day Mary Cochrane would admit the blood was hers – the result of a bloody nose.

The defense called an expert on pistols. He testified that the gun that was attributed to Lowenstein was a .22 caliber and that this type of gun would only cause a powder burn if fired within three feet of the target. To challenge the witness's ability to be an expert in guns, Moak asked what he knew about the "Governor." The witness went on to say that he had never heard of a gun called the "Governor" until that morning, but that a serial number such as 228 meant it was among the first manufactured. The expert neutralized Moak's challenge of his being an expert when he assured the court with that low a number he should not be expected to know too much.

The Defense

The defense, after its opening remarks, called Emil Lowenstein to the stand. His testimony reflected what was previously said in the text. He did much better on cross-examination than probably anyone expected, not yielding an inch on any significant point. Typical of Moak, the witness was asked a series of questions that would imply he was a criminal. These questions included the use of a variety of aliases, other arrests, and threats involving a gun. Moak never produced a witness who supported any of the questions, but the way they were asked together with Moak's gift for acting as if he had some hidden piece of information, had to have left the jury questioning Lowenstein's character.

The defense called 26 year-old Fanny Hume. She had been married for three years to a man who was in the shipping business. Her husband also kept the cigar store across from the prison. Her husband had gone to Atlantic City on business on August 5th so she was called upon to watch the store. She remembered Emil Lowenstein came in that night and purchased six cigars. She recognized him immediately because of his voice and because he had been in the store on other occasions.

Her cross-examination under Moak was typical of his behavior. He asked her about her living arrangements prior to her marriage. The implication being she was a woman of loose morals. Mrs. Hume was asked where she spent the night of August 5th - implying she may have spent it with Lowenstein. She replied she spent it with her parents and gave their address.

On behalf of the defense, Bond went to New York and Philadelphia to check the accuracy of Lowenstein's and others' testimony. He was also looking for witnesses for Lowenstein. On direct examination, Bond basically just collaborated the testimony of Lowenstein and Fanny Hume. Bond had been to the prison wall and seen the loose rock.

The next defense witness, Lucian Bond, also played into Moak's attack on Mrs. Hume. When Mrs. Hume was in Albany in December she stayed with Bond. When asked if Mrs. Bond was sick at the time of the December trip, Mrs. Hume replied yes. By implying the wife was ill, and therefore not able to chaperone her husband, Moak was successful in being able to raise the question of sleeping arrangements in front of the jury.

Lucian Bond became a lawyer in 1862 in Whitewater, Wisconsin. For 12 years before that he had lived in Washington County the village of Greenwich, New York. Bond left the practice of law for a while, first to become a life insurance agent, then a fire insurance agent. His final non-attorney position had been in the "non-explosive oil business until it exploded." Bond then returned to the practice of law joining a firm with John Nelson, Lowenstein's senior defense attorney and young Cady Herrick. In this case his role was more private detective than attorney.

The cross-examination was vicious. Moak was known for his attack on the defense's witnesses. In this case (as with Mrs. Washburn in the Billings's trial) Moak was way out of line. He implied that Bond, a fellow attorney, was making up evidence, using the money set aside for the defense for his personal travel and possibly taking advantage of his position to be with women. Moak never offered any supporting evidence to his allegations only smeared by question and innuendo. While on the stand Bond had to account for virtually every cent spent on the trial.

The defense rested having only called five witnesses.

The prosecution then brought witnesses to counter the testimony of the defense witnesses. The first was a fellow prisoner of Lowenstein's in St. Catharines. He only said that Lowenstein had told him the last time he saw Weston was on the streets of New York. The only value of the testimony was to demonstrate that Lowenstein often changed his story.

A major discussion occurred when Moak tried to place a witness on the stand to impeach Bond. There was a long, heated, emotional exchange and the judge ruled in favor of the defense. Moak never really lost in these rulings, as an issue raised never truly leaves a juror's mind.

Nelson's Summation

As defense attorney, John Nelson began his summary on February 6th. The limited rational demeanor of the trial and any semblance of justice went by the boards. Nelson had many years of experience in the courtroom. In sharp contrast, it was the first case for his protege Cady Herrick. Nelson's life of late had been challenging and to lighten his load he had on taken two partners, Lucian Bond and Herrick. Bond was the defense witness who Moak attacked so viciously while he was on the stand. Nelson was also visiting the bottom of a glass too often as had been previously demonstrated when this trial had to be quietly moved from the December term to January because of his "illness".

When the afternoon session began, Nelson was supposed to stand before the jury and set forth his summary. Unfortunately, Nelson's performance on this day was less than stellar. One reporter described Nelson's statements as "owing to his condition, it was so disjointed, pointless and incoherent that it was almost impossible to ascertain what he was driving at." Fortunately, the reporter for the *Argus* was able to discern enough to provide an overview of Nelson's bitter and angry remarks.

What could be grasped from Nelson's muddled summary was a personal attack on the prosecutor, Nathan Moak. The ever-arrogant Moak quite probably deserved the comments based on his behavior during the trial. To Nelson, the attack on Bond, while he was on the stand, was done with "meanness unparalleled."

Nelson started his slurred onslaught by comparing resources. Moak had demanded under oath that Bond account for how the $250 allowed for the defense of Lowenstein had been spent. As district attorney Moak was actually in control of the amount spent on the *defense,* but not in control of how it was spent. At the same time that Nelson had only $250, Moak had at his disposal, "all the resources of the county." To Nelson, Lowenstein was a "journeyman ...friendless and without means" who because of a lack of money had been deprived of justice.

Nelson apparently then tried to move to the issues. The first issue the jury had to decide was whether the murdered man was, in fact, John Weston. Nelson tried to show that there was not an assurance beyond a reasonable doubt that the body was that of Weston. Nelson felt there was only limited support of a positive identification. He made the clothing and a few personal marks appear as nothing. In fairness to Nelson, who was not having a good day, there was very little variety in the clothes people wore. Further, it needs to be noted that the percentage of people missing appendages was much higher at this time. With the Civil War over for only eight years there were many men living who had lost an arm or a leg. This is shown through many photographs of the field hospitals. It was a major flaw for the prosecution that the body was buried before it was properly identified. Nelson then cited several cases [Sarah Bloom – Newburgh] where a person had been tried and convicted for murder only to have the supposed victim found alive.

In fairness to the prosecution, the circumstantial evidence did seem to indicate the person was probably Weston. He went missing the day the person was murdered. Near the body there was a copy of the *Sun* dated the day Weston went missing. His height, weight and missing arm all matched that of the victim. The two congenital identifiers, the teeth and the finger that bent backward, were strong indicators that the body was probably that of Weston.

Nelson then appeared to turn his attention to the way Moak had portrayed the defendant in his opening statement. Nelson pointed out that Moak had said that he would show that Lowenstein was always borrowing money, yet had not put one witness on the stand who provided this testimony. Moak had said that when Lowenstein had his photograph taken he was wearing the new suit. Nelson showed the jury the photograph, which had Lowenstein in the old dark suit. Moak had also said the Lowenstein returned to Brooklyn, "lavished in jewelry." The defense had showed the total amount spent was less than $10. It was especially troubling for Nelson that Moak had badgered the defendant on the issue of a conviction for larceny, which never was proven to have happened.

Nelson then tried his best to deal with the points raised in the prosecution witnesses' testimony. Starting with Mary Weston's statement where she admitted that she made no protest when her husband said he was going away with Emil, Nelson tried his best to show the lack of logic to the primary prosecution witness's behavior.

The comments on Grunewald's testimony were devoted to the conflict with the color of the satchel the man was carrying. Grunewald had told the court the man he saw that morning was carrying a dark satchel, while Mary Weston had said her husband was carrying a drab satchel.

Nelson, in his disjointed remarks, tried to have the jury understand that the testimony of the two railroad conductors was hardly conclusive. These men had not positively identified either Weston or Lowenstein.

Nelson pointed out that no one had testified to seeing Lowenstein in Albany at any point. The grocer, Blackburn, had seen a one-armed man on Second Street with a second, taller man but the grocer did not identify the man as Lowenstein.

The best attack was saved for Mary Cochrane. According to Nelson, anything uttered from this woman's mouth should be looked upon with a great deal of suspicion. First, Nelson pointed out that Cochrane appeared on the scene about the same time as the alleged homicide. He then reminded the jury that she came to Albany and married the police officer who brought her here in custody. Nelson suggested that perhaps from the beginning Mary was in the employ of the police.

Nelson attempted to point out the lack of logic in Cochrane's testimony. First, she had taken the pistols from the Lowenstein's apartment to Mary Weston's apartment on Friday. She even picked them up again on Sunday, yet not a word about the pistols was said to Lowenstein until Monday. Why? Cochrane had told the court that Hannah was frightened at finding the guns in her possession. Why then would she take them and place them in the hands of the victim's widow? Would any wife who believed her husband involved in a serious crime give the weapon to the wife of the victim? Also, why would Cochrane agree to drop the pistol in the river, even if she did not know for certain of the crime? The next to last blow against Cochrane was that she claimed Lowenstein was nervous and pacing. Yet minutes later he was tired enough to fall asleep on the ferry - just so she could conveniently see a third gun in Lowenstein's jacket. The final assault was on Mary Cochrane's character. According to Nelson, "she came here day after day to hang the husband of her friend. If you believe her testimony the responsibility rests with you not with me."

As best he was able, Nelson then turned his attention to the behavior of Mary Weston. Through rhetorical questions he had tried to imply reasonable doubt to her testimony. He asked the jury, "do you believe that Mrs. Weston used every available means to get her husband back?" Nelson pointed out that Mary Weston said she was suspicious of Lowenstein, yet a half-hour after she confronted him she was dancing while he played the harmonica. He asked the jury, "Would your wife, supposing that you had either been murdered or disappeared, give away those pistols?" Would a woman (Mrs. Weston) who was struggling to sustain herself financially give away a pistol worth $15 to a man she had just met (Percival)?

There was a perplexing argument concerning the behavior of those involved made by Nelson during the protracted harangue. The women witnesses all testified that when Cornelia Weston confronted Lowenstein on Wednesday, the day after the murder, he looked nervous and trembled. Why then did he stay? Why did he buy the shop? Why would he later play the harmonica? Why would the ladies then dance for this man?

Nelson's finest moment came when he said to the jury, "I have never known a case like this, commenced in perjury and sustained by it."

It was the attack, probably deserved, on Moak that caused Nelson to get into trouble with the court. Nelson described Moak as a gentleman outside the court but "inside the courtroom he is a perfect and relentless devil." Nelson was putting forward a perception that would be shared by other attorneys in other trials. Whether true or not, there was prevailing perception that Moak felt "bound always to convict." Moak had a habit of "sneering at whatever did not please him."

Nelson, realizing his own problem, asked the court to give him a recess as he "was tired out." The court recessed until the next morning.

The junior counsel, Cady Herrick, who had proved himself a resourceful young attorney while examining the witnesses, sat through his senior's performance red-faced and appearing to the press to be humiliated. The reporter for the *Argus* said of Herrick that he was "dignified, courteous, and irreproachable."

Herrick Takes Over

The next day before court went into session John Nelson came into the courtroom and whispered into Cady Herrick's ear. Watched by every eye in the room the two men walked to the corridor. When Herrick came back into the courtroom he was alone. After the judges arrived he told the court that Mr. Nelson was not well and asked for a recess until the afternoon. The judge asked if Herrick could present the case that afternoon instead of the senior counsel. Herrick said that he was well aware of the issues, but he would need more time to put the facts together in a logical presentation. Moak, perhaps stinging from the personal assault the day before, joined with Herrick in asking for a recess with enough time so that the prisoner "received justice." After a long and almost repulsive set of professional courtesies the court recessed until the following Monday.

A Twist

On Monday morning, another twist developed. It was one more in a series for which this trial was becoming famous. It was noted that one of Albany's leading attorneys and state assemblymen, Col. Charles Spencer had taken a seat next to Herrick. It was obvious that the colonel planned to support Herrick in his closing remarks. This, however, was not the twist of the day. The twist was that only 11 of the jurors had come to court this morning. The twelfth had "been taken suddenly and violently ill." The judge declared a recess until the next day.

On Tuesday, the last juror was still not in attendance. A doctor's report said it would be Monday, February 16th, before the juror would be well enough to attend. The lawyers and judge had a long discussion then agreed to postpone the closing arguments until the next week.

The Trial Continues

Everyone was in attendance when Herrick started his summation at 3 o'clock in the afternoon on Monday the 16th. He started by apologizing to the jury for having to sit through a second summation by the defense and for his humble ability.

Herrick then joined his senior partner, Nelson, in putting down Moak. The difference in the two defense attorneys was the level of the approach. Herrick said Moak's behavior was "uncalled for and at times disgraceful." Herrick broke Moak's behavior into two sections. The first was subsequent to Nelson's remarks when Herrick felt Moak had been "honorable and magnanimous." The second, and far more important to the defendant, was at the beginning of the trial when Herrick felt Moak was "anything but honorable and fair." Herrick then examined the emotional argument that Moak had opened the court with, namely that he would gain nothing by a conviction (Moak would use this argument again in the Billings's Trial). Herrick pointed out that this was a major case with a huge following in the newspapers. It was also Moak's first capital case as district attorney. To Herrick, Moak knew that "disgrace in the event of a non-conviction would be infinite." Herrick summarized Moak's character and behavior as actuated by ambition grasping and inordinate. Herrick pointed out that Moak would "climb higher and higher at the disadvantage of a poor prisoner." Herrick went on to say Moak was not humble. Herrick would use very derogatory terms to describe Moak saying that he would "people all of hell and jump from the shoulders of a hanging man to (gain) a higher fame."

Herrick did an excellent job of summarizing the issue of the body's identification. He presented a clear picture to the jury that the victim of the homicide could just as easily not have been Weston. He then reminded the jurors that they were not to assume on the side of Lowenstein's guilt. He also reminded the jury that the defense was not required to find the guilty party, only to show that the defendant was not guilty.

Herrick noted that the switchman had admitted that his time frame for having heard the shots was shaped by Moak's opening statement. Herrick also noted it would be impossible for anyone to be in a field in West Albany at 2 o'clock in the morning and in Brooklyn by 8:30 the same morning.

The fact that Mrs. Weston had been allowed to use the power of the presence of her orphaned children troubled Herrick. He told the jury that the children were brought into court only to solicit support for her desire for the defendant's death. Herrick was kinder than his partner had been on the widow, only questioning her feelings toward the prisoner and her own husband. Like Nelson, Herrick wondered how much she really cared if her husband left, if she would not rise out of bed after her husband told her he was going off with Lowenstein.

Herrick addressed Lowenstein's behavior as presented by the women. He noted that no guilty man would stay in the room after being accused by the widow's sister-in-law. Even less likely would he stay if he had been "nervous and twitching." Who could believe that a guilty man would stay after that to play the harmonica so all the women could dance? Herrick asked the jury, "Why would a guilty man buy the shop after the accusation?"

The physical evidence was the next area Herrick struggled to examine. He pointed out the razor and the fact that Lowenstein had said he sold the razor to John Weston in front of Mrs. Weston. The fact that Moak had not put Mary on the stand to refute the testimony made it legally true.

Moak's general behavior concerning the physical evidence was challenged. Moak had, through the testimony of Mary Cochrane, put into evidence a knife and a bloody handkerchief. Later they had all learned that the damning blood on the handkerchief was the result of Cochrane's own nosebleed. In one of his most significant points, Herrick spoke of how the murder was very horrific with the victim's throat having being cut. Yet no one had said there was any evidence of blood on any of Lowenstein's clothes - the clothes he was still wearing three days after the murder.

Herrick peeked in a door he should have opened fully when he said to the jury, "I say that there is something terribly strange in the behavoir of these women. I say that Mary Cochrane knows more about this case than any living person." Like Nelson, Herrick felt the key to the case was somehow in the hands of Cochrane. He pointed out to the jury that she claimed to be Hannah's friend, yet had not visited in over a year. Then she suddenly showed up the day after the men went away and then stayed for a week. Herrick raised the question of Cochrane's role in taking the guns out and giving them to Mrs. Weston. She claimed she had moved the guns before there was any suspicion of Lowenstein's involvement in any crime, but why? Then Herrick reminded the court that Cochrane dropped the gun into the river. To Herrick, Mary was "not worthy of being believed under oath."

Herrick put it straight before the jury, "Upon such evidence it would be not only improper but criminal to convict this man."

Cady Herrick failed to put forward one very important question. With Weston's fear of powered vehicles, how could he have gotten to Albany? Everyone, including the prosecution's witnesses, said he would not ride a train or ferry. How could this man have gotten to Albany in a day without one of these two modes of transportation? Of equal importance was what could the motivation have been that would make a man confront his fear assuming he did take the train?

Moak Closes

There is little doubt that Moak's knowledge of the law and his behavior were both notable, but only one was admirable.

Moak's closing in this case was a classic in implied logic and should be studied by criminal lawyers. He started with what has become the "I am humble before you the jury" routine. He then exhibited, for the second time in the trial, his real skill as he patterned seemingly unrelated scraps of cloth into a quilt that looked as though it covered all the contingencies.

Summarizing the issue for conviction on circumstantial evidence was Moak's forte. Despite protest to the contrary, Moak was consumed by winning and only sought truthful events that supported his thinking. He would establish in his brilliant mind the sequence of events and then nothing could change his mind. He would never ask himself if there was another way to weave these threads. The true problem for his opponents was he was amazingly convincing in his beliefs.

Moak did an excellent job of explaining article by article how the clothes were a positive identification of the body. He put forward his theory of the case with equal zeal. The accuracy of his theory was the issue. Moak explained to the jury that the two husbands had planned to go away to make their fortune. Weston's fortune was to be through investment, Lowenstein's through murder. He reviewed how he felt the men came to Albany. How they were seen in Albany. Most important, he showed with train schedules how Lowenstein got back by 8:30 in the morning "in time to be seen by his grocer." He then talked of the spending spree, running away to Canada and Lowenstein's capture. To Moak, the facts had only one face and that face had an expression of guilt upon it.

When it came to defending himself for allowing Mrs. Weston to bring her child into the courtroom, Moak's explanation exceeded the gall of his initial behavior. The child's cough could be heard each day, a subtle reminder that he was now without a father. Moak dug into the emotional wallet of the jurors telling them that the child was dying. How could he separate a widow from the only thing she had left to hold on to, especially as it [the child] was near death? The child had died of whopping cough during the recess in the trial caused by Nelson's problem and the sick juror.

Moak shrugged off the bloody handkerchief. To Moak, it was a minimal piece of evidence to be taken for what it was worth. After all it had probably gotten in the trunk while the women carelessly gathered goods for the trip north.

As for the lack of blood on Lowenstein's clothes, Moak said he probably just washed it off in the stream. To Moak, the lack of blood proved nothing, but the choice of a barber's razor was all telling. Moak asked the jury, would not a barber use the tool he was most familiar with to commit the crime?

The following are the principal arguments Moak put forward as to the reasons Lowenstein should have been found guilty for the murder of John Weston. Note Moak, quite properly in a prosecution's closing, intermingled evidence with theory.

1. The reason Lowenstein took the razors from Grunewald's shop was to kill Weston, not to open a shop.
2. Lowenstein had to have been poor before the murder and had a burning desire for money; Moak's logic was based on Hannah's concern about their ability to pay for the play when they only had $2.20. Moak showed that days later Lowenstein had money enough to buy a shop.
3. The mark on the razor that was used to mask the murder matched the marks on the razors in Lowenstein's possession when he was captured.
4. Moak felt that he had shown that the satchel Lowenstein carried was the same one carried by Weston when he left on his last trip.
5. The two pistols, which Moak assured the jury were the ones used in the murder, could have only gotten into Lowenstein's apartment by his hands.
6. His rapid spending of money was key to Moak. The purchase of the new clothes, barber shop and having his picture taken were further proof.

The Defendant's Behavior

Lowenstein's reaction to confrontation as to the whereabouts of Weston or any other incriminating comments was an integral element for Moak. There was the confrontation by Cornelia Weston where she claimed he twitched and was nervous. There was the confrontation on Monday where his wife said, in front of Cochrane, he was found out. Then his threat to kill himself if she believed it to be true. To Moak, the coup de grace was Lowenstein's flight to avoid prosecution.

Moak traced Lowenstein's movements from the day he arrived back in New York City until he was arrested in Canada. Moak's explanation made every movement appear a further example of guilt.

Moak showed total disregard for Lucian Bond, referring to him as the "ex-insurance agent", "non-explosive man" and "the would-be-lawyer."

Moak defended Mary Cochrane by saying that Bond had followed her. Moak reminded the jury that if anything could have been found against her, "his (Bond's) slimy tongue would have uttered it." This quote showed Moak's venom toward Bond.

Judge Learned

The judge was relatively quick in his summation to the jury. The judge told the jury that their deliberations should fall within the following restrictions:

1. The jury must depend on its own recollection of the evidence and not upon the statements, theory, or remarks made by the attorneys. The personal controversy between the lawyers was just that and has nothing to do with the guilt of the defendant.
2. The jury must take the view of the evidence that is most favorable to the defendant.
3. That if the body found might be some other person than John Weston the jury must acquit.
4. That if the jury found that the defendant might not have killed the man found at West Albany, then the jury must acquit.
5. That the mere probability that the defendant is guilty is not sufficient to warrant a verdict of guilty.

In referring to Lowenstein's actions at the time of the probable homicide, Judge Learned said "actions are not conclusive evidence of guilt, but the actions of a man suspected of a crime" was important to consider. It was a question always to view and weigh in the minds of a jury whether a man knowing himself to be totally innocent of crime would run away as "this prisoner did in this case."

There was considerable resistance to the death penalty at this time. In closing, the judge reminded the jurors that they were not responsible for the penalty merely the determination of guilt or innocence.

The Verdict

The people of Albany County had been engrossed in this case since the discovery of the body of the one-armed man the previous August. Now, the community waited impatiently for the jury to make a legal decision in a case that the citizens had already decided for themselves. The newspapers were reporting that the general consensus among the people was that the jury would be unable to reach a verdict.

There were other perceptions alive and flourishing in Albany at the time that almost inevitably impacted the deliberations in the jury room. While the public starved for the jury's answer, the *Argus* ran a paragraph summarizing the feelings of many of the people who had attended the trial. The beginning of the quote speaks of those in attendance at the trial; the closing speaks to a general feeling in the community about war veterans. Referring to the people who attended the trial:

> from the expressions we have heard, [they would] render a judgement that would be prompt and decisive in avenging the cowardly and brutal murder of the one-armed soldier, whose life had been spared through all the horrors of war only to yield itself up to the pistol ball and steel of a sneaking assassin. The very manor in which the murder must have been committed stamps it as being without a parallel for studied and premeditated brutality and cruelty.

There were two other prejudices that were playing at the time. To understand how these played, a history refresher is required. As a result of the Civil War, we were thinking of ourselves as a country not just a collection of states. The mere fact that Lowenstein was an immigrant was an obstacle to justice. His broken English inevitably weakened his status. In 1873, the economy was in a major depression with many people out of work or underemployed. As has always been the case in this country, when the economy is down immigrants are considered to have taken jobs from "real" Americans. The second and probably more substantial obstacle was anti-Semitism. There are numerous references in the newspaper to the fact that Lowenstein was Jewish. There were even comments made that his wife was given housing based on the "practical Christianity of this city." Although anti-Semitism was almost never admitted, in 1870s Albany it must have played a role in the jury's deliberations.

Awaiting the Jury

To save space and time, the civil court was using the courtroom while the jury deliberated. Late in the morning, the sheriff's deputy in charge of the Lowenstein jury came into the courtroom and whispered in the judge's ear. The civil court, understanding the importance of what was happening, took an immediate recess.

Before the trial judge and his associate justices were able to resume their seats, the "report" flashed through those in attendance that the verdict was guilty. When Judge Learned walked into the room the only sound was the rustle of his shoes on the hardwood floor. There were only seconds between the entrance of the judges and that of the defendant. The stress and anxiety of the moment were plain in Lowenstein's "countenance." The silence was so intense, that even though the room was filled beyond capacity, the sounds of chairs scraping across the floor in the jury room overhead could be heard plainly.

As the jury entered the room, the sober expression on each member's face was a clear indication that he understood the importance of the task he had just completed. All gathered impatiently awaited the results. The name of each jury member was called then the clerk asked if they had reached a verdict. After hearing they had, the clerk asked the defendant and jury to both rise. The clerk's voice trembled as he said, "Jurors look upon the prisoner, prisoner look upon the jury. How say you gentlemen: is the prisoner at the bar guilty of the felony of murder in the first degree as charged in the indictment or not guilty?"

Foreman – "Guilty."

Within the deafening silence that followed, the scene in the courtroom played out in slow motion. Lowenstein, pale from the news, sank backward into his seat. Hannah seemed to take a moment to digest the news then, as if on cue, she let out a cry of anguish, the sound of which pierced the room. She raised her hands momentarily in an undefined gesture then fell backward in "a swoon". Lowenstein grasped a tumbler of water on his table, splashed its contents in her face, saving some to pour down her throat.

While Hannah was still unconscious, Moak rose and asked the court to take this time to fulfill its one remaining painful duty. Everyone knew that under the new law the punishment was hanging. In the midst of the confusion that surrounded him, Herrick said he did not object to the prosecutor's request, but only asked that the prisoner be given as long a period to prepare himself as possible.

To those present it was like looking down a pipe. The entire room seemed out of focus except for the judge and the scene around the defense table. Judge Learned broke the resounding silence calling, "Emil Lowenstein stand up." In the few intervening moments, Lowenstein had regained the calm demeanor that he had borne throughout the trial. Judge Learned then said, "Have you anything to say as to why the sentence of this court should not be passed upon you?"

Lowenstein's voice could barely be heard in the back of the room. In this soft voice he told the court that he was not guilty. Further, he claimed he had not been provided proper counsel so he should be granted a second trial.

The judge then began to close the session with a comment that on every occasion where a point of law was questioned, it had been answered in favor of the defendant. The judge said that although one counsel had broken down in his defense, he had been provided adequate counsel throughout the trial. Judge Learned told Lowenstein that a jury having considered all the evidence had found him guilty. The judge then made a telling comment describing the level of the evidence saying in the record, "however slight the circumstances." The judge then said he agreed with the verdict and sentenced Emil Lowenstein to be hanged on April 10, 1874.

Reactions

The doomed man, hearing the news, mechanically dropped once more into his chair. The color drained from his cheeks and his entire body trembled. His head slowly turned so that he could look upon the form of his unconscious young wife. Herrick shook the condemned man's hand. Then two jailers came forward to place shackles on Lowenstein's wrists. When he noticed the two men he turned back to his wife, bent down and kissed her at least a dozen times gently upon on the lips. This simple act seemed to recharge the condemned man. He rose and presented his wrists to the deputies. His wrists bound, he picked up his hat up from the table as if leaving a restaurant after an evening meal. Lowenstein was bound for the same cell that had been occupied by so many condemned criminals in Albany before him including, O'Brien, Hendrickson and Mary Hartung (the beautiful young women hung for the murder of her husband – motive to be with another man).

When Lowenstein left, the pent-up energy in the room suddenly burst free and the minor buzz that had been present since the verdict was handed down became a roar. Despite the fact that most agreed with the verdict, the scene they had witnessed moved some of the women to tears.

The Jury's Deliberations

The status of the jury during the deliberation is interesting. On the first ballot, taken shortly after they went into deliberations, the jury stood nine for conviction and three for acquittal. That evening, the jury met until midnight with the positions of every juror remained the same. The contention was over the testimony of Fanny Hume, the cigar sale clerk. To those three jurors her testimony that Lowenstein was in Philadelphia on the day of the murder was most convincing. The nine who felt a conviction was warranted kept hammering on the character of the witnesses and the probability of some of the witnesses – Hume - being mistaken. When a second ballot was taken the next morning, the vote had switched to 10 for conviction and two for acquittal. An hour more of discussion resulted in a vote of 11 to one. The one, seeing he stood alone, switched, saying to his fellow jurors that he and "Mrs. Hume were mistaken."

Charges against Nelson

The next action of the court was taken as soon as Lowenstein had left the courtroom. This action was against John Nelson, the defense attorney. Judge Learned said for the dignity of the court and respectability of the bar that charges must be filed against Nelson. The judge's order was that a trial be held for misconduct and that if convicted John Nelson's name would be "stricken from the roll of attorneys and counsellors (1870 spelling)." Moak tried to have the case assigned to a special prosecutor so it would not appear to be the result of any personal differences. The judge refused, saying he had ordered the charges filed and Moak could act professionally and present the case.

How the Case Broke

Now that the trial was over and the two Brooklyn detectives were back in the big city, Chief Malloy wanted the limelight. He told reporters that the case actually turned as a result of two clues. First was the discovery of the business card on Weston's body; the second was not known until the after trial. In an interview Malloy said that the ultimate lead was based on a question he asked Mary Cochrane. According to the ever-humble Malloy, after Moak and the Brooklyn detectives finished interviewing the three women the district attorney asked the Brooklyn detectives if they had any more questions. Overhearing the question and having "heard none of the examination," Malloy jumped in. He asked Mary if Lowenstein had said he would write to anyone. She explained that he was going to write to his wife at the place where she had worked as a domestic. She went on to say he was going to use her maiden name. This sent the detectives to search for the letter, which resulted in the arrest in Canada.

Silence

Over the course of the next week, Lowenstein made two comments that did little to build support for his cause, since they both implied he was a habitual liar. The first was that he claimed that he had written the local rabbi asking him to come to the jail for support. Lowenstein claimed that despite his plea the rabbi never came. An interview with the rabbi yielded a very different story. The rabbi said he never received such a request and if it had come he would have been prompt to attend anyone who wanted "religious instruction or consultation." Lowenstein's second statement had to do with his wife. He said that because they were destitute and no one in Albany would give her a place to stay, she might have to leave him in his final days. In checking, the paper found that one person had agreed to pay her room and board at any site in the city and at least two other people had literally opened their doors to her. Reading these contradictory reports in the newspapers, Lowenstein refused any more interviews.

Appeals

Hannah Lowenstein, Cady Herrick and Assemblyman Col. Charles Spencer utilized every avenue to push for a new trial. The case was even reviewed by Governor Dix. In the end it was all for naught as all the doors were closed with polite but definitive positions that the verdict would stand.

Lowenstein also tried to help himself. According to the *New York Times* on March 19th Lowenstein tried to escape from the Albany County Jail. In case his escape was not successful or a retrial not ordered, Lowenstein was trying every vehicle. So he converted to Catholicism. The Reverend Father Francis Neubauer spent all available time with the condemned man.

Preparations

With the hanging scheduled for Friday, April 10th, in the days, immediately proceeding the event, the local newspapers ran articles telling what preparations had been made and what precautions had been arranged. Four companies of the National Guard had been called up to surround the jail assuring that people would not try to press too close. The corridor in which the execution was to take place was cleaned and whitewashed.

Lowenstein had taken the sounds of the preparations in stride. He spent each day talking with his guards. Although generally solemn, Lowenstein showed tremendous fortitude in his last days; the sounds of the carpenter's hammer having no effect on his mood.

Although the execution was not scheduled until the afternoon, even by 8:00 o'clock in the morning there was a small crowd gathered in front of the jail. By 10:00 o'clock the National Guard in full winter uniform had placed pickets at regular intervals the entire perimeter of the city block. The Guard members all seemed to understand the solemn nature of their duty. To avoid problems, all of Maiden Lane from Lodge to Eagle Street was cordoned off to anyone who could not prove business on the street. These preparations were apparently warranted. Despite a snowstorm, by mid-afternoon more than 2000 people had gathered in the streets.

The evening of April 9th, Hannah had visited her husband for several hours. The two talked in whispered tones. At 8 o'clock that evening Hannah left for her Albany home. Shortly after Hannah departed, Father Neubauer went into Lowenstein's cell where he would remain the entire night praying and trying to help the condemned man through the long, tedious wait. In the deep black hours of the night, when only those with a real need are about, Lowenstein slept for two hours. At 7 o'clock in the morning the priest, a guard and Lowenstein set up an altar. The Sisters of Mercy arrived and stayed most of the morning. The priest said a mass at the makeshift altar for those who were gathered. Lowenstein's spirits and his resignation to the fate that awaited him impressed all those who saw him that morning.

Shortly before 8 o'clock Hannah arrived at the jail and was admitted to say her farewells to her husband. The scene between the two was very affectionate. Lowenstein kissed her softly, protesting in whispered tones his innocence. At 8 o'clock a hearty breakfast was served which the condemned man ate, remarking to his lovely wife that it would be his last. Her final good-byes were so emotional that Mrs. Lowenstein became faint and had to be helped all the way to the carriage that was waiting.

One of Lowenstein's former cellmates, an embezzler, came down for a brief visit. When he left he assured those gathered that Lowenstein was innocent of the crime.

Under the court's order, the execution could be between 10 a.m. and 4 p.m. In the morning Lowenstein requested that it be set for 2 o'clock in the afternoon. Those in charge granted his request.

At five after two, several guards entered the cell and found Lowenstein on his knees praying with the priest. While he was still on his knees a guard placed the noose around his neck and tightened it as low on his neck as possible. Lowenstein never flinched, trembled, or showed any sign of emotion as the death knot was secured. Lowenstein then pulled his collar up hiding, the rope from the view of any prisoner he might pass on his last walk.

Without any aid, Lowenstein rose and walked out of his cell for the last time. As the small group walked, the priest read from the Bible in muted tones. Lowenstein kept his gaze fixed on the cross in front of him. Accompanied only by the sounds of the locks and doors opening and closing, the small group joined the required witnesses in the corridor where the final act would occur. Lowenstein knelt and said a final prayer with the priest. The priest then asked if he had final words before the order of the law was enacted.

In a weak, almost inaudible voice, Lowenstein said:

> I wish to say that I am innocent of the crime for which I am about to suffer, I am condemned to die, and I am ready, but the time will come when my innocence will be proven. It may be long or it may be short, but it will be proved in the end. If I were guilty I would not deny it standing as I do before my God, on whom I call to witness my innocence. I believe God has forgiven all my sins, and as he is my witness, I am as innocent of this crime as an unborn babe.

One of the sheriff's deputy's then read the warrant ordering Lowenstein's death. As the deputy read the words, Lowenstein gazed upon the crucifix occasionally looking at the deputy. The warrant read, the deputy asked if he had any last words. In a voice described as a whisper he said, "Yes, I wish to say that although there have been a great many persons who have injured me, and who were false witnesses on my trial, I freely forgive them with all my heart, and I trust God, also will forgive them." A final prayer was said then Lowenstein gave the priest a kiss on the cheek. Lowenstein's face showed no expression as he prepared to take the journey that we must all take alone.

The hanging was done utilizing counter weights, not a trap door. The rope holding the weights up was cut and Lowenstein's limp body was snatched from the floor. The involuntary motions were described in detail. Let it be known that there were actions in his arms and hands for several painful moments. After two minutes and five seconds, his heart stopped beating. After nine minutes, his lifeless body was taken down, placed in a waiting coffin and removed to be taken to a church for services.

The Funeral

The funeral was set for 9 o'clock Saturday morning, April 11th. The church on Central Avenue was so crowded with people who wanted to look upon the body that all the seats were taken and people had to stand along the walls with others forced to stand outside the doors. Mrs. Lowenstein sat in the front row by the head of her husband's coffin. Six deputies, with whom Emil had become attached, accompanied her. They were to act as bearers.

After the mass it took over an hour for all those gawkers gathered for the dismal event to walk by the casket and gaze upon the remains. The last act was when Hannah bent forward and kissed the cold lips of her husband's body. Even those with dry eyes could not withstand the impact of this scene.

Lowenstein was buried in St. Mary's cemetery on Washington Avenue in Albany.

Postscript

Crimes reported in this series of true crime books either remain unproven or there is serious doubt as to the guilt of the party tried. Given these parameters, there will be those who wonder why this case was selected given that there was serious evidence implying that Lowenstein was, in fact, guilty.

Lowenstein was clearly not given a fair trial. By setting an extremely low amount of money for the defense, Moak had significant input as to who would be selected as the defense attorney. When Nelson was selected everyone knew he was a man with a drinking problem. Yes, Nelson had two partners, but their experience was extremely limited. Bond had never presented a case in court, having served only as a solicitor. Cady Herrick surprised everyone with his skills, but it was his first case. Even Cady did not think he had done an acceptable job on the defense.

As to Lowenstein's guilt, there are too many unresolved questions. Would any man about to die, and especially a recent convert, say that before his God he was innocent if he were not? Why would a man terrified of trains take a trip on one? Why did Mary Cochrane drop the pistol over the side of the boat? Why did the women who were suppose to be so concerned over Weston's whereabouts bring a male stranger (Percival) home? Why would they have given the gun to a man they had just met? Why did Hannah ask her husband to switch from speaking German to English when they were having the conversation in front of Mary Cochrane? Could it be that the women planned the murder from the beginning? Why did the bloody handkerchief suddenly get placed in the trunk?

Let me offer a rational logic accepting all the testimony in the case. The women, at least Hannah and Mary Cochrane, were of questionable backgrounds. Let's face it. They both married after only knowing the men less than three weeks, even in 1873 that would raise eyebrows. Hannah knew Mary Weston through her landlord, Joseph Weston. Mary Weston was unhappy in her marriage and suspected that her cheap husband planned to leave her. Worse yet, he may have stayed, and continue, to make her life miserable. Along comes Lowenstein a man with some worth, he has after all just returned from Europe. If he did in fact have money in the wall, he would have told Hannah. A man out to impress a woman (Emil) would not have been able to miss the opportunity to brag about his fortune.

The women began plotting to rid themselves of both men and to have the money. The plan was simple - they would kill one man and blame the other. The first step was to arrange for Weston to transfer the property into his wife's name. The second was to have both Weston and Lowenstein out of town on the same day so the blame would fall on Lowenstein. To complete the task they brought in Mary Cochrane. Cochrane was the one that arranged for the final trip. The actual arrangements included either Mary, or a friend of hers.

Keep in mind neither conductor remembered the men being together. Men on a business trip that was hours long would have sat together. Mary Cochrane, or a female friend of hers, was in the car with Weston. Like all couples on their way for a little tryst, they were trying to slip away unnoticed for their secret rendezvous. To avoid being seen together, Cochrane and Weston did not sit together. This was why Weston pinched Lowenstein's arm, not because they were going away together, but rather because they weren't and Weston did not want Lowenstein to forget he was his alibi.

Weston went to the woods for a quiet place to be alone with Mary. That number of shots was the sign of a woman, not a man. Would a man have used two guns full of bullets unless he was angry? Wouldn't a woman have used that number of bullets to be sure her victim was dead before she had to cut his throat with the razor? Why didn't anyone see blood on Lowenstein's clothes? Wasn't it just a little too convenient that the razor chosen to slit the victim's throat was the one given to Weston by Lowenstein? With all the razors Lowenstein had with him why would he use one with a mark? Could it be that the killer meant to leave that particular razor behind? Why else would the murderer take the real weapons - the guns - and leave the decoy - the razor - unless they meant to have it found?

Then Mary Cochrane showed up at the Weston house to tell them the job was completed. She needed to give Mary Weston her share of the money. The women on cue started on Lowenstein when he returned for Philadelphia. Little did they anticipate how fast he was going to start spending the money. They have to stop it, so they conveniently found the copy of the *Sun* with the article about the murder in Albany. They convinced Lowenstein to run, thus all blame would fall on him. Then Mary just happened to mention that Lowenstein promised to write his new bride. The rest is in the story.

Fiction? Only those gone on the long journey alone know for sure.

Index